Inclusionary Housing and Urban Inequality in London and New York City

Municipalities around the world have increasingly used inclusionary housing programs to address their housing shortages. This book problematizes those programs in London and New York City by offering an empirical, research-based perspective on the socio-spatial dimensions of inclusionary housing approaches in both cities. The aim of those programs is to produce affordable housing and foster greater socio-economic inclusion by mandating or incentivizing private developers to include affordable housing units within their market-rate residential developments.

The starting point of this book is the so-called "poor door" practice in London and New York City, which results in mixed-income developments with separate entrances for "affordable housing" and wealthier market-rate residents. Focusing on this "poor door" practice allowed for a critical look at the housing program behind it. By exploring the relationship between inclusionary housing, new-build gentrification, and austerity urbanism, this book highlights the complexity of the planning process and the ambivalences and interdependencies of the actors involved. Thereby, it provides evidence that the provision of affordable housing or social mixing through this program has only limited success and, above all, that it promotes – in a sense through the "back door" – the very gentrification and displacement mechanisms it is supposed to counteract.

This book will be of interest to researchers and students of housing studies, planning, and urban sociology, as well as planners and policymakers who are interested in the consequences of their own housing programs.

Yuca Meubrink currently works as academic coordinator of the interdisciplinary research group "Sustainable construction – for saving resources and climate protection" of Berlin-Brandenburg Academy of Sciences and Humanities. She previously worked as a research and teaching assistant in the study program Metropolitan Culture at the HafenCity University Hamburg, Germany from where she also received her Ph.D. She has been a visiting scholar at City University of New York and at Birkbeck, University of London. She is also a member of the editorial collective, sub\urban. zeitschrift für kritische stadtforschung – a peer-reviewed, open access journal. Yuca Meubrink studied North American Studies, Cultural and Social Anthropology and Journalism in Berlin, Germany.

Explorations in Housing Studies

Series editors:
Janet Smith, *University of Illinois, Chicago, USA*
Keith Jacobs, *University of Tasmania, Tasmania, Australia*
Mark Stephens, *University of Glasgow, UK*

Explorations in Housing Studies is a series of high-quality, research monographs which aim to extend and deepen both theoretical debate and empirical research in the housing studies field. The series is being introduced at a time when housing, in its various dimensions, is particularly closely intertwined with the impact of demographic change, economic instability, the shaping of life chances and wealth distributions, and with the uncertain impacts of environmental and technological change. This series aims to engage with these and related issues from a variety of perspectives and methodologies.

Evictions in the UK
Power, Housing, and Politics
Joe Crawford

Affordable Housing Preservation in Washington, DC
A Framework for Local Funding, Collaborative Governance, and Community Organizing for Change
Kathryn Howell

Home Beyond the House
Transformation of Life, Place, and Tradition in Rural China
Wei Zhao

Property, Planning and Protest
The Contentious Politics of Housing Supply
Quintin Bradley

Inclusionary Housing and Urban Inequality in London and New York City
Gentrification Through the Back Door
Yuca Meubrink

For more information about this series, please visit: https://www.routledge.com/Explorations-in-Housing-Studies/book-series/HOUSING

Inclusionary Housing and Urban Inequality in London and New York City

Gentrification Through the Back Door

Yuca Meubrink

LONDON AND NEW YORK

Designed cover image: Yuca Meubrink

First published 2025
by Routledge
4 Park Square, Milton Park, Abingdon, Oxon OX14 4RN

and by Routledge
605 Third Avenue, New York, NY 10158

Routledge is an imprint of the Taylor & Francis Group, an informa business

This book was first presented and defended as a doctoral thesis at HafenCity
University Hamburg, Germany.

British Library Cataloguing-in-Publication Data
A catalogue record for this book is available from the British Library

Library of Congress Cataloging-in-Publication Data
Names: Meubrink, Yuca, author.
Title: Inclusionary housing and urban inequality in London and New York
City : gentrification through the back door / Yuca Meubrink.
Description: Abingdon, Oxon ; New York, NY : Routledge, 2025. |
Series: Explorations in housing studies | Includes bibliographical references
and index.
Identifiers: LCCN 2024023957 (print) | LCCN 2024023958 (ebook) |
ISBN 9781032742731 (hardback) | ISBN 9781032742748 (paperback) |
ISBN 9781003468479 (ebook)
Subjects: LCSH: Housing policy--England--London. | Low-income
housing--England--London. | Gentrification--England--London. | Housing
policy--New York (State)--New York. | Low-income housing--New York
(State)--New York. | Gentrification--New York (State)--New York.
Classification: LCC HD7287.3 .M48 2025 (print) | LCC HD7287.3 (ebook) |
DDC 363.5/561--dc23/eng/20240614
LC record available at https://lccn.loc.gov/2024023957
LC ebook record available at https://lccn.loc.gov/2024023958

ISBN: 978-1-032-74273-1 (hbk)
ISBN: 978-1-032-74274-8 (pbk)
ISBN: 978-1-003-46847-9 (ebk)

DOI: 10.4324/9781003468479

Typeset in Times New Roman
by KnowledgeWorks Global Ltd.

For all those who fight for truly affordable housing

Contents

Figures

Maps

Tables

Boxes

Acknowledgments

Just as you say it takes a village to raise a child, it also takes a village to write a book. In this sense, I am deeply grateful to all those who have contributed to the creation and completion of this book.

First and foremost, I extend my deepest gratitude to all those who fight every day against all odds for more truly affordable housing, and who shared their experience with me – be they politicians, city planners, housing advocates, activists, or residents. You have been my main motivation to write this book. Your anonymity is safe with me.

I am deeply indebted to my mentors and advisors Alexa Färber, Monika Grubbauer und Margit Mayer whose guidance and wisdom have shaped my thinking and refined my ideas. Their expertise has been instrumental in bringing clarity and depth to the content of this book. Special thanks to my advisors Ida Susser in New York City and Paul Watt in London who, without knowing me, welcomed me with open arms and put me in touch with the right people.

I am very grateful to my friends, colleagues, and close family who have offered encouragement, feedback, and inspiration along the way. Your support has been a source of motivation and joy. I cannot name them all, but in particular I am grateful to Delphine Deryng, Juliane Ebert, Juan Garcia Basilio, Sarah Hostmann, Claudia Kapfer, Rebekka Korthues, Hendrik Mohrmann, Jule Mohrmann, Friederike Schröder, Hannes Trölsch and Aylin Winzenburg for always being there for me; Janina Kriszio and Inga Reimers for all the writing weekends in the countryside; and Urcu Meubrink, Matteo Lucas, Jonah Lucas and Christina Galic for making Hamburg a second home.

Special thanks are due to Matt Davis, Heike Derwanz, Kathrin Eitel, Justin Kadi, Lisa Vollmer, and the colloquium at the HafenCity University Hamburg, who provided constructive critiques on chapters or sections of the manuscript, and to Steven Morgana, the best proof reader I could have ever imagined.

I further thank my editorial colleagues at sub\urban.zeitschrift für kritische stadtforschung for providing me with a familiar space in which to discuss critical ideas.

I also express my appreciation to Caroline Church and Meghna Rodborne at Routledge for their excellent and reliable cooperation, and to my anonymous reviewers for taking the time to review the manuscript and provide helpful comments.

Lastly, I extend my heartfelt thanks to my mother, Almut Meubrink, for all her endless support over the years and for pushing my little son in his baby carriage through the streets of Berlin every day in all weathers so that I could finish this book. And I deeply thank my partner, Thomas Kahlbohm, for his constant encouragement, and reassurance through the highs and lows of writing this book, and his willingness to lend an ear whenever needed. I am truly happy to have him by my side.

Acronyms

ANHD	Association for Neighborhood and Housing Development
AMI	Area Median Income
ASH	Architects for Social Housing
BNBP	BNP Paribas (property consultancy company)
CB	Community Board
CIL	Community Infrastructure Levy
CPC	City Planning Commission
DoE	Department of Environment
FAR	Floor Aria Ratio
GLA	Greater London Authority
HfL	Homes for Lambeth
HPD	New York City Department of Housing Preservation and Development
IH	Inclusionary housing
IHP	Inclusionary Housing Program
LGA	Local Government Association
LHS	London Housing Strategy
MIH	Mandatory Inclusionary Housing
MLMP	More Light More Power campaign
NMN4S	Northern Manhattan Not For Sale campaign
NPPF	National Planning Policy Framework
NYCEDC	New York City Economic Development Corporation
NYCC	New York Communities for Change
POPS	Privately-Owned Public Spaces
R10	Residential Zoning District with Floor Area Ratio 10 (the highest FAR)
RAD	Rental Assistance Demonstration
RAFA	Real Affordability for All
REP	Resident Engagement Panel
RIBA	Royal Institute of British Architects
Section 106	Section 106 of the Town and Country Planning Act of 1990
SPV	Special Purpose Vehicles
ULURP	Uniform Land Use Review Procedure
ZQA	Zoning for Quality and Affordability

Maps

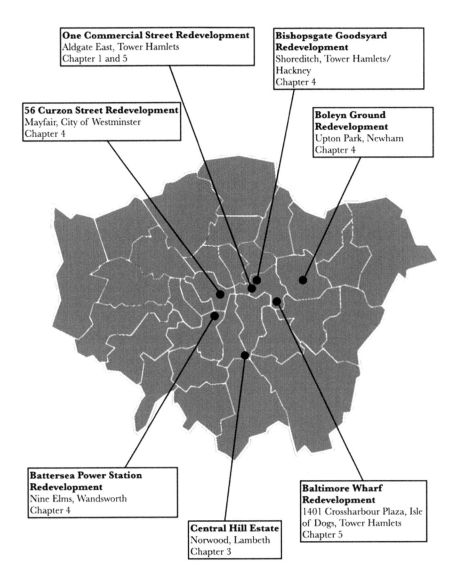

One Commercial Street Redevelopment
Aldgate East, Tower Hamlets
Chapter 1 and 5

Bishopsgate Goodsyard Redevelopment
Shoreditch, Tower Hamlets/ Hackney
Chapter 4

56 Curzon Street Redevelopment
Mayfair, City of Westminster
Chapter 4

Boleyn Ground Redevelopment
Upton Park, Newham
Chapter 4

Battersea Power Station Redevelopment
Nine Elms, Wandsworth
Chapter 4

Central Hill Estate
Norwood, Lambeth
Chapter 3

Baltimore Wharf Redevelopment
1401 Crossharbour Plaza, Isle of Dogs, Tower Hamlets
Chapter 5

Main case studies in London

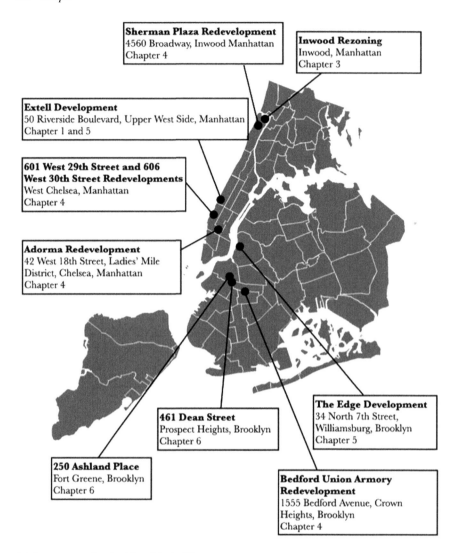

Sherman Plaza Redevelopment
4560 Broadway, Inwood Manhattan
Chapter 4

Inwood Rezoning
Inwood, Manhattan
Chapter 3

Extell Development
50 Riverside Boulevard, Upper West Side, Manhattan
Chapter 1 and 5

**601 West 29th Street and 606
West 30th Street Redevelopments**
West Chelsea, Manhattan
Chapter 4

Adorma Redevelopment
42 West 18th Street, Ladies' Mile
District, Chelsea, Manhattan
Chapter 4

461 Dean Street
Prospect Heights, Brooklyn
Chapter 6

The Edge Development
34 North 7th Street,
Williamsburg, Brooklyn
Chapter 5

250 Ashland Place
Fort Greene, Brooklyn
Chapter 6

**Bedford Union Armory
Redevelopment**
1555 Bedford Avenue, Crown
Heights, Brooklyn
Chapter 4

Main case studies in New York City

Introduction

Rethinking Inclusionary Housing in an Age of Austerity

A Tale of Two Doors: The "Poor Door" Phenomenon

In the summer of 2014, two glassy apartment towers – one in London and the other in New York City (NYC) – with separate entrances for rich and poor provoked outrage and protest at what is seen by many as socio-economic segregation. Leading newspapers on both sides of the Atlantic, such as *The Guardian* (Osborne 2014a) and the *New York Times* (Navarro 2014) as well as journalists, scholars, activists and politicians have all spoken out against what they saw to be a modern form of "housing apartheid" (Prince 2014), "social cleansing" (Low 2014) or, hinting to the Jim Crow[1] era, "separate but (un)equal" (Cohen 2014).

In New York, the public outrage centered on the development plans introduced by the real estate developer Extell Developers for a new apartment building on the Upper West Side in Manhattan. As part of the $3 billion Riverside South development project, the developer planned a 33-story luxury high-rise condominium with 219 units for sale at prices between 1.3 to almost 26 million US-Dollar (Schwartz 2016). To build higher than the zoning law allows and to receive tax incentives, Extell offered to include 20 percent affordable housing on-site. The catch, however, was that while the owners of the market-rate apartments would enter their homes through a luxury lobby from Manhattan's waterfront side that blends seamlessly into the glassy architectural structure of Riverside Boulevard, the tenants of the 55 "affordable" housing units would be separated from the market-rate residents by a separate, out of sight entrance. The local news blog *West Side Rag* first reported the development plans in August of 2013 and coined this phenomenon "poor door":

> A 33-story building slated to be built on Riverside Boulevard between 61st and 62nd street will have an entirely separate entrance for people of lower socioeconomic means: a door for the poor, or as we call it, a 'Poor Door'.
> (West Side Rag 2013)

When the city approved Extell's controversial plans for the luxury building on Riverside Boulevard in 2014, the controversy around the so-called "poor door" re-ignited. The developer used a loophole in the 421-a tax exemption program,[2] which counted affordable housing as on-site if it is built in the same zoning lot, albeit

DOI: 10.4324/9781003468479-1

with separate entrances. Appalled by the clear inequality of this, leading politicians including Manhattan Borough President Gail Brewer and New York City Mayor Bill de Blasio joined the discussion and condemned the practice, in spite of having voted in favor of the Extell development within the planning application process (Duran 2014; Gonen 2014). In 2015, as a response to the public outrage, the New York State Legislature enacted changes to the tax incentive program 421-a that banned the "poor door" practice by explicitly stating:

> ALL rental dwelling units in an eligible multiple dwelling must share the same common entrances and common areas as the market-rate units in such eligible multiple dwelling and shall not be isolated to a specific floor or area of an eligible multiple dwelling.
>
> (NYC Department of Housing Preservation and Development)[3]

Almost at the same time, in 2014, the "poor door" controversy hit London when *The Guardian* exposed the phenomenon in the British capital (Osborne 2014a). Located at the border between the City of London – the world's primary finance center – and Tower Hamlets – one of London's poorest boroughs – stood a 22-story, new-build residential tower with two separate entrances. Completed in 2012 at a cost of £140 million, the residential Relay Building[4] stands as a symbol of urban inequality in London:

> On my way to have a look at this mixed-income development, I go along Whitechapel Road which leads directly to the development. Whitechapel is a neighborhood in Tower Hamlets – one of the most deprived boroughs in London. It is a low-income neighborhood, undergoing substantial regeneration and host to a large Bangladeshi community. […] Here and there between the small shops, there are some old-looking pubs and more modern cafés. […] While I am still thinking about the mixture of Islamic culture and old, typical London pubs, it suddenly hits me: The two towers facing each other – one the Relay building – look like the entrance to another world. Behind these two buildings, I only see huge new-build towers one after another that are clearly part of the City of London. […]
>
> The Relay Building not only marks the border between the two boroughs, but it also symbolizes a line between West and East London, between rich and poor. The fact that the building has two separate entrances – one for the rich and one for lower-income tenants – underlines its symbolic significance. Only the 'poor door' is facing – somewhat ironically – the City of London, not Tower Hamlets. Maybe that is a sign of the developer's idea of "social mix" but maybe it is just an effect of convenient construction since the "poor door" is facing directly the wall of the next building.
>
> (Fieldnote 2015/06/08)[5]

The symbolic meaning of the Relay Building was further underlined when for nearly nine months a group of anarchists and activists held weekly protests in front of the "rich-door," blocking the entrance and forcing the residents of the market-rate apartments to enter through the "poor door" (Low 2014). While New York City's Mayor, Bill de Blasio, responded to political pressure by banning the "poor doors," London's Mayor, Boris Johnson, merely stated that he "does not like them" (Osborne 2014b). Nevertheless, he sees them as a functioning instrument both for the creation of new housing as well as for the social mix and thus did not plan to ban them, arguing that "they are something [he tries] to get out of the planning application if [he]can" (ibid.).

These two developments are, however, not isolated cases. Other cases in cities throughout North America, such as Washington D.C. (Withnall 2014), Toronto (The Huffington Post Canada 2014) or Vancouver (Testado 2015), have come under scrutiny. Nor is the practice entirely a new development in cities like New York and London. New York already had a raft of mixed-income developments with separate entrances for low-income tenants lacking access to the spacious, staffed lobbies, swimming pools and other amenities otherwise available to high-income residents (Grabar 2014; Susser 2012: 50). Particularly in London, The Guardian revealed that the "poor door" tendency has become "a growing trend in the capital's upmarket apartment blocks" (Osborne 2014a).

But why did the "poor door" practice suddenly spark such popular outcry in both cities while the segregation of people by streets, blocks or entire neighborhoods has generally been accepted by the wider public? The answer is quite simple. The 'poor door' represents inequality. In the midst of a prevailing affordable housing crisis, the catchy term perfectly captures the public's imagination by harkening the public to another era of each nation's history that – as has generally been assumed – has long been overcome. In the context of North America, the practice evokes the specter of Jim Crow laws in the South at the turn of the 20th century, a 21st-century version of the "separate but equal" doctrine that systemically segregated and discriminated against Black[6] people in the first half of the 20th century. Similarly, in the British context, and observed by Friedrich Engels almost two centuries earlier, the practice helps "conceal from the eyes of the wealthy men and women" the deplorable slum conditions of the poor (Engels [1844] 2000: 49). In other words, "poor doors" serve to hold a mirror to a delusional society that continues to aver that all its members are treated equally.

Real estate, seen only as an investment, has put housing markets under severe pressure and led to spiraling rents, land values and property prices in both New York City and London. As a result, housing discrimination and harassment have become widespread: social and affordable housing has continuously diminished and led to the accelerated displacement of low- and middle-income households. In short, both cities are plagued by ongoing housing affordability problems, which are generally marked by low vacancy rates, especially for lower-rent units, growing waiting lists for subsidized housing and high rates of homelessness. In this context, the "poor door" is the architectural manifestation of the growing social division between rich and poor.

However, on both sides of the Atlantic, certain journalists, scholars, economists, and developers have actually rallied in "defense of the 'poor door'" (Jacobus 2015). While they generally share with opponents of the "poor door" the view that the practice is "inherently jarring" (Glaeser 2015), they make mention of the fact that while such separate entrances generate outcry in the public, the public seems to have no issue with residential buildings built to cater to specific income groups (Lamberg 2015). Another issue that repeatedly came up in the press at the time – especially in London – was that managing and maintaining "affordable housing" units separately from the condominiums – symbolized by "poor doors" – boils down to a question of practicality for housing associations, and social landlords, and of feasibility for "affordable housing" tenants, for whom the service charges of common entrances and amenities would be unaffordable (Osborne 2014a; Wainwright 2014). Others have argued that the practice offers the best way forward to providing affordable housing in higher-income neighborhoods where NIMBYism – *Not In My Backyard* – has often prevented the construction of affordable housing (Jacobus 2015, Pomorski 2014). Further, many critical of "poor doors" have described the outrage over their use as a superficial one, since the deeper problem is the continuous undersupply of affordable housing (Yglesias 2014). Or, as the urban planning scholar Michael Edwards was quoted in The Guardian: "Of course these so-called 'poor doors' are shocking, but they are a symptom, not the problem" (Michael Edwards cited in Wainwright 2014). According to him, the real problem is that "[w]e've simply stopped building proper social housing, and until that's addressed then fiddling around with front-door arrangements is like rearranging deck chairs on the Titanic" (Edwards cited in Wainwright 2014).

Even though the "poor door" controversy has been rather short-lived in the press, it has mirrored discussions on prevailing political and socio-spatial tensions in both cities: the systematic affordable housing shortage, the cities' exorbitant housing prices, the spatial polarization of the rich and poor and the self-segregation of the rich as well as gentrification and displacement of the poor. Further, it has helped raise questions about current political strategies and arguments on how best to address the cities' severe housing problems such as social mix policies, the value of integration or the subsidization of expensive real estate. Symptom or not, the "poor door" signals a policy failure of the housing program that lies behind it: inclusionary housing (IH). And above all, it raises the question of how to advance equality in housing when the very programs designed to promote it are not effective in preventing processes such as gentrification and displacement from occurring, and in many ways offer a pathway for those processes to enter through, as it were, the "back door." It is this metaphorical 'back door' in inclusionary housing that this book seeks to examine.

Benevolent Planning Policy or "Recipe" for Gentrification?: Recent Approaches to Inclusionary Housing in London and New York City

While for many, the "poor doors" are a palpable symbol of socio-spatial inequality, the social mixing policies, as well as the programs that created them, have generally been valued as positive policy ambitions. In connection with the "poor door" debate, the inclusionary housing program itself has rarely been questioned – not even by the press.

In both cities, the 'poor door' phenomenon stems from planning practices called inclusionary housing. The term inclusionary housing refers to a planning program, regulation, or law that uses the planning system to produce affordable housing and foster greater social and economic inclusion by capturing value created through the marketplace (Calavita and Mallach 2010: 1). It mandates or incentivizes private developers to include affordable housing units within their market-rate residential developments. This can generally be done either by incorporating affordable housing as part of the same development – as has been done in the case of the "poor doors" –, by building affordable housing elsewhere within the city, or by contributing a payment in lieu of construction.

The earliest inclusionary housing programs[7] were enacted in Virginia, Maryland, and California in the United States in the 1970s to counter exclusionary zoning practices in generally white and affluent suburbs and to tackle the deepening affordable housing problems.[8] A major factor for the growth of inclusionary housing in the US was the cuts in federal funding for housing construction in the 1980s (Calavita 2006). By the 1990s, it had been increasingly implemented by major cities that were experiencing a rapid rise in housing prices such as Chicago, San Francisco, Washington DC, Denver, Baltimore, Philadelphia, and New York City (Mallach and Calavita 2010: 25). At this point, it also began to spread in Europe (Calavita 2006), first in England in 1990 and since then in one form or another in other parts of the world (Mallach 2010). In particular, the deregulation and privatization of social housing in England has led to the utilization of inclusionary housing.

In the last decade, due to increasing affordability problems, there has been a renewed interest among urban policymakers, planners, housing advocates, and urban scholars in the concept of inclusionary housing. In the context of predominant housing affordability problems, many countries or municipalities have adopted new, partly far-reaching IH legislations or programs in recent years as a means of producing affordable housing without direct public subsidies. As such, it is seen as a major planning and policy strategy to secure affordable housing, foster social inclusion, and tackle the housing affordability crises predominant in many urban areas today.

In New York City, inclusionary housing was first enacted only in Manhattan in 1987 as part of then-New York Mayor Edward Koch's (1978–1989) Ten-Year Housing Plan. While the Bloomberg administration expanded the program to all five boroughs, it was the self-proclaimed progressive Democrat Bill de Blasio, elected Mayor in 2013, who made the voluntary inclusionary zoning program mandatory in 2016. To ensure the housing program worked, de Blasio pushed through the biggest zoning changes in New York City since 1961. The program was part of a larger ambitious housing program, which sought to create 80,000 new low-cost homes and to preserve another 120,000 more homes – often referred to by de Blasio and other officials as "the country's most progressive housing program" (de Blasio 2016; Durkin 2016).

In England, inclusionary housing is known as Section 106 agreements because they are based on Section 106 of the Town and Country Planning Act (Section 106 or S106). In London, they have become the prime tool for creating affordable housing under the Boris Johnson administration (2008–2016). In 2016, Labour politician Sadiq Khan was elected Mayor of London. Known for being a social democrat, Khan's plan had been to use inclusionary housing to make affordable housing genuinely affordable, introducing new types of affordable housing across the spectrum of needs in 2018.

Despite the promising approaches of both Mayor's policies toward the creation of affordable housing, they were met with a level of public opposition: activists and housing advocates in both cities have accused the new requirements of not being far-reaching enough and exacerbating gentrification in low-income areas already under pressure from market forces (i.a. Architects for Social Housing 2017; Real Affordability for All 2016). Khan's Affordable Homes Programme has primarily been criticized for turning a blind eye to developers and housing associations for demolishing social housing and replacing it with other affordable housing tenures at much higher rents (Elmer 2019). Likewise, rather than seeing it as a progressive housing plan, activists and housing organizations have pilloried Mayor de Blasio's Mandatory Inclusionary Housing (MIH) Program as nothing but a gentrification plan. For them, building up to 80 percent market-rate housing in lower-income neighborhoods is nothing less than "a recipe for gentrification" (Farkas 2016).

In other words, while many politicians, housing advocates and mainstream academics alike praised both de Blasio's and Khan's housing programs for being progressive, many others criticized the very same programs for not doing enough to produce much-needed affordable housing or to foster social inclusion, of which the "poor door" is emblematic.

Researching Inclusionary Housing: Literature Review and Conceptual Framework

One Ambiguous Housing Program in the Wider Context of Privatization and Deregulation

Similarly, in the academic literature, inclusionary housing as a planning tool has avid supporters as well as its critics. There is a considerable body of literature on policies that pertain to inclusionary housing in the context of the USA (i.a. McClure 2008, Mallach 1984, Calavita and Mallach 2009, Schuetz, Meltzer, and Been 2011, Mukhija et al. 2015, Kontokosta 2016, McClure, Gurran, and Bramley 2017, Thaden and Wang 2017) and the UK (i.a. Crook and Whitehead 2002, Burgess, Monk, and Whitehead 2011; Monk 2010; Whitehead 2007, Crook and Monk 2011, Morrison and Burgess 2014, Crook, Henneberry, and Whitehead 2015, Gurran and Bramley 2017a) as well as internationally (i.a. Calavita and Mallach 2010, Austin, Gurran, and Whitehead 2014, Kam, Needham, and Buitelaar 2014, Helbrecht and Weber-Newht 2018).

Most of the scholars researching inclusionary housing policy in both the US and the UK consider it a very attractive political idea to provide low-income housing. It is seen as a benevolent local regulatory tool that holds the promise of solving several social problems such as the lack of affordable housing, social segregation, gentrification and its subsequent displacement of low-income households. Thus, this socially oriented regulation usually goes hand in hand with the paradigm of "social mix" and the political promise of a "city for all." Nico Calavita and Alan Mallach, for example, conclude in their comprehensive book on inclusionary housing that it "represents the best available means by which to link the provision of affordable housing to the compelling goal of social inclusion" (Calavita and Mallach 2010b: 382). In contrast to social housing estate development, inclusionary housing developments are geographically dispersed and thus aim at securing socially mixed communities and de-concentrating poverty (McClure 2008). In this sense, inclusionary housing is intended to work as an anti-gentrification and anti-displacement strategy since it places affordable housing in more affluent or gentrified areas where affordable housing development has become rather unlikely (Freeman and Schuetz 2016, Gurran and Bramley 2017a, Levy 2006, Tunstall 2012). Further, the creation of windfall profits by providing affordable housing through the marketplace is seen as a progressive way of profiting from real estate booms and ensuring that some of the private gains are given back to the public (Calavita and Mallach 2010, Helbrecht and Weber-Newth 2018, Monk 2010; Whitehead 2007). Overall, most scholars researching inclusionary housing consider it successful in delivering affordable housing (i.a. Hickey 2013; Monk 2010, Morrison and Burgess 2014, Li and Guo 2020, Whitehead 2007).

In terms of New York City, the 2016 enacted mandatory inclusionary housing program is seen as a "deepening political commitment towards fairer housing development" (Gurran and Bramley 2017b: 382) and as "emblematic of what planning for housing should be" (ibid.: 385). Yet despite all this positive policy attribution associated with inclusionary housing, concerns and criticism are numerous and on the rise (i.a. Angotti and Morse 2016a, Madden and Marcuse 2016, Newman 2018, Schuetz, Meltzer, and Been 2011; Stein 2018; Watt 2018a; Wolf-Powers 2019). On both sides of the Atlantic, many scholars question the implementation and the actual benefits of inclusionary housing. The main criticism is as follows:

First, numerous researchers have raised concern about the effects of inclusionary housing on housing production or the local housing market (i.a. Cheshire 2018, Bento et al. 2009, Mukhija et al. 2015, Schuetz, Meltzer, and Been 2011), while some are concerned that inclusionary housing might discourage new housing development as new developments seem to be less viable if developers are required to provide affordable housing units. This, they argue, results in fewer developments getting built, which in turn drives up local house and rent prices (Knapp, Bento and Lowe 2008). Others suggest that the effects of inclusionary housing are rather small or have no significant effects on the housing market (Schuetz, Meltzer, and Been 2011). Others still argue that inclusionary housing works best in high-rent neighborhoods where the potential to cross-subsidize affordable housing is higher, since higher financial returns can absorb the developer's cost of construction, and that in lower rent markets, subsidies and incentives are needed to mitigate the negative effects on developers (Mukhija et al. 2015, NYU Furman Center 2015). Meanwhile, some scholars have further criticized the concept for not challenging private market dynamics enough (i.a. Newman 2018, Stabrowski 2015) and have questioned the benefit of its distributional impacts (i.a. Stein 2018; Wolf-Powers 2019).

Second, researchers have raised concerns about the negotiation process of developer obligations. In England, one of the most common criticisms leveled at the negotiation process is its lack of transparency, particularly with regard to financial viability assessments. These are increasingly used as the basis for negotiating developers' contributions to individual development proposals and are primarily decisive in the question of how much affordable housing is created via Section 106 agreements (i.a. Colenutt, Cochrane, and Field 2015; Minton 2017: 34, Layard 2019). To put it simply, the assessment takes the total cost of a development project and subtracts it from the total projected income generated from selling the homes based on the current property value. Developers, therefore, often try to maximize the projected costs and minimize the projected sales value to make the development appear less viable, and like that, they can argue before the council that their project would not be profitable if they have to meet an affordable housing target (Wainwright 2015). One additional problem associated with these financial viability assessments is that the local councilors who are elected to decide on the development scheme are usually not allowed to see these assessments due to commercial confidentiality (i.a. Minton 2017: 35, Colenutt 2020: 115). In both cities, the process has further been criticized for the lack of guarantee that the affordable housing negotiated will actually get built. In particular, in London, after the credit crunch, developers frequently used their right to renegotiate the planning obligations, citing financial problems in order to reduce the number of affordable housing (Morrison and Burgess 2014).

Another criticism of the lack of transparency involved in the process is that community participation in the process is rather limited, and that community voices from primarily low-income communities are often ignored. Therefore, community representatives or residents are often frustrated about the lack of transparency involved in the negotiation process. In the eyes of the general public, many decisions seem to have been predetermined beforehand, as they are finalized behind "closed doors" or before the process officially starts (Angotti 2010; Watt 2018a).

Third, scholars questioning the programs' effectiveness in both producing affordable housing and fostering mixed communities (McAllister, 2017, Minton 2017; Watt 2018a, 2021) have contested the claim that these programs produce enough affordable housing and create income-integrated neighborhoods (Colenutt 2020: 118, Stein 2018). Studies and reports looking at London have found that inclusionary housing has in fact produced very little affordable housing, and that its affordability targets are insufficient to address the local communities' housing affordability problems (i.a. London Tenants Federation 2011, Ullman, Freedman-Schnapp, and Lander 2013).

Despite these wide-ranging concerns and criticisms, there has been very little discussion concerning the question of how inclusionary housing policies drive gentrification processes. From reviewing the literature, I have the impression that apart from some recent studies (Angotti and Morse 2016a, Layard 2018, Stabrowski 2015,

Stein 2018 and 2019), the wider academic debates on inclusionary housing fail to recognize the important insights to be potentially gained by linking inclusionary housing with gentrification processes. It is surprising when housing activists and local residents have time and again stressed how inclusionary housing leads to gentrification and displacement pressures.

Moreover, most scholars researching inclusionary housing have analyzed it in the wider context of privatization and deregulation. For example, in their comprehensive book on inclusionary housing, Mallach and Calavita emphasized that in order to understand the emergence and evolution of inclusionary housing policies, it is essential to analyze the changing roles of the public and private sectors and the growth of privatization and deregulation in both the housing and the planning system (Calavita and Mallach 2010c). Many scholars have followed Calavita and Mallach in analyzing the changes in the housing and planning system to understand how inclusionary housing emerged and is institutionally embedded across different countries (i.a. Alves 2022; Austin, Gurran, and Whitehead 2014, Gurran and Bramley 2017c, Kam, Needham, and Buitelaar 2014).

Although the literature on inclusionary housing takes into account the wider historical context of privatization and deregulation, it has until now had little to say about the influence of neoliberal urbanism on inclusionary housing, except for some recent case studies (i.a. Alves 2022, Fox-Rogers and Murphy 2015, Santoro 2019, Stabrowski 2015, Newman 2018; Stein 2016). And that even though the neoliberal urban restructuring of housing policy has been analyzed in detail on both sides of the Atlantic – in the context of the USA (i.a. Hackworth 2011, Marcuse and Keating 2006, Schwartz 2010) and NYC (i.a. DeFilippis and Wyly 2008, Kadi and Ronald 2016, Madden and Marcuse 2016) as well as the UK (i.a. Hodkinson and Robbins 2013, Hodkinson, Watt, and Mooney 2013; Malpass 2005; Murie 2009) and London (i.a. Hamnett 2003; Lees 2014; Watt 2009, 2021).

Following the global financial crisis of 2008, the effectiveness of the approach to deliver affordable housing through the planning system has come under close scrutiny by policymakers and academics alike on both sides of the Atlantic. Several scholars have discussed the impact of the financial meltdown on inclusionary housing approaches, pointing out how the recession immensely reduced the delivery of affordable housing (i.a. Crook and Monk 2011, Burgess and Monk 2012, Hickey 2013, Mallach and Calavita 2010, Morrison and Burgess 2014). However, less attention has been given to the impact of the austerity measures that were adopted by both national governments and devolved to local governments as a response to the global financial crisis of 2008 – measures that seriously affected the conditions of urban governance, and, as a result the provision of affordable housing via the planning system.

Therefore, in this study, I examine inclusionary housing within the context of austerity urbanism and policy-led gentrification. As such, I address two research gaps that I detected within the literature on inclusionary housing. My overall question guiding this research is, therefore, the following: In what way do inclusionary housing approaches in London and New York City intersect with gentrification and low-income household displacement in an age of austerity?

In the following, I build a conceptual framework by presenting the literature of inclusionary housing in relation to new-build gentrification, and to what has since become known as "austerity urbanism" (Peck 2012) before turning to define my own contribution to the ongoing debate.

Inclusionary Housing and Austerity Urbanism

Following the global financial crisis of 2008, falling house prices and reduced mortgage supply not only reduced the housing supply but also weakened the negotiation power of local authorities. As many developers requested to renegotiate affordable housing obligations citing financial viability issues, local authorities came under pressure to allow development to go ahead to meet their overall housing targets. Drawing on empirical research in England, Morrison and Burgess (2014), for example, highlighted various ways in which local authorities had to make compromises with developers that often ended in reduced planning obligations for developers. Burgess and Monk (2012) reported that about 40 percent of the renegotiated agreements in England reduced inclusionary housing goals.

The impact of austerity policies on inclusionary housing policies and practices has yet to be researched by scholars focusing on inclusionary housing. National austerity policies have involved fiscal retrenchments, the devolution of governmental risk and responsibilities to municipal and local tiers of government, as well as outsourcing and privatizing governmental services and cutbacks to social welfare. The impact of these policies is felt and seen most acutely in cities, where, as Jamie Peck describes it, it is in cities "where austerity bites" (Peck 2012: 629). Cities primarily host those groups such as the poor, working-class or minorities that are predominantly reliant on social services and, thus, the main target of austerity-driven welfare reforms (Donald et al. 2014; Meegan et al. 2014; Peck 2014). This evident urban dimension of the localized effects of these restrictive governmental budget cuts and welfare reforms is what Peck calls "austerity urbanism" (Peck 2014). These groups are also the ones that are reliant on the provision of affordable housing. Studying the impact of austerity policies on inclusionary housing policies and practices thus helps shed light on how the poor, working-class and people of color are affected by austerity measures.

In the context of the UK, the Conservative-led government implemented in 2010 drastic public cuts in spending and welfare reforms on the grounds that they were necessary to reduce the budget deficit, which sharply rose in the market crash. It was in this context that the Coalition government pushed forward with its political program of the "Big Society" and austerity localism. The program, in a word, redefined the relationship between citizens and the state through decentralizing power to local authorities, promoting charity-based welfare, and empowering communities to play a more active role in public service provision (Clarke and Cochrane 2013: 12, Hodkinson and Robbins, 2013: 64). According to Taylor-Gooby (2012: 61), these changes signal "the most far-reaching and precipitate attempt to achieve fundamental restructuring in an established welfare state in a larger Western economy in recent years" (Taylor-Gooby 2012: 61).

Numerous scholars have researched the impact of austerity measures in the UK on local authorities (i.a. Deas and Doyle 2013, Gardner and Lowndes 2016, Besussi 2016, Lowndes and Gardner 2016, Fuller and West 2017, McAllister 2018, Panton and Walters 2018, Penny 2017, Pill 2018), housing policies (i.a. Hodkinson and Robbins 2013, Gillespie, Hardy, and Watt 2021; Hamnett 2014; Watt 2018b) as well as the planning system (i.a. Colenutt 2020; Haughton and Hincks 2013). Even though the impact of austerity measures was significant in all aspects related to inclusionary housing – seen in local governments' lack of resources and capacities, and the deregulation of town planning, as well as cuts in social housing expenditures – inclusionary housing was rarely discussed explicitly in relation to austerity measures in the literature. Authors have instead mentioned inclusionary housing as a side note when discussing shifts in urban governance, housing and planning policy and practice. One of the most discussed issues has, for example, been the introduction of the policy of viability assessments into planning as a result of austerity measures, where it has significantly reduced the amount of affordable housing delivered through the planning system and increased the profits of the developers and landowners (i.a. Colenutt 2020; Colenutt, Cochrane, and Field 2015, Ferm and Raco 2020, Layard 2019; Minton 2017).

Most scholars who have researched inclusionary housing approaches in relation to these new shifts have described them as technocratic or post-political planning as opposed to being an explicit part of austerity urbanism.

In recent planning theory, planning scholars have, for example, proclaimed the rise of a new urban technocracy, in which private actors have become increasingly influential in urban planning systems, and thus have changed the nature of the decision-making process (i.a. Savini and Raco 2019). The legal scholar Antonia Layard (2019), for example, examines in this context the role of viability assessments in planning decisions. According to her, "few modern planning practices illustrate the growing quantitative technocracy in the English planning system as clearly as viability assessments for affordable housing" (Layard 2019: 213). Viability assessments are dominated by "commercial calculative practices" (ibid.: 214) that determine the question of profitability of development proposals, usually evaluated by private consultants instructed by developers or local authorities.

This influence of non-state actors in the planning process has often also been understood as a post-political condition (Mouffe 2005, Swyngedouw 2009) of urban governance, where "consensus rules and politics and political agency is virtually pre-ordained" (Beveridge et al. 2014: 67). Local authorities and urban planners subsequently only follow what real estate agents and experts dictate, thereby reducing their realm of political actions. However, the urban scholars Helbrecht and Weber-Newth (2018) argue that inclusionary housing can be seen as a possibility to "recover the politics of planning" (Helbrecht and Weber-Newth 2018). For example, they recognize the post-political context inclusionary housing is currently situated but argue that the negotiations around land value recapture and affordable housing provision can challenge the "dominant neoliberal post-political discourse in urban development" (Helbrecht and Weber-Newth 2017: 75, transl. by author).

In their view, inclusionary housing represents state intervention into private development as well as a tool for funding public infrastructure such as affordable housing and fostering social mixing. In this sense, the two authors follow the general argument that inclusionary housing delivers progressive and redistributive effects that I intend to challenge with this study.

In the context of the US, the term austerity has rarely been used officially, even though the US has similarly experienced the implementation of austerity measures, albeit in a more uneven and less explicit fashion than in the UK (Peck 2018). Jamie Peck argues that the practice of austerity has been more "normalized and localized" (Peck 2012: 627) in the US, as it has been forced upon local governments for the last 50 years, with the declarations of bankruptcy by Detroit, Michigan, and several Californian cities as only the most recent and explicit manifestations of austerity urbanism. The federal government's cuts in spending and welfare reforms have led local governments all over the US (but again unevenly) into financial difficulties, leading them to fundamentally restructure their local budgets and to privatize public services as a form of fiscal crisis management.

Critical urban scholars have thus placed austerity urbanism in the aftermath of the financial crisis of 2008 in a wider historical field of neoliberal reform and transformation, pointing out that it is not a new mandated program of restructuring (i.a. Peck 2012, Davidson and Ward 2018). According to Peck (2012: 629), the governing logic of austerity marks "a particular intensification of neoliberal restructuring strategies" in cities. As such, the management of New York City's fiscal crisis in 1975 became a blueprint for neoliberal restructuring of urban governance or what later would be called austerity urbanism, characterized by fiscal retrenchments, devolution of governmental risk and responsibilities, outsourcing and privatization of governmental services and cutbacks to social welfare. The difference between the 1970s and more recent adoptions of austerity measures is that today, they target an already neoliberalized (inter)governmental system (Peck 2020).

Kathe Newman (2018) is the only scholar who has explicitly discussed the origin and evolution of inclusionary housing in the context of austerity urbanism in the US. She explores the history of inclusionary housing in New York City, demonstrating how inclusionary housing reflects the new conditions of urban governance in an age of austerity (Newman 2018: 129). However, she has so far left the question unanswered of whether the most recently adopted mandatory inclusionary housing program by Mayor de Blasio can break out of the loop of neoliberalism and produce and preserve affordable housing across the income spectrum of need (Newman 2018: 142).

Following Newman, I place my research in the context of austerity urbanism to explore in what way the most recent inclusionary housing approaches highlight or break with the neoliberal paradigm of public-private urban governance relations. By tracing the evolution of inclusionary housing in London and New York City and assessing local authorities' planning practices in negotiating inclusionary housing while coping with the austerity measures placed on them, I demonstrate how local governments contribute to gentrification and displacement.

Inclusionary Housing and New-Build Gentrification

Urban scholars researching the relationship between social mix policies, urban re-generation and gentrification have long argued that social mix policies promote and spur gentrification processes (i.a. Lees 2008, Bridge, Butler, and Lees 2012, Davidson 2012). Indeed, a wealth of existing literature on gentrification and con-temporary social mix policies already involves complex analyses and theoretical debates on social mix as a policy concept, the factors and processes leading to inner-city regeneration as well as the (mainly negative) economic, social and cul-tural impacts it has on incumbent residents and their communities. Nevertheless, in the literature on gentrification and social mix, inclusionary housing policies are rarely mentioned, and in those rare cases where they are, the policies are merely mentioned as one form of social mix policy among many others (i.a. Hodkinson and Robbins 2013, Lees 2008, Madden and Marcuse 2016, Rosen and Walks 2016, Watt 2009).

In the gentrification literature, it has also been debated whether new construc-tion activities fall under the definition of gentrification. Due to the lack of direct displacement of low-income groups, some scholars have argued that new-build development does not fall into the category of gentrification (Lambert and Broddy 2002, Boddy 2007, Hamnett 2003). As a response, other urban scholars have coun-ter-argued that new-build activities do in fact count as gentrification, as they can lead to both direct and indirect displacement (Davidson and Lees 2005, 2010). Since then, the concept of new-build gentrification[9] has been picked up in a wide range of studies describing new urban transformation processes across the globe, such as in London (ibid.), Tokyo (Lützeler 2008), Berlin (Holm 2010; Marquardt et al. 2013), cities in Switzerland (Rérat et al. 2010), Shanghai (He 2008), Cape Town (Visser and Kotze 2008) and post-socialist cities such as Leipzig in Germany and Łódź in Polen (Holm, Marcińczak, and Ogrodowczyk 2015).

As it takes different forms across time and place, there is no clear definition of new-build gentrification, but reviewing the central arguments in the exist-ing gentrification literature, some defining features emerge. Davidson and Lees (2005) defined gentrification – including new-build gentrification – in the widest sense, as a process comprising of four basic elements: "(1) reinvestment of capital, (2) social upgrading of locale by incoming high-income groups, (3) landscape change, and (4) direct or indirect displacement of low-income groups" (Davidson and Lees 2005: 1170). In the following, I recapitulate some of the arguments given by previous researchers on new-build gentrification and inclusionary housing.

In terms of reinvestment of capital, a central theme within the literature is that new-build gentrification is often associated with state-led gentrification, in which the state is involved as a major driving force behind the social transformation of formerly neglected or low-income neighborhoods. Prime examples of this are the replacement of social housing estates with new mixed-income communities (Watt 2009, 2021), or large-scale residential development on brownfield sites in city cent-ers such as along the Thames in London, which has led to social upgrading along the waterfront despite affordable housing requirements (Davidson and Lees 2005).

Across the new-build gentrification literature, the state is often described as taking an active role in neighborhood change, promoting socially mixed communities and urban densification (Hedin et al. 2012; Murphy 2008; Ortega 2016). Davidson and Lees described this as a "negotiated process of gentrification in which the state engages with developers to produce regeneration cooperatively" (Davidson and Lees 2005: 1175). In other words, the state engages with developers to direct large-scale economic capital into formerly neglected areas or low-income neighborhoods.

The few studies that explicitly examine the relationship between inclusionary housing and gentrification support the theory that new-build gentrification is often a state-initiated process that is negotiated between the state and developers. Stein (2018), who also examined Mandatory Inclusionary Housing in New York City, found that it is used as a state-led geographical strategy for capital accumulation in areas that were not yet experiencing gentrification (Stein 2018: 7). This process, which he called "planning gentrification" (Stein 2019), is planned by the state, produced by the developer and ultimately consumed by the condominium residents. More empirical and comparative studies are, however, needed to provide a more detailed account of the role of the state in relation to new-build gentrification and inclusionary housing.

The new-build gentrification literature has further pointed out how new residential development involves the social upgrading of affected neighborhoods and various forms of displacement. Davidson and Lees argue that the massive influx of a large population of high-income earners into formerly neglected neighborhoods has a gentrifying effect on the surrounding communities (Davidson and Lees 2005: 1184). In this case, it matters little if the development does not involve direct displacement, as both indirect displacement and displacement pressures are likewise factors related to gentrification (Marcuse 1985). Furthermore, policy programs that aim at social mixing or urban densification have further set in motion indirect displacement or opened up low-income neighborhoods to displacement pressure (i.a. Lees, Loretta, Tim Butler, and Gary Bridge 2012, Stabrowski 2014). Many new-build gentrification studies have associated the process also with significant amounts of direct displacement (Bromley and Mackie 2009, He 2010). Davidson described new-build gentrification as "a more commodified process" (Davidson 2018: 258) in which the gentrifier is the purchaser or renter of a usually luxury apartment. Studies on new-build gentrification thus show that these gentrifiers usually represent the local elite from the financial, technological, and service sectors and – as high-income residents – are more interested in living in high-end apartment buildings situated in urban centers (Rérat et al. 2010) than in the socio-cultural diverse neighborhoods as the classical gentrifier (Glass 1964).

Studies that have focused on the relation between gentrification and inclusionary housing have already provided some insights into how neighborhoods change as a result of inclusionary housing. In New York City, Angotti and Morse (2016a) examined neighborhood change following city-initiated rezonings[10]. They note that inclusionary zoning[11] in practice meant 80 percent of new housing was dedicated to luxury housing, translating to an influx of upscale residents in the area. In turn, this led to gentrification pressures in and substantial displacement of low-income communities predominately populated by people of color (Angotti and Morse 2016: 70). The case study of Greenpoint-Williamsburg (DePaolo and Morse 2016), included in the book, underlines this argument. Other authors who have also investigated neighborhood change in Greenpoint-Williamsburg after the 2005 waterfront rezoning supported the theory that affordable housing created through inclusionary zoning was not able to prevent, but rather facilitated gentrification and displacement of the residing low-income communities (Stabrowski 2015, Susser 2012). While these examples provide some insight into neighborhood change as a result of state-initiated upzonings, more research is needed in the context of developer-initiated gentrification as a result of inclusionary housing development projects.

With respect to what Davidson and Lees call landscape change, the new-build gentrification literature reveals some typical spatial patterns: New residential development occurs as small- or large-scale development throughout the city in already gentrified neighborhoods, making the neighborhoods even more expensive and homogeneous enclaves (Holm 2010; Lees 2003), or in lower-income neighborhoods (Davidson 2008), or on formerly industrial brownfield areas redeveloped for residential use (Davidson and Lees 2010). According to Holm et al. (2015: 167), the spatial context of new-build gentrification has, however, not been analyzed systematically.

Similarly, only a few studies have empirically explored the spatial distribution of affordable housing through inclusionary housing (Hickey 2013, Kontokosta 2015, Li and Guo 2020, NYU Furman Center 2015, Morrison and Burgess 2014, Whitehead 2007). With respect to England in particular, existing research has emphasized that the discretionary nature of the negotiation process has often led to a great variation in the spatial distribution of inclusionary housing developments (i.a. Morrison and Burgess 2014, Li and Guo 2020, Whitehead 2007).

Overall, the literature does not provide a clear picture of the spatial distribution of inclusionary housing developments. Particularly in the US, some reports state that inclusionary housing works best in areas with high rent, as the additional zoning density can cross-subsidize affordable housing and thus not require direct public subsidies (Hickey 2013; Kober 2020; NYU Furman Center 2015). Schwartz et al. (2012) examined eleven inclusionary housing programs across the Unites States and found that most of the affordable homes created through inclusionary housing were located in low-poverty neighborhoods. They, however, found that five out of the eleven programs studied provided "affordable housing" for households earning up to 100 or 120 percent of the Area Median Income (AMI) and that most of the provided homes were for sale, thus serving relatively more-advantaged households than low-income ones (Schwartz et al. 2012). Kontokosta (2015) studied inclusionary housing policies in the two US counties of Montgomery County, Maryland, and Suffolk County, New York, between 1980 and 2000. She found that there was significant variation in the spatial distribution of inclusionary housing homes across the two cases studied (Kontokosta 2015: 588). Nevertheless, her results indicate that inclusionary housing in Montgomery County has been more often sited in low-poverty areas, whereas in Suffolk County, they have been predominantly placed in low-income neighborhoods with high Black and Hispanic populations (ibid.: 586).

More recent studies in New York City and London also pointed out that inclusionary housing developments are more likely to be placed in disadvantaged neighborhoods (Angotti 2016a; Li and Guo 2020; Stein 2018).

After going over the arguments given by previous research, it is evident that more empirical and comparative research is needed on the various practices and effects of inclusionary housing within and across contexts as well as its relationship to new-build gentrification. Although inclusionary housing takes different forms in different contexts and places, through tracing out its defining features, it is possible to examine how inclusionary housing produces urban change and neighborhood class-based transformations. The question of where and how affordable units are built under inclusionary housing can in this way also help to study the socio-spatial context of new-build gentrification. Other questions that concern the patterns of mix produced between the different tenure types, or the actual beneficiaries of the affordable housing created, provide insight into the 'reality' of mixing within new-build income developments or apparent wider neighborhood diversity. Similarly, unraveling how inclusionary housing policies have become incorporated into middle-class and luxury housing development can help to understand how new-build gentrification has become part of broader politico-economic processes through state planning – a process about which we still know too little, according to Davidson (2018: 259) but which the present study will aim to shed light on.

Gentrification through the Back Door: Conceptualizing the Socio-Spatial Practices and Effects of Inclusionary Housing

In reviewing the literature on inclusionary housing, there is surprisingly scarce discussion and evidence on the way that inclusionary housing intersects with gentrification and displacement in an age of austerity. This book's ambition, therefore, is to close this research gap by providing an empirical research-based perspective on the socio-spatial dimension of the political policy strategies, processes and consequences of inclusionary housing approaches in New York City and London.

The intention is to significantly advance the critique of inclusionary housing by showing how inclusionary housing policies are accepted and implemented – often uncritically – by various levels of governance in the face of evidence that suggests limited success of such policies' provision of affordable housing or social inclusion and, above all, their promotion of the very gentrification and displacement mechanisms they are intended to counteract.

By posing the research question of how inclusionary housing intersects with gentrification and displacement in times of austerity, I raise important questions about how inclusionary housing policy strategies and practices are implicated in the social and spatial transformation of particularly lower-income inner-city neighborhoods, and, therefore of the larger city itself in an age of austerity.

To this end, the overall research question is guided by three sub-questions that will be dealt with throughout this book: first, regarding the political policy strategies, the question will be in what way do inclusionary housing policies in both cities promote new-build gentrification? Second, in terms of inclusionary housing practices, in what way do local and planning authorities contribute to gentrification, thereby preparing the ground for later displacement? And thirdly, the question of how new-build mixed-income developments influence gentrification and displacement processes.

The literature review further reveals that inclusionary housing has rarely been placed in the wider context of austerity urbanism or new-build gentrification. The goal of this book is, thus, to tread new ground in the study of inclusionary housing. Placing it within these two debates allows a rethink of the role of the local state in the socio-spatial dimension of inclusionary housing. With respect to austerity urbanism, I explore the changing "realities" of urban governance and the way these might affect local governments' approaches and socio-spatial practices as well as their effects on inclusionary housing.

In the context of new-build gentrification, local authorities are seen as major drivers of neighborhood upgrading, commonly known as state-led gentrification, often driven by "rhetorically and discursively disguised [...] social mix policies" (Lees, Butler, and Bridge 2012: 1) that aim at bringing middle-income households into low-income neighborhoods. Although inclusionary housing policies embody social mix policies like few others, they have been rarely examined explicitly in relation to gentrification efforts in the literature as outlined above.

In this book, I apply the concept of state-led gentrification to the context of inclusionary housing policies and practices in order to examine the role of the local state as a catalyst of the socio-spatial restructuring of the city. However, instead of focusing on the local state itself, as in the concept of state-led gentrification, I focus on the process, that is, on *how* the local state – alongside other private actors – contributes to gentrification through its inclusionary housing policies. For this purpose, as my central thesis, I introduce a new concept to critically explore inclusionary housing in the context of urban austerity: *gentrification through the back door*.

Although the idea of *gentrification through the back door* is a rather metaphorical one, it is based on a visible, palpable and concrete structure: the "poor doors." The idea of *gentrification through the back door* is further substantiated by "real" experiences of residents, housing activists and rather progressive housing advocates who have accused inclusionary housing of being a Trojan horse for gentrification and displacement. For them, these doors exhibit the "polarized patterns of gentrifying affluence and relative poverty" (Evans 2014: 127) on a micro-spatial level.

I started this study as ethnographic research on 'poor doors' in London and New York City. This ethnographic focus on "poor door" practices helped me to critically look at the housing program behind these practices. In other words, it was literally through the 'poor door' that led me to a broader analysis of inclusionary housing.

It is, therefore, the study of these actual physical doors as well as peoples' "real" experiences with said doors that allowed me to see "poor doors" as a metaphor for the myriad problems with inclusionary housing. This metaphor evokes how inclusionary housing regulations and practices result in mixed-income developments that are characterized by exclusion rather than inclusion. Put simply, I intend to use this concept of *gentrification through the back door* to examine the way inclusionary housing policies and practices produce and shape space according to certain goals and logic pursued by specific political as well as private actors.

There are various ways inclusionary housing leads to *gentrification through a back door*. As such, in the chapters that follow, I present detailed accounts of these various socio-spatial practices and effects of inclusionary housing in New York City and London. In other words, each chapter depicts a way of how inclusionary housing policies and practices, disguised as benevolent programs by local governments, offer an indirect channel to radical and often negative neighborhood transformations, and in doing so, together, the chapters will contribute to the critical debate around inclusionary housing in greater depth than what is found in the current literature.

This study also delves into a variety of other topics and debates related to urban transformation and development, such as post-neoliberalism, land value capture, financialization of housing, urban design and vertical urbanism. The state of research on these topics is discussed in more detail in the respective chapters.

Finally, I will approach inclusionary housing through a comparative historical, political, geographical as well as ethnographic case study of its policies, practices and effects in London and New York City.

Approaching Inclusionary Housing: Methods and National and Local Context

Comparing Inclusionary Housing in New York City and London

New York City and London represent the Anglo-American hegemony in urban studies, from which many urban theories have spread to the rest of the world. As such, they have been models for urban development and gentrification processes and "testing grounds" for neoliberal urban policies (DeFilippis and Wyly 2008, Fainstein 2010, Hamnett 2003).

Comparing London and New York City is, therefore, neither very innovative nor something novel in the field of urban studies. They have been the subject of many urban comparisons, in particular in the context of "global cities," housing neoliberalization, urban redevelopment and gentrification (Fainstein 1994; Harloe, Marcuse, and Smith 1992; Lees 1994, Carpenter and Lees 1995, Sassen 2001, Marom and Carmon 2015).

More recently, urban scholars have, therefore, called for more comparative urban studies that include cities from the Global South in order to break with the universalizing northern theory formation (i.a. Lees 2018, McFarlane 2010, Peck 2015, Roy 2009, Robinson 2015). Research on inclusionary housing is a case in point: Inclusionary housing has been studied extensively in the context of the Global North, notably in the US and UK, but there exists a huge research gap in the context of cities from the Global South that have implemented this planning instrument, such as Brazil, China, Colombia, India, Israel, and Malaysia.

So why study New York and London – again? First, I focus on New York and London because these two cities provide the most prominent examples of the "poor door." In both cities, recent inclusionary housing approaches have been used as progressive public policy responses to the affordable housing shortage, and they have been framed in the context of urban austerity as an economic necessity and an instrument for social justice. Despite different inclusionary housing approaches in each city, the "poor door" occurs as a repeated urban outcome of such approaches. Thus, I use the seemingly serial reproduction of the "poor door" as a reason to question the socio-spatial strategies, practices and effects of recent inclusionary housing approaches in both cities.

Second, inclusionary housing has been extensively studied and compared on the national level (i.a. Austin, Gurran, and Whitehead 2014, Calavita 2006, Helbrecht and Weber-Newth 2018, Kam, Needham, and Buitelaar 2014) or across different jurisdictions within a national framework, in particular the US (Mallach 1984, Calavita and Mallach 2009, Schuetz, Meltzer, and Been 2011, Mukhija et al. 2015, Kontokosta 2016, McClure et al. 2017, Thaden and Wang 2017, Wang and Balachandran 2021) and the UK (Crook and Whitehead 2002, Burgess et al. 2011; Monk 2010; Whitehead 2007, Crook and Monk 2011, Morrison and Burgess 2014, Crook et al. 2015). Inclusionary housing, however, has rarely been discussed in the context of cities, with the exception of some recent studies of Bogota and São Paulo (Santoro 2019), Montreal, Vancouver, and Toronto (Mah and Hackworth 2011), Gothenburg and Stuttgart (Granath Hansson 2019), and cities in China (Huang 2015). Despite several research studies comparing the US and the UK in their approaches to inclusionary housing (Calavita 2006; Gurran et al. 2008), New York City and London have yet to be compared. Most of the comparative research on inclusionary housing between the UK and the US focuses on the origin and evolution of inclusionary housing and highlights both the similarities and national differences in their governance, housing and planning systems. In acknowledging contextual differences, a comparison between New York City and London offers potential for cross-urban learning by allowing a deeper analysis of the contemporary particularities of the spatial practices and effects of inclusionary housing between but also within these two cities.

In the US context, critically examining NYC's inclusionary housing policy means criticizing one of the most progressive housing policies. This has led to criticism of my research on several occasions. Most recently at a conference themed "Comparative Urbanism: Global Perspectives" in Atlanta, Georgia, in 2019, I presented some preliminary results of my research, and after my presentation in the Q&A round, some of the American participants argued that New York City was miles ahead of most other cities in the country in terms of its housing policies and addressing the need of its poor. By criticizing New York's inclusionary housing policies, I am questioning one of the most progressive policy agendas in the country, and, in the view of certain Americans, that is problematic. Their views, however, only substantiated my choice of case studies. Because of the notability of New York's housing policy within the US, it is essential to think outside the "national box." Thus, comparing New York City's inclusionary housing policies and practices to London's – where the program has produced far more "affordable housing" than in New York City, albeit not enough and mostly unaffordable for low-income households – can generate new insights into the field of inclusionary housing in both cities. Moreover, the stated progressive goals of inclusionary housing provide a further opportunity to examine cases such as New York City's newly implemented inclusionary housing program, which could serve as a model for other local governments.

Third, New York and London are ideal for the exploration of the spatial dimensions of inclusionary housing practices because of the existence of similar recent trends in housing and urban development: Both cities are struggling with how to mitigate their respective housing affordability crises, characterized by escalating housing prices, deteriorating housing affordability, overcrowding of dwellings, insecure housing tenures, longer social housing waiting lists and increasing homelessness. In the context of gentrification, the process has accelerated in both cities over the past decade. Studying how inclusionary housing and new-build gentrification intersect in both cities sheds more light not only on inclusionary housing practices but also on the factors leading to gentrification.

National and Local Conditions in Comparative Perspective

Together with Tokyo, New York City and London are regarded as preeminent global cities, performing a vital role within the contemporary world system (Sassen 2001). Both cities are very similar in size, population, density, economic strength, diversity, and desirability, and have undergone similar, though of course not identical, processes of urban restructuring and change. At the same time, they have strikingly different national traditions of welfare state, different local government and planning systems as well as different approaches to land value recapture and definitions of affordable housing. In the chapters to come, I will touch upon some of these different traditions, structures as well as definitions in my analysis of inclusionary housing.

In the following, differences as well as similarities between national contexts and local conditions are highlighted due to their importance in understanding the particularities of inclusionary housing in New York City and London.

Traditions of Welfare State Provision

Although both countries differ in their traditions of welfare state provision, both countries have adopted inclusionary housing programs. Alan Mallach, however, points out that "the specific approach characterized as an inclusionary housing program is largely an American phenomenon" (Mallach 1984: 21). He argues that the dominant ideology in the US has always been – even at the peak of federal housing programs – the belief that the provision of affordable housing is a private sector responsibility (ibid.: 22). This is in line with what Tony Crook describes as different attitudes to privatism (Crook 1996: 52). He argues that England generally had bigger ambitions in confronting private interests and implemented much bigger federal housing programs in the heyday of the welfare state during the 1940s and 1950s. Privatism in the US has much deeper roots, where the welfare state has never reached the same extent in the US as it did in England. It is, therefore, also not surprising that even though inclusionary housing has its roots in the American context, it has been used more productively in England than in the US (Calavita 2006).

Local Governance Structure

With respect to governance structures, New York City is governed by a mayor and the City Council. The mayor determines the city's overall political direction, and the City Council is the law-making body of the city. It determines the city budget, monitors city agencies and reviews matters on a variety of issues such as land-use. In contrast to New York City's political institutions, London's governing bodies are fairly new, having been established only in 2000[12]. Since then, London has been governed by the Mayor of London and the London Assembly that together form the Greater London Authority (GLA), which derives its powers primarily from the Greater London Authority Act of 1999 and 2007. The Greater London Authority is, among other things, responsible for the London Plan – the statutory spatial development strategy for the Greater London area that sets out mayor guidelines in areas such as housing or planning that the 32 London Boroughs must follow.

Since the UK is a unitary state in which the central government is supreme, all local authorities are required to prepare comprehensive local development plans to outline strategic planning policies for their areas that abide by the rules and goals laid out in the central government's higher development plans (Crook 1996: 63). In contrast, the US is a federal government system. This means every US state has considerable autonomy over how to control its land. The states usually delegate their power and responsibilities given to them by the US Constitution to their counties or municipalities which has traditionally strengthened local governments and made it easier for local authorities to adopt policy agendas that are opposed by the national administration in power (Fainstein 1994: 81). This "local parochialism" (Crook 1996: 63) in effect means that New York City can produce its own zoning ordinances without necessarily having to abide to higher authorities or other zoning ordinances.

Planning System

Another essential distinction between the two countries is their strategic approach to land use planning. In the US, inclusionary housing is generally referred to as inclusionary zoning, since zoning has been the primary means of local authorities to regulate land use for nearly a century. Zoning regulations dictate how land is divided spatially and rigidly for specific uses and prescribe, among other things, setbacks, sizes, and heights of the built environment. These zoning plans, however, differ from development plans. Zoning plans in the US are designed to specify what kind of development is allowed where, without necessarily having to abide to higher authorities or policy frameworks. As such, they are much more rigid and binding than development plans in the UK (Crook 1996: 52).

Even though development plans are guided by a national policy framework in the UK – in contrast to the US – local authorities generally have great discretionary power in granting or refusing planning permission if planning applications do not conform to higher policy frameworks. And while in both countries, the goals of the land use regulatory system are generally the same, as in most land use frameworks, the UK differs from the US in that it has one clear additional planning goal: It tries to meet expected housing needs by implementing the policy framework that is determined at the national and regional level (Monk 2010: 134). Thus, in the UK, it is more accepted that the planning system plays an important role in meeting local or regional housing requirements for low- to middle-income households since it is supported on the national level (Austin et al. 2014: 469).

Nevertheless, after the 1980s and the privatization approach of the Thatcher government in Great Britain, the reliance on the market in providing services that formerly belonged to the public sector, such as the provision of social housing, represented a shift towards US housing policies. Since then, there have been notably more similarities than in the past between the American and English planning systems. Not only has the need to deliver affordable housing through the planning system moved them closer to one another, but "the US has become more negotiative while the English system more rule-bound" (Crook 1996: 67). This means that local development plans now have a stronger policy frame in England than previously, whereas in states or cities in the US where inclusionary housing programs were implemented, there are more and more site-by-site negotiations between local planning authorities and developers (ibid.). Since zoning ordinances generally protect rather than confront private interests (ibid.: 52), it is harder in the US to place housing requirements within the zoning ordinances. Thus, some states or cities, among them New York City, predicate the provision of affordable housing on the condition of upzoning. In other words, inclusionary housing gets triggered if a developer wants to change the zoning plans, such as building denser or higher in a certain area.

Approaches to Land Value Recapture

The concept of "land value recapture" is not a new concept, but in the last two decades, it has gained popularity in planning practices as a tool for local governments to compensate for the dwindling subsidies from higher levels of government in the US, Europe and elsewhere internationally (i.a. Fainstein 2012, McAlister et al. 2018). It describes policies intended to "secure societal benefits from increases in land value that can arise from changes to land use rights through the planning system and/or investment in public infrastructure" (McAllister et al. 2019: 316). The idea behind the concept is that the landowner or developer should not benefit from the increased property values generated by public action. Since they did not produce the increase in land value through their private investment, it belongs to the society at large and, thus, should be recaptured for public benefit. There are various land use regulations or policies that embody the concept of land value recapture, of which inclusionary housing is just one variant. Other forms are land use exactions, impact fees or taxes.

In England, the recapture of the increased land value, better known as betterment or planning gain, has become part of the "planning consensus" in the UK (Calavita and Mallach 2010: 369). Since England nationalized development rights in 1947, the public sector owns the development rights, which means that developers must obtain planning obligations for all kinds of developments or their change in use. It also means that local authorities have the power to control development and to set specific obligations as a precondition for planning approval (Monk 2010; Whitehead 2007, Crook 1996). Since the Town and Planning Act of 1990, developers in England have been further required to contribute to the public infrastructure (e.g. public parks, roads, schools, affordable housing) to mitigate the impact of their development and to eliminate windfall profits for the landowner. The legally binding planning obligations placed on the developer ensure that the developer makes a contribution to the community when it is assumed that the development will have a significant impact on the local area. In this way, the increase in land value is recaptured for public benefit, "making landowners pay for its costs" (Calavita 2006: 9). In other words, in this site-by-site decision-making process, in cases where a developer refuses to make affordable housing contributions, or the contributions are considered unreasonably low, local authorities generally have the power to deny planning permission on the grounds of "material consideration."

In contrast, land value recapture is not part of the planning culture in the US. The development rights are part of the property rights that are safeguarded by the US Constitution – more specifically in the Fifth Amendment – that prohibits that "private property is [sic] taken for public use, without just compensation"[13]. This makes it difficult to recapture development values without providing "just compensation." Local authorities in the US have therefore applied the concept of land value recapture to specific zoning techniques or various types of exactions such as impact fee, linkage fee or payment in lieu but rarely framed it explicitly as a land value recapture tool (Kim 2020: 1). Nevertheless, city administrations always fear that real estate groups might challenge inclusionary housing laws as infringing on private property rights.

In New York City, the recapture of value from real estate development arises – similar to London – as a condition for planning permission. There are, however, considerable differences between London and New York City when this process is triggered that are important to mention here, impacting as they do the way inclusionary housing requirements are negotiated during these procedures.

In New York City, the majority of development is done "as-of-right," which means the proposed development matches the given zoning regulations of the area and the developer can build without having to go through a public land use review process, which is called Uniform Land Use Review Procedure (ULURP). This review process provides a formalized opportunity for the public to provide feedback on a proposed rezoning and it sets a mandated timeline for the local Community Board, the Borough President, the City Planning Commission (CPC)[14] and the City Council to review, host hearings and ultimately vote on the proposed land use change. In other words, it is the process through which a rezoning is either approved or disproved. While local agencies such as the local Community Board as well as the Borough President only have advisory functions, the main decision-making power lies with the City Planning Commission and the City Council. Thus, if a developer seeks planning permission to build a larger or taller building or wants to expand the residential floor area and so make it denser than the current zoning permits, then a formalized 215-day mandatory process of public review and participation is triggered. Additionally, the URLURP is triggered if a developer wants to convert a non-residential property into an apartment building that would otherwise not be permitted under the current zoning. In both cases, the development would be subject to the Mandatory Inclusionary Housing rules, unless the proposed building includes the creation of less than ten residential units or 12,500 square feet ($\approx 1160m^2$) of floor area.

In contrast to New York City, planning obligations known as Section 106 agreements in London can be applied to every new development proposal that involves the creation of more than 10 residential units or 1,000 square meters of floor space, since the state owns the development rights independent of private ownership. Section 106 agreements are linked to a planning application when it is considered that the new residential building will put significant pressure on the social, physical, and economic infrastructure of the local area. Even though both planning procedures function on a case-by-case decision-making process, in contrast to the ULURP process in New York City, the decision-making process of planning applications in London is less formalized and based on a rather discretionary system. Further, the decision-making power of planning applications in London usually lies with the local planning authority. The Mayor can only take over a planning application if the development proposal is considered to have a potential strategic importance to the city or if there are sound reasons for intervention. In both cities, the process is also accompanied by a formal public hearing procedure. Despite the inclusionary housing regulations being mandatory in New York City, the scope and scale of developer contributions are still greatly determined in both cities by what is negotiated with city and local governments.

Definitions of Affordable Housing and Housing Affordability

The term affordable housing represents a programmatic shift in American and British housing policy since the 1980s: Publicly funded social housing programs have been substituted by public-private funded affordable housing programs that serve lower- and middle-income housing rather than the poorest or those on welfare (Gurran and Whitehead 2011, Stone 2006). The urban scholars David Madden and Peter Marcuse argue that the keyword of today is affordable housing, and that inclusionary housing is the prime example of this shift in housing policy (Madden and Marcuse 2016: 137). The provision of a certain number of 'affordable housing' by private developers is one of the main planning ideals of inclusionary housing. Since, in both cities, affordable housing is commonly regarded as a benefit for the community, the question of how much value can be recaptured from market-rate development and redirected back to local communities is very much tied to the question of how much affordable housing can be recaptured.

The definition of what affordable housing is, however, often questioned – in particular by the local community groups fighting against local development proposals. With regard to housing policy, affordable housing is generally based on certain norms or percentages of median incomes or general housing costs and encompasses not only social and low-income households but also moderate- to middle-income households that have difficulties finding an apartment in the speculative market.

In both cities, affordable housing is roughly defined as that which costs one-third or less of a household's income. In New York City, the income eligibility for these lower-income units is based on a measurement called Area Median Income (AMI). The median income is defined each year for all cities in the US by the US Department of Housing and Urban Development. The New York City region considered for this measurement includes the five boroughs and the rather affluent suburbs of Westchester, Rockland, and Putnam County. The 2021 AMI for New York City, for example, is $119,3400 (100% AMI) for a family of four. The term affordable housing includes a wide range of income categories, from very low-income (30-50% AMI) to middle-income (up to 165% AMI). The actual median household income in New York City was, however, only $70,590 in 2020. In the Bronx, for example, that figure is $42,140 (as of 2019), about 40 percent less than the citywide median household income (NYU Furman Center 2020).

In London, affordable housing is defined as for those whose needs are not met by the market. It is divided into social rented, affordable rented and intermediate housing as specified in the National Planning Policy Framework (NPPF) of 2012. The income eligibility is determined with regard to local incomes and local house prices. In short, social rented housing is owned by local authorities or private registered landlords, and the rents are determined through the national rent regime. Affordable rented housing is let by local authorities or private registered providers. The rent is subject to rent controls that require a rent of no more than 80 percent of the local market rent. Intermediate housing is low-cost homes for sale and rent that generally include shared ownership models. The annual income for intermediate homes is in the range of £18,100–£66,000 (up to £80,000 for families) (Greater London Authority 2016: policy 3.10). The estimated median household income is, however, about £40.000 a year as of 2012/13 (GLA 2016), so approximately half of the highest eligible income for families.

One problematic aspect of the term "affordable housing" is that the definition applied by the city's governments refers to different types of affordable housing, rather than housing that is actually affordable for local communities. According to Paul Watt, the "[c]ommon sense usage of the word 'affordable' links it to people's capacity to pay for a particular good or service, a notion that is largely absent from the usage of 'affordable housing' in policy circles" (Watt cited in London Tenants Federation 2011: 3). In other words, affordable housing and affordability do not mean the same thing (ibid.: 4).

The term "housing affordability" is as manifold as the term "affordable housing." Housing affordability is the ratio of housing costs to the tenant's income. A general rule for affordability is that housing costs should not exceed one-third of the tenant's income (Gurran and Bramley 2017b: 339). Affordability, however, has less to do with housing than with the relationship between housing and people (Stone 2006:153). It expresses "the social and material experiences of people, constituted as households, in relation to their individual housing situations" (ibid.: 151). In this sense, what is considered affordable is particularly subjective. The institutionalized notion as well as the standardized norms of what is considered to be "affordable housing" often are at odds with individual experiences. In other words, what is considered to be "affordable housing" in policy terms might not be considered affordable for those eligible for it.

Throughout this research study, I will discuss the tensions that arise between the two terms. To distance myself from the more institutionalized version of affordable housing and to underline that most of the affordable housing is not affordable for the local low-income community, hereinafter, I will put the term in quotation marks.

A Comparative Research Strategy

According to Philip Booth (2011), one of the first questions one has to ask oneself is why one wishes to undertake a comparative approach at all (Booth 2011: 14). My overall motive for this book is based in the appalling "poor door" practice that emerged in New York City and London at almost the same time. I first found out about this practice while reading The Guardian, and I immediately wondered about the underlying policy and practices of this urban phenomenon. Thus, my reason for undertaking this comparative study was to make sense of this recurrent phenomena in both cities, and I assumed that they could be "explained by a 'deeper level' common process or cause" (Pickvance 2001: 18).

To explore the similarities of this phenomenon and the underlying policies and practices that give rise to it, my overarching research strategy is the universalizing comparative analysis. According to sociologist Charles Tilly, the universalizing comparison aims to "establish that every instance of a phenomenon follows essentially the same rule" (Tilly 1984: 82). My primary analytical goal is to underpin the common patterns and effects of inclusionary housing practices in what are otherwise two different national housing and planning systems and cultures.

As it is the case in many comparative studies (Booth 2011: 19), I draw upon more than just one comparative research strategy. To fully grasp the common pattern and effects of inclusionary housing, I found it helpful to also explore local variations between and within specific urban places as well. Therefore, I incorporated some elements of what Tilly called "variation-finding comparative analysis" into my analysis. According to Tilly, the variation-finding approach aims to put "different instances at various locations within the same system, on the way to explaining their characteristics as a function of their varying relations to the system as a whole" (Tilly 1984: 82). In the chapters to come, a selection of various sites and instances in both New York City and London will serve as case studies through which to better understand inclusionary housing in the wider context of austerity urbanism and new-build gentrification. In chapter three, for example, I explore the variations of several development projects in different neighborhood contexts within each city to demonstrate how city and local governments act differently depending on the local context. These forms of variations, however, can be observed in both cities and by pointing out these variations, I am able to demonstrate the analogous patterns of inclusionary housing practices in both cities. In other chapters, I show certain degrees of variations of otherwise common features and practices between the two cities. These variations are identified to demonstrate that despite these variations in inclusionary housing policies and practices, the effects of inclusionary housing are mostly consistent.

A Mixed-Method Approach

The comparison is undertaken according to two different methodological perspectives: diachronic and synchronic (Chrisomalis 2006). First, inclusionary housing is analyzed diachronically by tracing the history of inclusionary housing policies in both cities from the 1970s to 2020. I look at the evolution of inclusionary housing policies in the context of the development of the national and local planning and housing systems. Methodologically, this involves a critical reading of housing and planning-related data, empirical housing studies and secondary literature, alongside strategic policy documents, which present the inclusionary housing strategies in the two cases of London and New York City. I evaluate the most recent housing plans with those that preceded them and then proceed to compare their similarities and differences.

Second, I use a synchronic approach to compare the implementation as well as the impact of current inclusionary housing policies in both cities. For this, I work predominantly with case studies. Case studies provide depth, present analytic details (Flyvbjerg 2006), and show complexity (Mabry 2008: 217). Since inclusionary housing projects are negotiated on a side-by-side basis in both cities, generalization is difficult. The cases studied are, thus, strategically selected to illustrate different aspects of inclusionary housing practices and their impact on the surrounding neighborhood and its residents in both cities.

In addition to evaluating strategic policy and planning documents, as well as government reports and press coverage of specific inclusionary developments, I mostly applied an ethnographic research approach. During my several fieldwork phases in both cities between 2014 and 2017[15], I held various conversations and conducted interviews with residents, leading activists, housing advocates and some local planners and politicians in both cities. Furthermore, various dérives and systematic observations were undertaken by me to obtain a feeling for and an understanding of new-build inclusionary housing developments and their surrounding neighborhoods and communities.

One of the main methods of my empirical research has been participant observations: Not only did I participate in various demonstrations and other forms of protests, activist organizational meetings and community informational events, but I spent countless hours in local governmental sessions and committee meetings to be able to get some insight into planning processes that are often not transparent. In that way, I add some "anthropological flesh" (Watt 2017: 16) to the understanding of the practices and social implications of inclusionary housing approaches in a cross-national perspective of two cities – something that distinguishes it from other existing cross-national overviews of inclusionary housing programs.

The purpose here is not to paint a complete picture of each country's or cities' land-use planning or inclusionary housing approaches, but rather to better grasp the principles that shape affordable housing provision in London and New York City today. By drawing on empirical research into specific cases of inclusionary housing projects and by focusing on the "everyday" of the decision-making processes, I aim to shed light on how these two cities have come to arrive at something like a 21st-century version of "housing apartheid" (Cohen 2014).

In contrast to Philip Booth (2011), I do not see comparative analysis in urban policymaking as a way to "look for solutions to problems" (Booth 2011: 13) and "to see whether there are policies and practices that might be borrowed from other places" (ibid.: 14) and possibly improved. As Calavita and Malach (2010) have pointed out in their introduction to their edited volume on inclusionary housing, this research is not interested in "suggesting that one's country's effort or form of inclusionary housing is 'better' or 'worse' than another's" (Calavita and Malach 2010c: XV). Instead, this book is about assessing the policy aims and the ways it has been implemented, and the effects it has on the ground in these two cities. It is an attempt to dispel the common myth surrounding the public debates in London and New York that inclusionary housing programs are essential for solving the affordable housing crisis (Angotti 2016a).

In doing so, this book is written for housing advocates, city and neighborhood planners, as well as politicians at the city government level and, most of all, for housing activists. That said, it is also written for those who face similar housing conditions and contradictions. It is a way of saying that one is not alone in this fight for social and truly affordable housing.

Empirical Research Limits and Data Hurdles

As in general, with all qualitative comparative research, I ran into difficulties in the matching up of comparable data. Descriptive statistics vary from city to city or do not exist at all in either of the two cities. The statistics that are publicly available are often big data tables, such as huge lists of issued planning permissions, which are difficult to comprehend and analyze in their complexity. Reports and studies that have provided data on housing constructions, for example, have also often provided different findings or have been contradictory. Freedom of Information Act requests I made with authorities in London often were answered unsatisfactorily, whereas in New York City, I often received the requested information. And not surprisingly, developers and housing associations in both cities have been less than helpful in providing statistics and much less open to being interviewed.

Additionally, save for some public meetings and records, the whole decision-making process behind individual inclusionary housing projects is very non-transparent, and many negotiations between local planning agencies and developers take place behind closed doors. Whereas in New York, public committee meetings are filmed and publicly archived, which makes it easier to at least access public testimonies, in London, it is very difficult to retrace decision-making processes since none of the data is made public or archived other than from some final planning permissions documents or cases in which developers re-negotiated planning permissions.

The case-by-case planning procedures and the discretionary decision-making process make it further difficult to generalize ideas and formulate broader principles and norms based on a case-based analysis. This has been the case particularly in London, where inclusionary housing is less rule-bound and more discretionary than in New York City.

According to anthropologist Alexa Färber (2021), these data hurdles and empirical research limits are often perceived by the researcher as shortcomings. Instead, in most cases, they express complexity rather than pointing to weaknesses within the research. She argues that although they might lead to "comparing unequal material densities" (Färber 2021), they "are illuminating and sharpen the understanding of individual research fields" (ibid.). In my case, this means the difficulties that I encountered with big data tables and with gathering information on every step taken in the decision-making process was an indication of the opacity of the research subject. This opacity further highlighted the power and control those local governments and developers have over the knowledge and decision-making process for ongoing as well as past development projects.

This issue of opacity may also explain why scholars have rarely studied inclusionary housing from the perspective of a comparative, qualitative, case-based research approach. Studying inclusionary housing from this perspective, thus, presents hurdles in formulating general principles and norms. Yet, it is particularly important to pay more attention to these discretionary processes and their effects, as it allows for a more nuanced picture of the dynamics of inclusionary housing policies and practices.

Summary of the Chapters

The following chapters of this book each provide evidence of how inclusionary housing approaches in both cities intersect with gentrification and displacement mechanisms. Each chapter discusses one of the above-mentioned sub-hypotheses.

In Chapter 1, I provide historical background on the evolution of inclusionary housing policies in both cities and reflect on their political, economic and institutional embeddedness. I discuss the link between inclusionary housing policies and austerity measures and describe three circles of inclusionary housing regulations that have emerged in both cities to highlight how inclusionary housing policies serve the interest of the real estate sector rather than the interest of the people it is intended to serve, thereby promoting urban growth and real estate development which is likely to lead to gentrification and displacement of lower-income communities.

Chapters 2 and 3 explore two different situations in which inclusionary housing applies: In the first situation, discussed in Chapter 2, the city or local government facilitates inclusionary housing by identifying a neighborhood to rezone (New York City) or a housing estate to redevelop (London) as a strategic investment opportunity. The second situation, discussed in Chapter 3, arises when a developer wants to build a residential building that will have a considerable impact on the surrounding local area. I argue that in both situations, inclusionary housing practices of both city and local governments tend to contribute to gentrification. In Chapter 2, I show how inclusionary housing enhances the large-scale urban regeneration of housing estates in London and of the few remaining lower-income neighborhoods in New York City. I draw on in-depth research of two case studies – one in each city – in which city and local governments engage in entrepreneurial urban regeneration efforts to create the conditions to advance the implementation of inclusionary housing policies. These practices present two different ways of how inclusionary housing is used by local governments as a pathway to state-led gentrification and displacement. In Chapter 3, I focus on developers' planning applications to local authorities and examine the public negotiation process of four application cases in each city. I demonstrate how governmental actors have adopted different dynamics in imposing inclusionary housing requirements on developers, depending on the wealth of the neighborhood.

Chapters 4 and 5 address the main objects of inclusionary housing: the provision of "affordable housing" and the fostering of "social mixing." I explore the localized effects of "mixing" different tenure types within development projects and the experiences of residents in obtaining and living in a so-called affordable housing apartment. I argue that inclusionary housing contributes to a certain exclusion of low-income tenants by limiting the possibility of social mixing and the accessibility as well as affordability of "affordable housing" units. In Chapter 4, I explore the design practices and outcomes of new-build mixed-income developments, where I argue that various design practices studied are exclusionary in one way or another and advance a vertical enclosure movement. I call this process vertical segregation by design in which affluent households come to dominate the space within the development over lower-income households. In Chapter 5, I examine the "real life" experiences of residents, housing advocates and managers of new-build mixed-income developments. My findings indicate that lower-income households are more excluded from affordable housing than certain income percentages and targets suggest.

In the Conclusion, I summarize the overall objective and findings of this study. I thereby question the assumption that inclusionary housing is the right planning tool to address the current housing crisis in both cities, as it further entrenches a system of private property relation, which not only systematically excludes lower-income people but also accelerates gentrification and displacement pressures in the name of apparent public benefit. I further ask what wider use the concept of *gentrification through the back door* might have in other contexts of social mix or 'affordable housing' policy.

In the Afterword, I comment on the latest developments of inclusionary housing policies in both cities and briefly discuss them in relation to the COVID-19 pandemic.

Fieldnotes

Meubrink, Yuca. Dérive along Whitechapel Road in the direction of the Relay Building, Whitechapel Road and One Comercial Street, Tower Hamlets, London, June 8, 2015.

Notes

1 The Jim Crow Laws enforced racial segregation in the American South between 1874 and 1954. In theory, the separation of whites and African Americans was justified by 'separate but equal' treatment and facilities such as in education, transport or housing, but in reality, the treatment and facilities were very unequal and African Americans were treated inferior to whites. The practice was declared unconstitutional within the landmark Supreme Court case Brown v. Board of Education in 1954.
2 The 421-a program is a tax exemption program that is set on the state level but only applies to New York City. It was first implemented in 1971 to incentivize real estate to build in the city again at a moment of urban decline.
   A developer could stand to enjoy tax exemptions for as long as 35 and in some cases even 40 years if they simply set aside 20 percent of units in a given development for households earning up to 60 percent of AMI. Over the decades, it has become a central means of the city to subsidize affordable housing. In 2017, the program has been re-named the Affordable Housing New York Program.
3 For more information see NYC HPD's website: https://www1.nyc.gov/site/hpd/services-and-information/tax-incentives-421-a.page.
4 The Relay Tower was formerly known as One Commercial Street. However, its actual address is on Whitechapel High Street, despite its former name.
5 This fieldnote has been edited for publication.
6 I capitalize *Black* in this context to emphasize its importance, even though it is subliminal, and only made clear by lower-casing *white* as the "other." Another reason to capitalize *Black* but not *white* is that *capitalizing White* would give the impression that whites form a single ethnic group which is questionable. For more information see the editor's note of the Columbian Journalism Review in 2015: https://www.cjr.org/analysis/language_corner_1.php (last accessed: June 14, 2022).
7 In the US, it is often called 'inclusionary zoning'. Throughout this thesis, I will, however, use the more general term inclusionary housing.
8 While in Virginia inclusionary housing was soon ruled by the Supreme Court to violate Virginia's Constitution, it was upheld in Montgomery, Maryland, and Pablo Alto, California. The most "successful" inclusionary housing program in terms of affordable housing production is probably the Moderately Priced Dwelling Unit (MPDU) program enacted in 1973 in Montgomery County, Maryland. Almost 50 years old, the program has produced around 15,000 affordable units since its inception (Mallach and Calavita 2010: 23).
9 The term "new-build gentrification" is not commonly used in the academic context of New York City and US policy. However, I will apply the term also to the New York City context throughout the book because it clarifies that new-build development can be considered gentrification. An alternative would be to simply use the word gentrification.
10 A rezoning is a change in land use in a particular area, generally to facilitate policy initiatives, such as preserving neighborhoods through *downzoning* or promoting economic development through *upzoning*. An upzoning usually increases the buildable floor area,

allowing for taller and denser buildings. A downzoning, on the other hand, reduces the buildable floor area. For more information see glossary of zoning terms of the NYC Department of City Planning: https://www1.nyc.gov/site/planning/zoning/glossary.page.

11 As MIH was only implemented in 2016, the argument refers to the results of some 421a and voluntary inclusionary housing programs in specific developments.

12 London reorganized its overall structure three times since the mid-1960s. First, in 1965, the London County Council (LCC) – in charge only for the inner boroughs – was replaced by the Greater London Council (GLC). The second reorganization of the local administration structure was in 1986 when the GLC fell victim to the policies of the Thatcher government – interestingly, almost parallel to the abolition of the Board of Estimates in New York but for entirely different reasons. The central government pushed for an approach to using the market to facilitate development that further marked the reorganization of the relation between the state, the private sector and civil society. During the 21 years of the GLC existence, London never had as much local autonomy as the government of New York, but together with the boroughs it was responsible for the construction of roads, social housing and leisure facilities as well as land-use planning, among other things. The dissolution of the Greater London Council left London without a municipal administration to govern its metropolitan area and mainly shifted the governing power to the central government or its 32 rather small boroughs. The Greater London Authority (GLA) was established in 2000.

13 U.S. Const. amend. V

14 The New York City Planning Commission has a total of 13 appointed members. The mayor appoints the Chair, who is also the Director of Department of City Planning and six other members. Each of the five Borough Presidents appoints one member and the NYC Public Advocate also appoints one member. Except for the chair, who acts on behalf of the mayor, the other 12 commission members are elected for five-year terms. For more information see: https://www1.nyc.gov/site/planning/about/commission.page (last accessed: June 13, 2022).

15 I spend roughly seven months in New York City in the years of 2016 and 2017, and five rather short phases in London between 2014 and 2017, adding up to about four months in total.

References

Alves, Sónia. 2022. "Divergence in Planning for Affordable Housing: A Comparative Analysis of England and Portugal." *Progress in Planning* 156 (February): 100536–57.

Angotti, Tom. 2010. "Land Use and the New York City Charter." submitted to the New York City Charter Commission.

———. 2016a. "Land Use Zoning Matters." In *Zoned Out! Race, Displacement, and City Planning in New York City*, edited by Angotti, Tom, and Sylvia Morse, 18–45. New York: UR.

Angotti, Tom, and Sylvia Morse, eds. 2016a. *Zoned Out! Race, Displacement, and City Planning in New York City*. New York: UR.

Architects for Social Housing. 2017. "The Good Practice Guide to Resisting Estate Demolition: ASH Response to the GLA." *Architects for Social Housing* (blog). March 8. https://architectsforsocialhousing.co.uk/2017/03/08/ash-good-practice-guide-to-resisting-estate-demolition-2/.

Austin, Patricia M., Nicole Gurran, and Christine M. E. Whitehead. 2014. "Planning and Affordable Housing in Australia, New Zealand and England: Common Culture; Different Mechanisms." *Journal of Housing and the Built Environment* 29 (3): 455–72.

Bento, Antonio, Scott Lowe, Gerrit-Jan Knaap, and Arnab Chakraborty. 2009. "Housing Market Effects of Inclusionary Zoning." *Cityscape: A Journal of Policy Development and Research* 11 (2): 7–26. https://scholarworks.boisestate.edu/econ_facpubs/5.

Besussi, Elena. 2016. "Extracting Value from the Public City. Urban Strategies and the State-Market Mix in the Disposal of Municipal Asset." In *Urban Austerity. Impacts of the Global Financial Crisis in Europe*, Barbara Schönig Und Sebastian Schipper. Berlin: Theater der Zeit, 89–102.

Boddy, Martin. 2007. "Designer Neighbourhoods: New-Build Residential Development in Nonmetropolitan UK Cities—The Case of Bristol." *Environment and Planning A: Economy and Space* 39 (1): 86–105.

Booth, Philip. 2011. "Culture, Planning and Path Dependence: Some Reflections on the Problems of Comparison." *The Town Planning Review* 82 (1): 13–28.

Bridge, Gary, Tim Butler, and Loretta Lees. 2012. *Mixed Communities: Gentrification by Stealth?* Bristol: POLICY PR.

Bromley, Rosemary D.F., and Peter K. Mackie. 2009. "Displacement and the New Spaces for Informal Trade in the Latin American City Centre." *Urban Studies* 46 (7): 1485–1506.

Burgess, Gemma, and Sarah Monk. 2012. *Capturing Planning Gain – The Transition from Section 106 to the Community Infrastructure Levy*. London: Royal Institution of Chartered Surveyors. https://www.cchpr.landecon.cam.ac.uk/Research/Start-Year/2011/Impact-recent-financial-crisis-planning-affordable-housing-England/Capturing-Planning-Gain-Transition-S106-to-Community-Infrastructure-Levy.

Burgess, Gemma, Sarah Monk, and Christine Whitehead. 2011. "Delivering Local Infrastructure and Affordable Housing Through the Planning System: The Future of Planning Obligations Through Section 106." *People, Place and Policy Online* 5: 1–11.

Calavita, Nico. 2006. "Inclusionary Housing in the US and Europe." Presented at 42nd ISoCaRP Congress. http://www.isocarp.net/Data/case_studies/737.pdf.

Calavita, Nico, and Alan Mallach. 2009. "Inclusionary Housing, Incentives, and Land Value Recapture." *Land Lines*, 7.

———. eds. 2010. *Inclusionary Housing in International Perspective: Affordable Housing, Social Inclusion, and Land Value Recapture*. Cambridge, Mass: Lincoln Institute of Land Policy.

———. 2010a. "An International Perspective on Inclusionary Housing." In *Inclusionary Housing in International Perspective. Affordable Housing, Social Inclusion, and Land Value Recapture*, edited by Calavita, Nico, and Alan Mallach, 1–14. Cambridge, Massachusetts: Lincoln Institute of Land Policy.

———. 2010b. "National Differences and Commonalities: Comparative Analysis and Future Prospects." In *Inclusionary Housing in International Perspective. Affordable Housing, Social Inclusion, and Land Value Recapture*, edited by Calavita, Nico, and Alan Mallach, 359–86. Cambridge, Massachusetts: Lincoln Institute of Land Policy.

———. 2010c. "Preface." In *Inclusionary Housing in International Perspective. Affordable Housing, Social Inclusion, and Land Value Recapture*, edited by Calavita, Nico, and Alan Mallach, XV–XVI. Cambridge, Massachusetts: Lincoln Institute of Land Policy.

Carpenter, Juliet, and Loretta Lees. 1995. "Gentrification in New York, London and Paris: An International Comparison." *International Journal of Urban and Regional Research* 19 (2): 286–303. https://doi.org/10.1111/j.1468-2427.1995.tb00505.x.

Cheshire, Paul. 2018. "Broken Market or Broken Policy? The Unintended Consequences of Restrictive Planning." *National Institute Economic Review* 245 (August): R9–19. https://doi.org/10.1177/002795011824500111.

Chrisomalis, Stephen. 2006. "Comparing Cultures and Comparing Processes: Diachronic Methods in Cross-Cultural Anthropology." *Cross-Cultural Research* 40 (4): 377–404. https://doi.org/10.1177/1069397106287926.

Clarke, Nick, and Allan Cochrane. 2013. "Geographies and Politics of Localism: The Localism of the United Kingdom's Coalition Government." *Political Geography* 34: 10–23.

Cohen, Rick. 2014. "Rich Door/Poor Door Affordable Housing Controversy in New York City." *NPQ - Nonprofit Quarterly*, July 31, 2014. https://nonprofitquarterly.org/policysocial-context/24594-rich-door-poor-door-affordable-housing-controversy-in-new-york-city.html.

Colenutt, Bob. 2020. *The Property Lobby: The Hidden Reality Behind the Housing Crisis.* Policy Press.

Colenutt, Bob, Allan Cochrane, and Martin Field. 2015. "The Rise and Rise of Viability Assessment." *Town and Country Planning* 84 (10): 453–58.

Crook, Antony (D. H.) 1996. "Affordable Housing and Planning Gain, Linkage Fees and the Rational Nexus: Using the Land Use Planning System in England and the USA to Deliver Housing Subsidies." *International Planning Studies* 1 (1): 49–71. https://doi.org/10.1080/13563479608721643.

Crook, Tony, John Henneberry, and Christine Whitehead. 2015. *Planning Gain: Providing Infrastructure and Affordable Housing.* Wiley-Blackwell.

Crook, Tony, and Sarah Monk. 2011. "Planning Gains, Providing Homes." *Housing Studies* 26 (7–8): 997–1018. https://doi.org/10.1080/02673037.2011.619423.

Crook, Tony, and Christine Whitehead. 2002. "Social Housing and Planning Gain: Is This an Appropriate Way of Providing Affordable Housing?" *Environment and Planning A: Economy and Space* 34 (7): 1259–79. https://doi.org/10.1068/a34135.

———. 2019. "Capturing Development Value, Principles and Practice: Why Is It so Difficult?" *Town Planning Review* 90 (4): 359–81.

Davidson, Mark. 2018. "New-Build Gentrification." In *Handbook of Gentrification Studies*, edited by Loretta Lees and Martin Phillips, 247–61. Cheltenham, UK; Northampton, MA USA: Edward Elgar Publishing.

Davidson, Mark, and Loretta Lees. 2005. "New-Build 'Gentrification' and London's Riverside Renaissance." *Environment and Planning A: Economy and Space* 37 (7): 1165–90. https://doi.org/10.1068/a3739.

———. 2010. "New-Build Gentrification: Its Histories, Trajectories, and Critical Geographies." *Population, Space and Place* 16 (5): 395–411. https://doi.org/10.1002/psp.584.

Davidson, Mark, and Kevin Ward. 2018. "Introduction." In *Cities Under Austerity: Restructuring the US Metropolis*, edited by Mark Davidson and Kevin Ward, 1–26. SUNY Press.

de Blasio, Bill. 2016. "Statement from Mayor de Blasio on Progress under NYC's New Mandatory Inclusionary Housing Law," December 16. https://www1.nyc.gov/office-of-the-mayor/news/954-16/statement-mayor-de-blasio-progress-under-nyc-s-new-mandatory-inclusionary-housing-law.

Deas, Iain, and Jennifer Doyle. 2013. "Building Community Capacity Under 'Austerity Urbanism': Stimulating, Supporting and Maintaining Resident Engagement in Neighbourhood Regeneration in Manchester." *Journal of Urban Regeneration and Renewal* 6 (January): 365–80.

DeFilippis, James, and Elvin Wyly. 2008. "Running to Stand Still: Through the Looking Glass With Federally Subsidized Housing in New York City." *Urban Affairs Review* 43 (6): 777–816. https://doi.org/10.1177/1078087407312179.

DePaolo, Philip, and Morse Sylvia. 2016. "Williamsburg: Zoning Out Latinos." In *Zoned Out! Race, Displacement, and City Planning in New York City*, Tom Angotti and Sylvia Morse. New York: UR, 72–94. https://www.urpub.org/books/zonedout.

Donald, Betsy, Amy Glasmeier, Mia Gray, and Linda Lobao. 2014. "Austerity in the City: Economic Crisis and Urban Service Decline?" *Cambridge Journal of Regions, Economy and Society* 7 (1): 3–15. https://doi.org/10.1093/cjres/rst040.

Duran, Paula. 2014. "Gale Brewer Calls on City to End 'Poor Doors.'" *Observer*, July 25. https://observer.com/2014/07/gale-brewer-calls-on-city-to-end-poor-doors/.

Durkin, Erin. 2016. "City Council Strike Deal on Support for Affordable Housing Plan." *New York Daily News*, March 14. http://www.nydailynews.com/new-york/de-blasio-city-council-strike-affordable-housing-deal-article-1.2564407.

Elmer, Simon. 2019. "How Sadiq Khan's Housing Policy Is Making London's Housing Crisis Worse." *VICE*, January 30, 2019. https://www.vice.com/en/article/43zvdw/how-sadiq-khans-housing-policy-is-making-londons-housing-crisis-worse.

Engels, Friedrich. 2000. "The Great Towns. From The Condition of the Working Class in England in 1844 (1845)." In *The City Reader*, edited by Richard T. LeGates and Frederic Stout, 47–55. New York: Routledge.

Evans, Graeme. 2014. "Living in the Mix. Mixed Use and Quality of Life." In *Wellbeing: A Complete Reference Guide: Volume II: Wellbeing and the Environment*, Rachel Cooper, Elizabeth Burton, Cary L. Cooper. South Gate, Chichester, West Sussex: Wiley-Blackwell.

Fainstein, Susan. 1994. *The City Builders: Property Development in New York and London*. Oxford, New York: Blackwell.

———. 2012. "Land Value Capture and Justice." *Value Capture and Land Policies*, January, 21–40.

Färber, Alexa. 2021. "The Anthropology of Urban Comparison: Urban Comparative Concepts and Practices, the Entrepreneurial Ethnographic Self and Their Spatializing Dimensions." *Forum: Qualitative Social Research* 22 (3).

Farkas, Ava. 2016. "MIH: 'Progressive' Gentrification." *The Tenant*, April 12. https://thetenant. org/mih-progressive-gentrification/.

Ferm, Jessica, and Mike Raco. 2020. "Viability Planning, Value Capture and the Geographies of Market-Led Planning Reform in England." *Planning Theory & Practice* 21 (2): 218–35. https://doi.org/10.1080/14649357.2020.1754446.

Flyvbjerg, Bent. 2006. "Five Misunderstandings About Case-Study Research." *Qualitative Inquiry* 12 (2): 219–245. https://doi.org/10.1177/1077800405284363.

Fox-Rogers, Linda, and Enda Murphy. 2015. "From Brown Envelopes to Community Benefits: The Co-Option of Planning Gain Agreements Under Deepening Neoliberalism." *Geoforum* 67, 41–50. https://doi.org/10.1016/J.GEOFORUM.2015.09.015.

Freeman, Lance, and Jenny Schuetz. 2016. "Producing Affordable Housing in Rising Markets: What Works?" *SSRN Electronic Journal*, January. https://doi.org/10.2139/ssrn. 2851175.

Gardner, Alison, and Vivien Lowndes. 2016. "Negotiating Austerity and Local Traditions." In *Rethinking Governance. Ruling, Rationalities and Resistance*, Mark Bevir and R. a. W. Rhodes. Routledge, 125–43. https://doi.org/10.4324/9781315712949-17.

Gillespie, Tom, Kate Hardy, and Paul Watt. 2021. "Surplus to the City: Austerity Urbanism, Displacement and 'Letting Die.'" *Environment and Planning A: Economy and Space* 53 (7): 1713–29. ps://doi.org/10.1177/0308518X211026323.

Glaeser, Edward. 2015. "There Are Worse Things in Housing Policy than Poor Doors." *NYU Furman Center*, March 2015. https://furmancenter.org/research/iri/essay/there-are-worse-things-in-housing-policy-than-poor-doors.

Glass, Ruth. 1964. *London: Aspects of Change*. London: MacGibbon & Kee.

Gonen, Yoav. 2014. "De Blasio Voted for Luxury Building 'Poor Door.'" *New York Post*, July 29. https://nypost.com/2014/07/28/de-blasio-voted-for-luxury-building-poor-door-as-councilman/.

Grabar, Henry. 2014. "New York City's Appalling 'Poor Door' Fiasco." *Salon*, August 8. https://www.salon.com/2014/08/03/new_york_citys_appalling_poor_door_fiasco/.

Granath Hansson, Anna. 2019. "Inclusionary Housing Policies in Gothenburg, Sweden, and Stuttgart, Germany: The Importance of Norms and Institutions." *Nordic Journal of Surveying and Real Estate Research* 14 (1): 7–28.

Greater London Authority. 2016. "A City for All Londoners." Greater London Authority. https://www.london.gov.uk/sites/default/files/city_for_all_londoners_nov_2016.pdf.

Gurran, Nicole, and Glen Bramley. 2017a. "Planning, Housing Supply and Affordable Provision in Britain." In *Urban Planning and the Housing Market: International Perspectives for Policy and Practice*, Nicole Gurran and Glen Bramley. London: Palgrave Macmillan UK, 123–63. https://doi.org/10.1057/978-1-137-46403-3_1.

———. 2017b. "Planning for Inclusionary Housing in New and Renewing Communities." In *Urban Planning and the Housing Market: International Perspectives for Policy and Practice*, Gurran, Nicole, and Glen Bramley. London: Palgrave Macmillan UK, 363–85. https://doi.org/10.1057/978-1-137-46403-3_12.

———. 2017c. "Introduction: The Twenty-First Century Urban Housing Agenda." In *Urban Planning and the Housing Market: International Perspectives for Policy and Practice*, Gurran, Nicole, and Glen Bramley. London: Palgrave Macmillan UK, 1–12. https://doi. org/10.1057/978-1-137-46403-3_5.

Gurran, Nicole, Vivienne Milligan, Doug Baker, Laura Bugg, and Sharon Christensen. 2008. *"New Directions in Planning for Affordable Housing: Australian and International Evidence and Implications."* Australian Housing and Urban Research Institute (AHURI). https://www.ahuri.edu.au/research/final-reports/120.

Gurran, Nicole, and Christine Whitehead. 2011. "Planning and Affordable Housing in Australia and the UK: A Comparative Perspective." *Housing Studies* 26 (7–8): 1193–1214. https://doi.org/10.1080/02673037.2011.618982.

Hackworth, Jason. 2011. *The Neoliberal City: Governance, Ideology, and Development in American Urbanism.* Cornell University Press. https://www.degruyter.com/document/doi/10.7591/9780801461590/html.

Hamnett, Chris. 2003. *Unequal City: London in the Global Arena.* London; New York: Routledge.

———. 2014. "Shrinking the Welfare State: The Structure, Geography and Impact of British Government Benefit Cuts." *Transactions of the Institute of British Geographers* 39 (4): 490–503.

Harloe, Michael, Peter Marcuse, and Neil Smith. 1992. "Housing for People, Housing for Profits." In *Divided Cities: New York and London in the Contemporary Period*, edited by Susan Fainstein, Ian Gordon and Michael Harloe, 175–202. Oxford: Blackwell.

Haughton, Graham, and Stephen Hincks. 2013. "Austerity Planning." *Town and Country Planning: The Quarterly Review of the Town and Country Planning Association* 82 (January): 23–28.

He, Shenjing. 2010. "New-Build Gentrification in Central Shanghai: Demographic Changes and Socioeconomic Implications." *Population, Space and Place* 16 (5): 345–61. https://doi.org/10.1002/psp.548.

Hedin, Karin, Eric Clark, Emma Lundholm, and Gunnar Malmberg. 2012. "Neoliberalization of Housing in Sweden: Gentrification, Filtering, and Social Polarization." *Annals of the Association of American Geographers* 102 (2): 443–63.

Helbrecht, Ilse, and Francesca Weber-Newth. 2018. "Recovering the Politics of Planning." *City* 22 (1): 116–29. https://doi.org/10.1080/13604813.2018.1434301.

Hickey, Robert. 2013. *New Challenges and Opportunities for Inclusionary Housing.* Washington DC: Center for Housing Policy.

Hodkinson, Stuart, and Glyn Robbins. 2013. "The Return of Class War Conservatism? Housing under the UK Coalition Government." *Critical Social Policy* 33 (1): 57–77.

Hodkinson, Stuart, Paul Watt, and Gerry Mooney. 2013. "Introduction: Neoliberal Housing Policy – Time for a Critical Re-Appraisal." *Critical Social Policy* 33 (1): 3–16. https://doi.org/10.1177/0261018312457862.

Holm, Andrej. 2010. "Townhouses, Urban Village, Car Loft Berliner Luxuswohnanlagen Als ‚dritte Welle' Der Gentrification." *Geographische Zeitschrift* 98 (2): 100–115.

Holm, Andrej, Szymon Marcińczak, and Agnieszka Ogrodowczyk. 2015. "New-Build Gentrification in the Post-Socialist City: Łódź and Leipzig Two Decades after Socialism." *Geografie* 120 (January): 164–87. https://doi.org/10.37040/geografie2015120020164.

Huang, Youqin. 2015. *Bolstering Inclusionary Housing in Chinese Cities.* The Paulson Institute.

Jacobus, Rick. 2015. „In Defense of the ‚Poor Door'". *Shelterforce*, October, 14. https://shelterforce.org/2015/10/14/in_defense_of_the_poor_door/.

Kadi, Justin, and Richard Ronald. 2016. "Undermining Housing Affordability for New York's Low-Income Households: The Role of Policy Reform and Rental Sector Restructuring." *Critical Social Policy* 36 (2): 265–88. https://doi.org/10.1177/0261018315624172.

Kam, George de, Barrie Needham, and Edwin Buitelaar. 2014. "The Embeddedness of Inclusionary Housing in Planning and Housing Systems: Insights from an International Comparison." *Journal of Housing and the Built Environment* 29 (3): 389–402. https://doi.org/10.1007/s10901-013-9354-5.

Knapp, Gerrit-Jan, Antonio Bento and Scott Lowe. 2008. *Housing Market Impacts of Inclusionary Zoning.* College Park, MD: National Center for Smart Growth Research and Education.

Kober, Eric. 2020. *"How Has De Blasio's Inclusionary Zoning Program (MIH) Fared?"* New York City: Manhattan Institute. https://www.manhattan-institute.org/deblasios-mandatory-inclusionary-housing-program.

Kontokosta, Constantine E. 2014. "Mixed-Income Housing and Neighborhood Integration: Evidence." *Journal of Urban Affairs* 36 (4): 716–741.

——. 2015. "Do inclusionary zoning policies equitably disperse affordable housing? A comparative spatial analysis". *Journal of Housing and the Built Environment* 30. https://doi.org/10.1007/s10901-014-9430-5.

Lamberg, Carol. 2015. "Housing Priorities: Quality Is More Important than the Number of Entrances." The Dream Revisited: The Poor Door Debate. NYU Furman Center. https://furmancenter.org/research/iri/essay/housing-priorities-quality-is-more-important-than-the-number-of-entrances.

Lambert, Christine, and Martin Boddy. 2002. *Transforming the City: Post-Recession Gentrification and Re-Urbanisation.* ESRC Centre for Neighbourhood Research.

Layard, Antonia. 2018. "Property and Planning Law in England: Facilitating and Countering Gentrification." In *Handbook of Gentrification Studies*, edited by Loretta Lees and Martin Phillips, 444–66. Cheltenham, UK ; Northampton, MA USA: Edward Elgar Publishing.

——. 2019. "Planning by Numbers: Affordable Housing and Viability in England." In *Planning and Knowledge: How New Forms of Technocracy Are Shaping Contemporary Cities*, Raco, Mike, and Federico Savini. Bristol: Policy Press, 213–24. https://policy.bristoluniversitypress.co.uk/planning-and-knowledge.

Lees, Loretta. 1994. "Gentrification in London and New York: An Atlantic Gap?" *Housing Studies* 9 (2): 199–217. https://doi.org/10.1080/02673039408720783.

——. 2003. "Super-Gentrification: The Case of Brooklyn Heights, New York City." *Urban Studies* 40 (12): 2487–509. https://doi.org/10.1080/0042098032000136174.

——. 2014. "The Death of Sustainable Communities in London?" In *Sustainable London? The Future of a Global City, Rob Imrie and Loretta Lees*. Bristol: Policy Press, 149–71. https://doi.org/10.1111/anti.12020.

Lees, Loretta, Tim Butler, and Gary Bridge. 2012. "Introduction: Gentrification, Social Mix/ Ing and Mixed Communities." In *Mixed Communities: Gentrification by Stealth?*, Gary Bridge, Tim Butler, and Loretta Lees. Bristol: POLICY PR, 1–16.

Levy, Diane K. 2006. "Keeping the Neighborhood Affordable: A Handbook of Housing Strategies for Gentrifying Areas." The Urban Institute. https://www.semanticscholar.org/paper/Keeping-the-Neighborhood-Affordable%3A-A-Handbook-of-Levy/fba730bc3093fc761e303012e1461e0b0bb812de.

Li, Fei, and Zhan Guo. 2020. "Will Mandatory Inclusionary Housing Create Mixed-Income Communities? Evidence From London, UK." *Housing Policy Debate* 30 (6): 972–93. https://doi.org/10.1080/10511482.2020.1787482.

London Tenants Federation. 2011. "The Affordable Housing Con." London Tenants Federation. http://www.londontenants.org/publications/other/theafordablehousingconf.pdf.

Low, Chris. 2014. "Developers Installed a 'Poor Door' and a 'Rich Door' on a London Apartment Building." *VICE*, August 25. https://www.vice.com/en/article/av4ywp/one-commercial-street-poor-door-protest-101.

Lowndes, Vivien, and Alison Gardner. 2016. "Local Governance Under the Conservatives: Super-Austerity, Devolution and the 'Smarter State.'" *Local Government Studies* 42 (3): 357–75. https://doi.org/10.1080/03003930.2016.1150837.

Lützeler, Ralph. 2008. "Population Increase and 'New-Build Gentrification' in Central Tōkyō." *Erdkunde* 62 (4): 287–99.

Mabry, Linda. 2008. "Case Study in Social Research." In *The SAGE Handbook of Social Research Methods*, Pertti Alasuutari, Leonard Bickman and Julia Brannen. London: SAGE Publications Ltd, 214–27. https://doi.org/10.4135/9781446212165.

Madden, David, and Peter Marcuse. 2016. *Defense of Housing: The Politics of Crisis.* London; New York: Verso.

Mah, Julie, and Jason Hackworth. 2011. "Local Politics and Inclusionary Housing in Three Large Canadian Cities." *Canadian Journal of Urban Research* 20 (1): 57–80.

Mallach, Alan. 1984. *Inclusionary Housing Programs: Policies and Practices.* New Brunswick, NJ: Rutgers Univ Center for Urban.
———. 2010. "The Global Reach of Inclusionary Housing." In *Inclusionary Housing in International Perspective. Affordable Housing, Social Inclusion, and Land Recapture, Nico Calavita and Alan Mallach.* Cambridge, MA: Lincoln Institute of Land Policy, 323–58.
Mallach, Alan, and Nico Calavita. 2010. "United States: From Radical Innovation to Mainstream Housing Policy." In *Inclusionary Housing in International Perspective: Affordable Housing, Social Inclusion, and Land Value Recapture*, edited by Nico Calavita and Alan Mallach, 15–78. Cambridge, MA: Lincoln Institute of Land Policy.
Malpass, Peter. 2005. *Housing and the Welfare State: The Development of Housing Policy in Britain.* Houndmills, Basingstoke, Hampshire; New York: Red Globe Press.
Marcuse, Peter. 1985. "Gentrification, Abandonment, and Displacement: Connections, Causes, and Policy Responses in New York City." *Urban Law Annual." Journal of Urban and Contemporary Law* 28 (1): 195–240.
Marcuse, Peter, and W. Dennis Keating. 2006. "The Permanent Housing Crisis: The Failures of Conservatism and the Limitations of Liberalism." In *A Right to Housing: Foundation for a New Social Agenda*, edited by Rachel G. Bratt, Michael E. Stone, and Chester Hartman, 139–62. Temple University Press, http://www.jstor.org/stable/j.ctt1bw1kqb.10.
Marom, Nathan, and Naomi Carmon. 2015. "Affordable Housing Plans in London and New York: Between Marketplace and Social Mix: Housing Studies: Vol 30, No 7." *Housing Studies* 30 (7). https://www.tandfonline.com/doi/abs/10.1080/02673037.2014.10008 32?journalCode=chos20.
Marquardt, Nadine, Henning Füller, Georg Glasze, and Robert Pütz. 2013. "Shaping the Urban Renaissance: New-Build Luxury Developments in Berlin." *Urban Studies* 50 (8): 1540–56. https://doi.org/10.1177/0042098012465905.
McAllister, Pat, Edward Shepherd, and Peter Wyatt. 2018. "Policy Shifts, Developer Contributions and Land Value Capture in London 2005–2017." *Land Use Policy* 78 (November): 316–26. https://doi.org/10.1016/j.landusepol.2018.06.047.
McClure, Kirk. 2008. "Deconcentrating Poverty with Housing Programs." *Journal of the American Planning Association*, January. https://doi.org/10.1080/01944360701730165.
McClure, Kirk, Nicole Gurran, and Glen Bramley. 2017. "Planning, Housing Supply and Affordable Development in the USA." In *Urban Planning and the Housing Market: International Perspectives for Policy and Practice*, edited by Nicole Gurran and Glen Bramley, 165–200. London: Palgrave Macmillan UK. https://doi.org/10.1057/978-1-137-46403-3_6.
Meegan, Richard, Patricia Kennett, Gerwyn Jones, and Jacqui Croft. 2014. "Global Economic Crisis, Austerity and Neoliberal Urban Governance in England." *Cambridge Journal of Regions, Economy and Society* 7 (February): 137–53. ttps://doi.org/10.1093/cjres/rst033.
Minton, Anna. 2017. *Big Capital: Who Is London For?* UK: Penguin.
Monk, Sarah. 2010. "England: Affordable Housing Through the Planning System: The Role of Section 106." In *Inclusionary Housing in International Perspective. Affordable Housing, Social Inclusion, and Land Recapture*, edited by Nico Calavita and Alan Mallach, 123–68. Cambridge, MA: Lincoln Institute of Land Policy.
Morrison, Nicky, and Gemma Burgess. 2014. "Inclusionary Housing Policy in England: The Impact of the Downturn on the Delivery of Affordable Housing Through Section 106." *Journal of Housing and the Built Environment* 29 (3): 423–38.
Mouffe, Chantal. 2005. *On the Political.* London; New York: Routledge.
Mukhija, Vinit, Ashok Das, Lara Regus, und Sara Slovin Tsay. 2015. "The Tradeoffs of Inclusionary Zoning: What Do We Know and What Do We Need to Know?" *Planning Practice and Research.* https://www.tandfonline.com/doi/abs/10.1080/02697459.2015.1008793.
Mukhija, Vinit, Lara Regus, Sara Slovin, and Ashok Das. 2010. "Can Inclusionary Zoning Be an Effective and Efficient Housing Policy? Evidence from Los Angeles and Orange Counties." *Journal of Urban Affairs* 32 (2): 229–52. https://doi.org/10.1111/j.1467-9906.2010.00495.x.

Murie, Alan. 2009. "The Modernisation of Housing in England." *Tijdschrift Voor Economische En Sociale Geografie* 100 (September): 535–48. https://doi.org/10.1111/j.1467-9663.2009.00557.x.

Murphy, Laurence. 2008. "Third-Wave Gentrification in New Zealand: The Case of Auckland." *Urban Studies* 45 (12): 2521–40. https://doi.org/10.1177/0042098008097106.

Navarro, Mireya. 2014. "'Poor Door' in a New York Tower Opens a Fight Over Affordable Housing." *The New York Times*, August 26. https://www.nytimes.com/2014/08/27/nyregion/separate-entryways-for-new-york-condo-buyers-and-renters-create-an-affordable-housing-dilemma.html.

New York City Department of Housing, Preservation and Development. n.d. "Tax Incentives: 421a." NYC Department of Housing Preservation and Development. https://web.archive.org/web/20190808115734/https:/www1.nyc.gov/site/hpd/developers/tax-incentives-421a-main.page (last accessed: 03/03/2022).

Newman, Kathe. 2018. "Urban Governance and Inclusionary Housing in New York City." In *Cities Under Austerity: Restructuring the US Metropolis*, David Davidson and Kevin Ward. Albany: SUNY Press, 127–42. https://www.amazon.com/Cities-under-Austerity-Restructuring-Metropolis-ebook/dp/B079M955KQ/ref=sr_1_2?keywords=austerity+cities&qid=1559857008&s=books&sr=1-2.

NYU Furman Center. 2015. "*Creating Affordable Housing Out of Thin Air: The Economics of Mandatory Inclusionary Zoning in New York City*." New York City: NYU Furman Center. http://furmancenter.org/files/NYUFurmanCenter_CreatingAffHousing_March2015.pdf.

———. 2020. "*Citywide Data. The State of New York City's Housing and Neighborhoods*." NYU Furman Center. https://furmancenter.org/stateofthecity/view/citywide-data.

Ortega, Arnisson Andre C. 2016. "Manila's Metropolitan Landscape of Gentrification: Global Urban Development, Accumulation by Dispossession & Neoliberal Warfare Against Informality." *Geoforum* 70 (March): 35–50. https://doi.org/10.1016/j.geoforum.2016.02.002.

Osborne, Hilary. 2014a. "Poor doors: the segregation of London's inner-city flat dwellers." *The Guardian*, July 25. https://www.theguardian.com/society/2014/jul/25/poor-doors-segregation-london-flats.

———. 2014b. "Boris Johnson Rules out 'poor Door' Ban on London Housing Developments." *The Guardian*, July 28. https://www.theguardian.com/society/2014/jul/28/boris-johnson-rules-out-poor-door-ban-london-housing-developments.

Panton, Mark, and Geoff Walters. 2018. "'It's Just a Trojan Horse for Gentrification': Austerity and Stadium-Led Regeneration." *International Journal of Sport Policy and Politics* 10 (1): 163–83. https://doi.org/10.1080/19406940.2017.1398768.

Peck, Jamie. 2012. "Austerity Urbanism. American Cities under Extreme Economy." *City* 16 (6): 626–55.

Peck, Jamie. 2014. "Pushing Austerity: State Failure, Municipal Bankruptcy and the Crises of Fiscal Federalism in the USA." *Cambridge Journal of Regions, Economy and Society* 7 (1): 17–44. https://doi.org/10.1093/cjres/rst018.

———. 2018. "Situating Austerity Urbanism." In *Cities Under Austerity: Restructuring the US Metropolis*, edited by Davidson, Mark, and Kevin Ward, xi–xxxiii. SUNY Press.

———. 2020. "Austerity Urbanism." In *Oxford Bibliographies in Urban Studies*, Dilworth, R. Oxford Bibliographies. https://www.oxfordbibliographies.com/view/document/obo-9780190922481/obo-9780190922481-0001.xml.

Penny, Joe. 2017. "Between Coercion and Consent: The Politics of 'Cooperative Governance' at a Time of 'Austerity Localism' in London." *Urban Geography* 38 (9): 1352–73. https://doi.org/10.1080/02723638.2016.1235932.

Pickvance, Chris. 2001. "Four Varieties of Comparative Analysis." *Journal of Housing and the Built Environment* 16: 7–28. https://doi.org/10.1023/A:1011533211521.

Pill, Madeleine. 2020. "The Austerity Governance of Baltimore's Neighborhoods: 'The Conversation May Have Changed but the Systems Aren't Changing.'" *Journal of Urban Affairs* 42 (1): 143–58. https://doi.org/10.1080/07352166.2018.1478226.

Pomorski, Chris. 2014. "The Worst Thing About the 'Poor Door' Might Be Its Naysay-ers." *Observer*, August 27. https://observer.com/2014/08/the-worst-thing-about-the-poor-door-might-be-the-nay-sayers/.

Real Affordability for All. 2016. "A Tale of One Housing Plan. How Bill de Blasio's New York Is Abandoning the Same Low-Income New Yorkers Left behind during the Bloomberg Years." Real Affordability for All. https://alignny.org/resource/a-tale-of-one-housing-plan/.

Rérat, Patrick, Ola Söderström, Etienne Piguet, and Roger Besson. 2009. "From Urban Wastelands to New-Build Gentrification: The Case of Swiss Cities." *Population, Space and Place* 16 (5). https://www.academia.edu/1852179/From_urban_wastelands_to_new_build_gentrification_The_case_of_Swiss_cities.

Rosen, Gillad, and Alan Walks. 2015. "Castles in Toronto's Sky: Condo-Ism as Urban Transformation." *Journal of Urban Affairs* 37 (3): 289–310. https://doi.org/10.1111/juaf.12140.

Santoro, Paula Freire. 2019. "Inclusionary Housing Policies in Latin America: São Paulo, Brazil in Dialogue With Bogotá, Colombia." *International Journal of Housing Policy* 19 (3): 385–410. https://doi.org/10.1080/19491247.2019.1613870.

Sassen, Saskia. 2001. *The Global City: New York, London, Tokyo*. Princeton, N.J: Princeton University Press.

Savini, Federico, and Mike Raco. 2019. "The Rise of a New Urban Technocracy." In *Planning and Knowledge: How New Forms of Technocracy Are Shaping Contemporary Cities*, Mike Raco and Federico Savini. Bristol: Policy Press, 3–17. https://policy.bristoluniversitypress.co.uk/planning-and-knowledge.

Schuetz, Jenny, Rachel Meltzer, and Vicki Been. 2011. "Silver Bullet or Trojan Horse? The Effects of Inclusionary Zoning on Local Housing Markets in the United States." *Urban Studies* 48 (2): 297–329. https://doi.org/10.1177/0042098009360683.

Schwartz, Alexandra. 2016. "The 'Poor Door' and the Glossy Reconfiguration of City Life." *The New Yorker*, January 22. http://www.newyorker.com/culture/cultural-comment/the-poor-door-and-the-glossy-reconfiguration-of-city-life.

Schwartz, Alex F. 2010. *Housing Policy in the United States*. New York: Routledge.

Schwartz, Heather, Lisa Ecola, Kristin Leuschner, and Aaron Kofner. 2012. *Is Inclusionary Zoning Inclusionary? A Guide for Practitioners*. RAND Corporation. https://www.rand.org/pubs/technical_reports/TR1231.html.

Stein, Samuel. 2016. "Chinatown: Unprotected and Undone." In *Zoned Out! Race, Displacement, and City Planning in New York City*, Tom Angotti and Sylvia Morse. New York: UR, 122–41. https://www.urpub.org/books/zonedout.

———. 2018. "Progress for Whom, Toward What? Progressive Politics and New York City's Mandatory Inclusionary Housing." *Journal of Urban Affairs* 40 (6): 770–81. https://doi.org/10.1080/07352166.2017.1403854.

———. 2019. *Capital City: Gentrification and the Real Estate State*. London; Brooklyn, NY: Verso.

Stabrowski, Filip. 2014. "New-Build Gentrification and the Everyday Displacement of Polish Immigrant Tenants in Greenpoint, Brooklyn." *Antipode* 46 (3): 794–815.

———. 2015. "Inclusionary Zoning and Exclusionary Development: The Politics of 'Affordable Housing' in North Brooklyn." *International Journal of Urban and Regional Research* 39 (6): 1120–36.

Susser, Ida. 2012. *Norman Street: Poverty and Politics in an Urban Neighborhood*, Oxford University Press. http://www.oxfordscholarship.com/view/10.1093/acprof:oso/9780195367317.001.0001/acprof-9780195367317.

Taylor-Gooby, Peter. 2012. "Root and Branch Restructuring to Achieve Major Cuts: The Social Policy Programme of the 2010 UK Coalition Government." *Social Policy & Administration* 46 (1): 61–82.

Testado, Justine. 2015. "Another Case of 'Poor Door' for Proposed Vancouver High-Rise." *Archinect*, May 8. https://archinect.com/news/article/126953722/another-case-of-poor-door-for-proposed-vancouver-high-rise.

Thaden, Emily, and Ruoniu Wang. 2017. "Inclusionary Housing in the United States: Prevalence, Impact, and Practices." Lincoln Institute of Land Policy. https://www.lincolninst. edu/sites/default/files/pubfiles/thaden_wp17et1_0.pdf.

The Huffington Post Canada. 2014. "This Toronto Condo Has Separate Entrances for Richer, Poorer." *The Huffington Post Canada*, September 4. https://www.huffingtonpost. ca/2014/09/04/poor-doors-toronto-condo_n_5767226.html.

Tilly, Charles. 1984. *Big Structures, Large Processes, Huge Comparisons*. New York: Russell Sage Foundation.

Tunstall, Rebecca. 2012. "Mixed communities and urban policy: Reflections from the UK" In *Mixed Communities: Gentrification by Stealth?*, Gary Bridge, Tim Butler, Loretta Lees. Bristol: Policy Press, 35–42.

Ullman, Seth, Michael Freedman-Schnapp, and Brad Lander. 2013. "Inclusionary Zoning in New York City: The Performance of New York City's Designated Areas Inclusionary Housing Program since its Launch in 2005." Office of Council Member Brad Lander. https://www.scribd.com/doc/160544058/Inclusionary-Zoning-in-New-York-City-The-performance-of-New-York-City-s-Designated-Areas-Inclusionary-Housing-Program-since-its-launch-in-2005.

Visser, Gustav, and Nico Kotze. 2008. "The State and New-Build Gentrification in Central Cape Town, South Africa." *Urban Studies* 45 (12): 2565–93. https://doi.org/10. 1177/0042098008097104.

Wainwright, Oliver. 2014. "'Poor Doors': Not the Worst Thing about Social Housing." *The Guardian*, July 30. http://www.theguardian.com/artanddesign/architecture-design-blog/2014/jul/30/poor-door-social-housing-apartheid.

———. 2015. "Revealed: How Developers Exploit Flawed Planning System to Minimise Affordable Housing." *The Guardian*, June 25. http://www.theguardian.com/cities/2015/ jun/25/london-developers-viability-planning-affordable-social-housing-regeneration-oliver-wainwright?CMP=share_btn_tw.

Watt, Paul. 2009. "Social Housing and Regeneration in London." In *Regenerating London*. Routledge.

———. 2017. "Social Housing and Urban Renewal: An Introduction." In *Social Housing and Urban Renewal. A Cross-National Perspective*, edited by Watt, Paul, and Peer Smets, 1–36. UK: Emerald Publishing.

———. 2018a. "Social Housing Not Social Cleansing': Contemporary Housing Struggles in London." In *Rent and Its Discontents. A Century of Housing Struggle*, edited by Grey, Neil, 117–35. London: Rowman & Littlefield.

———. 2018b. "Gendering the Right to Housing in the City: Homeless Female Lone Parents in Post-Olympics, Austerity East London." *Cities* 76 (June): 43–51. https://doi.org/ 10.1016/j.cities.2017.04.005.

———. 2021. *Estate Regeneration and Its Discontents: Public Housing, Place and Inequality in London*. Bristol: Policy Press.

West Side Rag. 2013. "New UWS Development Could Have Separate Entrance for Poorer People." *West Side Rag*, August 12. https://www.westsiderag.com/2013/08/12/new-uws-development-could-have-separate-entrance-for-poorer-people.

Whitehead, Christine. 2007. "Planning Policies and Affordable Housing: England as a Successful Case Study?" Housing Studies 22 (1)." *Housing Studies* 22 (1): 25–44.

Withnall, Adam. 2014. „'Poor Door' Controversy Extends to Washington DC as Affordable Housing 'Wing' given Entrance on Different Street - next to the Loading Bay. " *The Independent*, August 4. https://www.independent.co.uk/news/world/americas/poor-door-controversy-extends-to-washington-dc-as-affordable-housing-wing-given-entrance-on-different-street-next-to-the-loading-bay-9646069.html.

Wolf-Powers, Laura. 2019. "Reclaim Value Capture for Equitable Urban Development." *Metropolitics, May* 28.

Yglesias, Matthew. 2014. "In Defense of the NYC 'Poor Door.'" *Vox*, July 31. https://www. vox.com/2014/7/31/5954355/poor-door-inclusionary-housing.

1 Building the Way Out of the Crisis?

The Evolution of Inclusionary
Housing Policies in London and
New York City under Conditions
of Austerity

Over the last 50 years, New York City and London have both experienced persistent housing affordability problems. In addition, they have become prime targets for national austerity measures and the neoliberalization of housing policies. In this context, both city governments have increasingly turned to the private market to shoulder part of the wider societal costs of housing development, adopting Inclusionary Housing Programs (IHPs) as the primary vehicles through which they seek to create much-needed affordable housing.

More recently, while the global financial and economic crisis of 2008 set the stage for further cutbacks and an intensification of austerity urbanism (Peck 2012), tenants and local activists in both cities have been fighting for the provision of more decent and affordable housing across the income spectrum, demanding and proposing concrete policy alternatives that could break out of the neoliberal cycle. Against this backdrop, in both cities, a seemingly new generation of left-oriented city officials rose to office, in part because of their touted "progressive" housing agendas and "proximity" to urban activist movements. Bill de Blasio in New York City and Sadiq Khan in London have embraced inclusionary housing as one of the main "progressive" tools for addressing the cities' prevailing crises in affordable housing.

While surely many hoped that these recently adopted inclusionary housing policies would be characterized as what has been called in the literature – particularly the German literature – post-neoliberal housing policy[1] (i.a. Kadi, Vollmer, and Stein 2021; Rinn 2018; Schipper 2015, 2021; Vogelpohl and Buchholz 2017), most tenant organizations and local community coalitions wondered from the very beginning whether the programs would bring the desired effects.

In this chapter, I take a close look at the evolution of inclusionary housing in London and New York City from the 1970s until 2020, just before the outbreak of the COVID-19 pandemic, to assess their takes on inclusionary housing and evaluate the extent of which both city governments have broken with the market-based policy instituted by their predecessors, and, in doing so, have been able to counteract the prevailing housing affordability problems. I, thereby, trace the history of inclusionary housing in both cities by embedding it in a broader debate about the core principles of austerity urbanism and neoliberal housing policy such as the national cuts in spending, the continuous disinvestment in social and public rental housing, the market-based restructuring of low-income housing, increased power

DOI: 10.4324/9781003468479-2

and influence of private real estate and financial capital in housing production and planning procedures, as well as gentrification efforts to attract middle- and upper-classes to city centers (i.a. Hodkinson, Watt, and Mooney 2013; Jacobs 2019; Kadi and Ronald 2016). I further touch upon, but do not fully engage in, the more recent debate on post-neoliberalism. This has not primarily to do with the fact that the debate revolves mainly around German cities, but rather because, although some announce a noteworthy post-neoliberal shift (Vogelpohl and Buchholz 2017), most scholars within this debate do not see a general departure from neoliberal housing policies (Kadi, Vollmer, and Stein 2021 2021; Rinn 2018; Schipper 2021).

Inclusionary housing policies only date back to the 1980s in New York City and the early 2000s in London, but have evolved in both cities to the point where it is possible to place the development of the program in chronological order. While most scholars researching inclusionary housing would agree that the programs in both cities evolved over time, little attempt has been made so far to chronicle, much less theorize the changes. As such, I discern three phases of inclusionary housing that appear in both cities, with New York City being somewhat ahead of London (Figure 1.1). These three phases show how inclusionary housing has been adapted to changing economic and political conditions on the local, national, and global scale. Despite the considerable differences in the two cities' housing programs, due in large part to their different housing and planning systems, I intend to highlight the broader similarities and common trajectories as well as some particularities of inclusionary housing in these two cities. In doing so, I illustrate how inclusionary housing reflects the broader conditions of urban governance in the context of austerity.

This periodization is based on primary as well as secondary readings of London and New York City and may not necessarily have wider application, nor is it exhaustive in relation to the evolution of inclusionary housing. Even though I do not claim that these phases are globally applicable, the broader economic and political events of the last five decades probably influenced inclusionary housing practices in other Western countries. However, the specific dates or length of these phases might vary from place to place. This, however, is open for empirical verification. Moreover, not all countries have these kinds of programs.

I am also aware that there are other periodizations in the field of political economy of housing policy that take a similar approach, though not in relation to inclusionary housing. One influential example is Hackworth and Smith's (2001) article on *The Changing State of Gentrification*, in which they propose three waves of gentrification as well as their expansions to a fourth (Lees et al. 2008) and fifth wave of gentrification (Aalbers 2019). My periodization should in no way be taken as a contradiction to these studies. Rather, it is meant as a complement in the sense that the second and third phases of inclusionary housing can be assigned to Hackworth and Smith's third wave, which is characterized by state-led gentrification, as well as Aalbers fifth wave of gentrification in which the state's role in gentrification is supplemented by finance (ibid.).

I analyze the evolution of inclusionary housing policies as part of government's responses to the austerity measures imposed on local authorities and the deepening affordability problems in housing by discussing each mayor's housing plans and

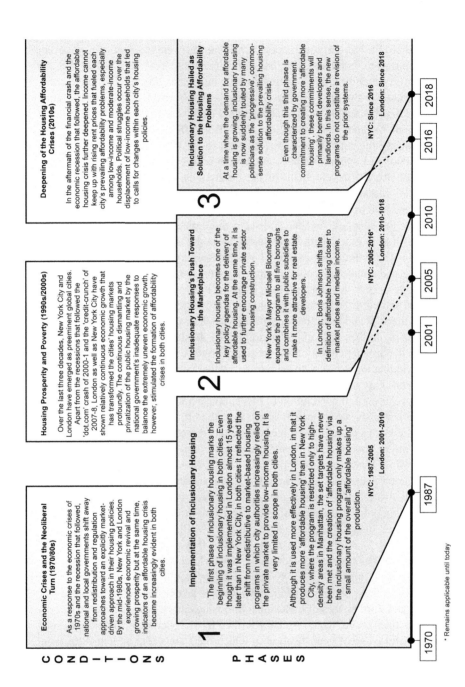

Figure 1.1 Periodization of inclusionary housing in New York City and London.

strategies. In the last decades, the neoliberal reconfiguration of state-market-civil society relations in London and New York has strengthened the role of the mayor in providing strategic housing plans. In New York City, it was under the Koch administration (1978–89) that a comprehensive housing plan was implemented for the first time, including the city's first IHP. Inclusionary housing was then further developed under the administrations of Michael Bloomberg (2002–13), and Bill de Blasio (2014–21). In London, inclusionary housing was implemented under London's first Mayor, Ken Levingston (2000–08) and then adjusted under the administrations of Boris Johnson (2008–16) and Sadiq Khan (since 2016).

I discuss the three phases of inclusionary housing in three main sections. Each section begins with a discussion of the particular constellations of the economic and political conditions as well as the changes the cities' housing and planning systems have undergone within that defined period. While I acknowledge the important differences between the two cities' national and local developments and conditions, I show in each section that both cities have undergone similar housing trends and reforms that are marked by neoliberalization and austerity urbanism. The second part of each of the three sections is divided into two subsections that outline each city's particular take on inclusionary housing and highlight its commonalities in that defined phase. A final section focuses on answering the question of whether the recent takes on inclusionary housing in both cities present a break with the market-based policy-making of their predecessors.

First Phase of Inclusionary Housing

Setting the Stage: The Economic Crises of the 1970s and the Neoliberal Turn in Housing Policy in New York City and London

London's and New York's developments in the last decades have been parallel in many ways. Both cities went through an economic recession in the 1970s, even though it hit New York harder than London, which experienced the recession over a longer period. In both cases, as a response to the recessions, national and local governments shifted away from redistribution and regulation approaches toward an explicitly market-driven approach in their housing policies (Gordon and Harloe 1991: 378). It was against this backdrop that inclusionary housing was created first in New York City and later in London. I briefly depict the conditions that led in both cities to the implementation of the first IHPs, which will be introduced in the next subsection.

New York City is known to be the poster child for fiscal crisis management and institutional restructuring at the urban scale (Harvey 2005: 44; Davidson and Ward 2018: 9). In the 1970s, New York faced a combined urban and fiscal crisis.[2] By 1975, the city was not able to pay for its operating expenses nor to borrow more money and faced the prospect of defaulting on its obligations and declaring bankruptcy. President Gerald Ford announced that he would not bail the city out, prompting the New York City *Daily News* to publish the infamous headline: "Ford to City: Drop Dead" (Phillips-Fein 2017: 1).

To solve New York City's fiscal crisis, New York State stripped the city government of all financial responsibility and created several business-dominated bodies that had the task to oversee NYC's budget and future spending. According to David Harvey (2005), the management of this fiscal crisis "pioneered the way for neoliberal practices" (Harvey 2005: 48). The shifting of control of public policy from the mayor to these newly created agencies to guarantee fiscal solvency provided an opportunity for external actors to dictate New York City's policy and opened the doors for private market investment. From there on, the city dramatically rolled back spending on a broad array of public services. In other words, these new agencies enacted a regime of de facto urban austerity that continues in many respects to this very day.

In the long run, this crisis and its management shaped New York City's priorities in favor of real estate and finance capital. As a development strategy to encourage developers to invest in the city, New York City as well as the state adopted a pro-development strategy of tax credits and tax exemption programs that would not require direct expenditures from the government. Noteworthy in this context is the city-run but state-funded 421a property tax exemption program mentioned in the Introduction. New York State created the program in 1971 at a time when almost no one was developing residential buildings in the city. It became a crucial tax exemption program for Koch's housing plan because it aimed at giving property tax breaks to developers of residential buildings. In the beginning, it was used to subsidize all residential buildings, but later it was only used to stimulate the creation of affordable housing. In the course of this chapter, we will come back to this program since it played a key role in the implementation of de Blasio's mandatory IHP in 2016.

After the combined urban and fiscal crisis in New York, the city experienced an economic revival and growing prosperity, but at the same time by the mid-1980s indicators of an affordable housing crisis became increasingly evident (again): housing prices and rents were beginning once again to rise rapidly throughout the city, homelessness had become a growing and increasingly visible problem and over 175,000 households were on the Housing Authority's waiting list for public housing (Fainstein 1994: 106; NYU Furman Center 2006). Even though the city's population was growing again, there was no low-income housing being created, mainly due to the fact that the Nixon administration had put a hold on new public housing construction and the Reagan administration in Washington, as well as the New York State authority, further began to reduce its redistributive strategies in urban housing markets.

It was in this context that New York City introduced its first IHP. It was implemented as a "density bonus" program in 1987 in conjunction with Mayor Koch's housing plan that was designed to stimulate real estate growth while at the same time generating low-income housing through the marketplace.

The fiscal and urban crisis of the 1970s that hit "New York had no direct parallel in London" (Gordon and Harloe 1991: 380). None of the central elements that led to the combined urban and fiscal crises of New York, such as residential abandonment, loss of tax revenues, near fiscal bankruptcy, and deep cuts in public employment, played a major role in London during the 1970s. This does not mean that London or the UK as a whole did not experience a state of crisis during the 1970s. Between the early 1960s and the mid-1980s, London lost about 800,000 jobs, which made up about 18 percent of total employment. The loss was mainly in the manufacturing sector due to the closures of inner-city factories. The population in London fell from about 8 million to about 6.5 million during that time. The main difference to New York here is that the decline in population and employment in London extended over a longer period, while in New York the decline had been limited to the early and mid-1970s. In other words, "London government escaped the fiscal crisis that hit New York City" (Gordon and Harloe 1991: 393), albeit against the backdrop of a longer period of decline.

As in New York City or pretty much anywhere in the US at the time, the economic crisis of the 1970s also marked the ending of the long post-war boom in the UK and had profound implications for the housing sector in London: by the mid-1970s, national housing policy had already re-directed its course, subsidies for local authorities had been cut back, and grants for the improvement of private housing were increased. The central government considered real estate development as a strategy to stimulate economic growth, and thus encouraged local authorities to become facilitators rather than providers of housing (Crook 1996: 55). The construction of new council housing that dominated post-war housing policies was no longer a priority. This break in council housing policy was exacerbated when Margaret Thatcher's government pursued a policy of privatization and implemented the "Right to Buy" scheme in 1980, which gave those living in council houses the ability to buy their homes. Since then, more than 300,000 homes have been passed onto private ownership through the "Right to Buy" scheme (Mayor of London 2021).

The Thatcher government further transferred capital grants for the provision of new low-cost homes to independent non-profit housing associations that had to buy land on the open market. However, this resulted in a drastic increase in land prices that then stirred public concern over affordability and the difficulty for lower-income households to access the housing market, especially in areas of tight planning constraints (Pawson and Mullins 2010).

Local authorities at the time attempted to use the planning system specifically to secure affordable housing. In need of low-income housing, local authorities started to use their considerable discretion power to negotiate binding agreements with developers that restricted their developments to higher density as a possible way of meeting local housing needs. Since this process of bargaining and negotiating was, however, very informal, it created public concern and debate since it undermined the national development plan system and used sites that were not suitable for residential development.

It was during this time that the Thatcher government implemented the Town and Country Planning Act of 1990. This act reflected the central government's balancing act between keeping the real estate market "hot" and dealing with growing inequality: it combined the stimulation of real estate growth through the provision of subsidies for developers with the provision of affordable housing. This act fundamentally changed the planning arrangements, notably in terms of delivering affordable housing through the planning system. In other words, it was the birth of inclusionary housing politics in England.[3]

Due to the absence of London's municipal government at the time,[4] it was not until the turn of the century, however, that inclusionary housing was implemented in London. Since 1986, the central government, in the form of the Department of Environment (DoE), acted mainly as London's executive authority. The DoE, however, did not play an assertive role in producing comprehensive development plans in London. It rather restricted its actions to being an appeal body when, for example, developers were denied planning permission by local authorities (Fainstein 1994: 85). In 2000, when the Greater London Authority (GLA) was established, the city gradually reasserted its role in designing and implementing its own programs to address its severe housing problems.

In short, inclusionary housing policies emerged in both cities, at a time when the capacity of the local state to act was limited. For the local state, it provided a way to respond to the housing crisis, but following neoliberal logic, by providing affordable housing through the very marketplace that had caused the affordability problems in the first place.

Development Rather than Welfare: Origins of Inclusionary Housing in New York City and London

The first phase of inclusionary housing marks the beginning of inclusionary housing in both cities. Even though it was implemented in London almost 15 years later than in New York City, in both cities it reflected the shift from redistributive to market-based housing programs in which city authorities increasingly relied on the private market to provide low-income housing.

New York City: The Rise of Inclusionary Housing in the Wake of Urban Renewal

The story of inclusionary housing in New York City starts in 1987. The increasingly heated housing market and the changed urban governance relations in New York City had set the conditions for the implementation of a voluntary IHP that would stimulate the private sector provision of low-income housing.

The first IHP in New York City was implemented as part of Mayor Edward Koch's housing plan: in 1987, after years of pressure from grassroots organizations to tackle the housing problem, Mayor Edward Koch (1978–1989), a Democrat, launched an ambitious Ten-Year Housing Plan to stimulate "affordable housing" construction and rehabilitation. He used new housing policy and financing strategies to fulfill the housing goals laid out in the Plan: he used about $5 billion of the city's capital budget to invest in low-income housing (Schwartz 1999). According to a speech given by the mayor in 1985, the proposed plan was "a comprehensive strategy for maintaining the City's existing housing and producing new housing for a broad range of income groups throughout the city" (Koch 1985). The specific "aim was to renovate 82,000 units in occupied *in rem*[5] buildings, rebuild 47,000 units in vacant *in rem* buildings, build 37,000 new units and upgrade 87,000 apartments in privately owned buildings" (NYU Furman Center 2006: 3).

While the 1980s marked an overall transformation of the regulatory framework of New York's housing market, Koch's housing plan mirrored this interim phase. It entailed redistributive programs that are more characteristic of the post-war years, but it also entailed a range of programs that heralded the market-based housing policies of the years to come (Kadi and Ronald 2016: 273).

The so-called *in rem* housing program, for example, can be characterized as one of the last redistributive housing programs in New York City. It aimed at rehabilitating vacant tax-foreclosed housing or properties of which the city took ownership and then rented out at low cost. By 1979, the city had, for example, taken ownership through tax foreclosure of over 100,000 units, most of them in abandoned buildings (Braconi 1999). It is for this reason that one can consider Koch's housing plan as one of the last "spending-intensive supply-side initiatives" (Kadi and Ronald 2016: 273).

However, the plan marked the beginning of a shift from direct public funding of low-income housing to subsidies for private developers, relying heavily on the private market to provide and maintain low-income housing. [6] Inclusionary housing represented one of these new market-based housing policy approaches. Its introduction was one of the main pillars of Koch's housing plan.

Inclusionary housing was primarily introduced as a density bonus program that allowed new residential developments in high-density areas to take a density bonus and increase the maximum allowable Floor Area Ratio (FAR), more commonly known as density, from 10.0 to 12.0, in exchange for creating or preserving permanently "affordable housing" units at or below 80 percent of the AMI. In other words, for each square foot of "affordable housing," the city granted 3.5 square feet of additional floor area. Since the maximum allowable FAR is determined at 12.0, which generally results in a 20 percent density bonus, the "affordable housing" being generated was less than 5 percent. The granted density bonus was substantially reduced when additional public subsidies were used in order to avoid "double-dipping" by developers (Association for Neighborhood and Housing Development (ANHD) 2015: 9).

The idea of the program was to use the strength of the real estate sector in these urban areas to produce below-market-rate housing and to counteract the urban sprawl by redirecting growth from the suburbs to the inner cities through redevelopment and densification. As such, the program only applied to Manhattan, predominantly in lower and mid-Manhattan, since nowhere else was a maximum allowable FAR of 10.0 deemed possible (ANHD 2015: 9). That is why the program is also known as the R10[7]-IH program.

Reflecting Koch's housing plan, Jonathan Soffer – author of *Ed Koch and the Rebuilding of New York City* (2010) – called Koch's housing plan "primarily an economic development program, not a welfare program" (Soffer 2010: 295). That is, the neoliberalization of housing that has affected the rest of the country since the 1980s didn't stop in New York City. Even though the Dinkins and Giuliani administrations by and large continued Koch's ten-year plan in the decade to come – including the IHP – New York's rental market has been continuously deregulated, leading to a shrinking of the protected rental stock (Kadi and Ronald 2016: 277). According to Kadi and Ronald (2016), there have been mainly three policy measures that led to the deregulation of the rental market: first, on the federal level, funding for supply-side programs like project-based Section 8[8] was cut. Second, on the New York State level, funding for the Mitchell-Lama[9] rental units was discontinued and rent regulation was weakened when the Giuliani administration introduced the policy measure "luxury decontrol" in 1993, which was extended in 1997. The measure allowed apartments with a monthly rent of $2,000 or more to be unaffected by rent control (Kadi and Ronald 2016: 277). Third, on the local level, supply-side funding was also reduced, together with the overall spending of the city's budget on housing, which dropped by about three-fourths of the annual budget by the mid-1990s. In addition, as part of the Koch housing plan, the *in rem* units were sold to private developers.

With respect to the newly adopted inclusionary housing or R10-IH program, as it is often called, it failed to generate much "affordable housing," mainly due to the fact that it stood in competition with the Privately-Owned Public Spaces (POPS) program. This was another density bonus program, where the city granted a density bonus to developers in exchange for a publicly accessible plaza or atrium (Marcus 1992: 722). Since the costs of producing a public space are much smaller than the costs of producing "affordable housing," developers almost always chose the POPS program over R10-IH (Stein 2018: 5). The POPS program led to a range of architectural peculiarities – a public plaza or atrium, for example, in the entrance area or on the roof of a privately owned house.

By the early 2000s, inclusionary housing had not only been increasingly implemented by other major US cities that also were experiencing rapid rise in housing prices, such as Chicago, Boston, and San Francisco (Mallach and Calavita 2010: 25), but had also spread to a growing number of countries and cities in Europe, starting with England in 1990.

London: Inclusionary Housing Set against London's Global Economic Success

Unlike the US, where the implementation of inclusionary housing varies from state to state and municipality to municipality, it was adopted in England on the national level in 1990 and about a decade later in London.

The Town and Country Planning Act of 1990 and the amended Planning and Compensation Act of 1991 gave local authorities, through Section 106 (short: S106), the power to negotiate with developers the provision of community infrastructure such as "affordable housing" in the way specified in a local development plan. That is why in England inclusionary housing is generally just called Section 106.

The act affected the planning system profoundly, as it represented a "general move from a regulatory to a negotiation style of development control" (Cullingworth and Nadin 2006: 200). In other words, this approach introduced by the Conservatives "is one of negotiations rather than formal taxation" (Whitehead 2007: 34). The success of this new planning system, therefore, depends on local planning authorities to reach an agreement with developers on the planning obligations (ibid.). On the one hand, this new act certainly further institutionalized the 1947 Act concept of planning gain by giving local authorities the power to negotiate planning obligations. On the other hand, it only served to further erode the already compromised 1947 Act and the idea of a national betterment tax (Ward 2004: 237).

In the beginning, the new law proved to be not as successful as policymakers hoped it would be. By 1997, only about half of English local authorities had implemented development plans that defined the need for additional "affordable housing" (ibid.). Nevertheless, it almost doubled in the following years, and by 2001, the number of local authorities that had implemented inclusionary housing was close to 90 percent (ibid.: 238).

It was not until 2000 that London gradually reasserted its role in designing and implementing its own programs to address its severe housing problems. In 2000, the GLA was established as the new regional governance body of Greater London and the City of London. The first elected Mayor of London, Ken Livingstone, who ran as an Independent, determined in 2001 that Section 106 agreements should be a key source for the provision of "affordable housing." This made the planning system mainly responsible for the contribution to the provision of "affordable housing" in London (GLA 2004: 67).

Against the backdrop of London's economic success while experiencing severe housing problems, Livingstone put a clear emphasis on the provision of additional "affordable housing" as well as on the promotion of mixed and balanced communities (ibid.: 61). Due to his closeness to property developers, he deemed inclusionary housing the right means to create the "affordable housing" needed, as he thought he would be able to "get more 'affordable housing' out of property developers than [...] out of government" (Horwitz and Robinson 2015: 89).

Just a few months before his re-election in 2004, he announced his Spatial Development Plan that came to be known as the London Plan, in which he laid out – among other things – his housing policy approach. His housing target for new housing was 30,000 additional dwellings per year, of which 50 percent should be "affordable housing." The Plan further introduced a new definition of "affordable housing" that was designed "to meet the full spectrum of housing need" (GLA 2004: 61). "Affordable housing" was divided into social and intermediate housing: social housing "is on the basis of housing need, and rents are no higher than target rents set by the government for housing association and local authority rents" (ibid.). In contrast, intermediate housing, which can include shared ownership, sub-market rent provision, and key worker housing, "is substantially below open market levels and is affordable by households on incomes of less than £40,000" (ibid.). The overall ratio of "affordable housing" to be achieved was supposed to be 70 percent social housing and 30 percent intermediate housing (ibid.: 63) (Table 1.2). That meant that, similar to NYC, the moderate and lower middle classes were now included in what was called "affordable housing."

The London Plan also disclosed how market-driven and urban growth-oriented Ken Livingstone's housing policy was. He stressed that residential development should be encouraged rather than restrained by local authorities and prompted the boroughs to "take a reasonable and flexible approach on a site-by-site basis" (ibid.: 65). He further encouraged the boroughs as well as private actors such as house builders or housing associations to "take a more pro-active approach in pre-application discussions, public consultation and negotiations over planning agreements" (ibid.: 65).

Morrison and Burgess (2014) argue that overall Section 106 has "success-fully" (Morrison and Burgess 2014: 430) contributed to the creation of "afford-able housing" before the financial meltdown of 2008. They largely attribute it "to the fact that until 2007 there was buoyant demand and rising house prices, producing high development values that enabled developers to agree and fulfill obligations" (ibid.: 424).

However, according to the Annual Monitoring Report by the GLA in 2009, the "affordable housing" target of 30,000 has never been met. Between 2004/05 and 2007/08, a total of about 50,000 affordable homes were delivered in London, which comes down to about 35 percent of the total net number of new homes. The breakdown between social rent and intermediate housing was evenly split between the two, contrary to the set target that envisaged 70 percent social housing and 30 percent intermediate homes (GLA 2009). This tendency to favor moderate- to middle-income households over those in need of social housing would be rein-forced by Boris Johnson's take on inclusionary housing.

In summary, in this first phase, inclusionary housing as a policy was very lim-ited in scope in both cities. Although it was used more effectively in London, in that it produced more "affordable housing" than in New York City, where the program was restricted only to high-density areas in Manhattan, the set targets were never met and the creation of "affordable housing" via the IHP only made up a small amount of the overall "affordable housing" production.

During the 1990s and the turn of the century, both cities' economies were rela-tively strong and the housing markets were increasingly heated. At the same time, the demand for low-income housing was increasingly high, leading officials in both cities to change the rules of inclusionary housing.

Second Phase of Inclusionary Housing

Housing Prosperity and Poverty in New York City and London:
From the Economic Boom Years of the 1990s and Early 2000s
to the Financial Crisis of 2008

Over the last three decades, New York City and London have emerged as preemi-nent "global cities" (Sassen 2001). Apart from the recessions that followed the "dot.com" crash of 2000–1 and the "credit-crunch" of 2007–8, London and New York City have shown relatively continuous economic growth that has transformed the cities' housing markets profoundly. Indeed, some of the most severe effects of handing power to market forces could be seen in the housing field.

House and rent prices were largely unruffled by the "dot.com" stock market crash of 2000 that stretched until 2003, climbing continuously until the credit crunch in 2007. During the decades-long period of growth, from the 1980s to 2007, social polarization deepened and housing affordability increasingly became a prob-lem. Soaring houses as well as rent prices, a real estate construction boom, and increased mortgage access led to an increase in indebted households and a rise in homelessness (Mulliner and Maliene 2013).

In London, house prices grew almost continuously, and average house prices nearly tripled between 1997 and 2007 (GLA 2009), increasing by an annual rate of about 9 percent (Marsden 2015: 19). The privatization of social housing – once the largest tenure in London – through *Right to Buy* as well as the increasing unaffordability of house prices expanded (again) the private renting sector, which grew from 13 percent of the overall housing sector in 1991 to 20 percent in 2007 (ibid.: 29). It was estimated that there were about 1.8 million owner-occupied households, including 750,000 in "affordable" homes and 650,000 households in the private renting sector in 2007 (ibid.: 7). In the early 1990s, local authorities more or less stopped building new social housing and depended for the supply of new "affordable housing" almost entirely on the private market and housing associations (ibid.: 8). At the same time, housing affordability became the biggest issue cited by Londoners (ibid.: 11). This problem was amplified by a continuously growing population that increased from 6.8 million in 1991 to about 7.6 million in 2007 (GLA 2020). The number of households on local authority waiting lists almost doubled from 1997 to 2007 with over 350,000 households compared to 179,000 ten years earlier (GLA 2009: 23). Furthermore, about 210,000 households were overcrowded with the majority in social rent housing (ibid.).

Despite the continuous dismantling and privatization of the public housing market, the homeownership rate in New York City increased only modestly between 1990 and 2005 and was still less than half the rate of the rest of the country. However, it varied widely within the various ethnicities ranging from 44 percent for whites to just 16 percent for Hispanics and 15 percent for Blacks (NYU Furman Center 2007: 1). Though Blacks and Hispanics together made up only about one-third of total homeowners, they obtained almost 51 percent of all refinance loans and 69 percent of all subprime refinance loans in 2006 (ibid.: 2). As a result, these communities were most affected by the foreclosure crisis in New York City. Furthermore, the building boom increased substantially: between 2000 and 2006, the construction rate grew approximately 12 percent annually, peaking at 25,659 new units completed in 2007 – the highest rate seen in 20 years. Most of the units were constructed in Manhattan, followed by Brooklyn and Queens (NYU Furman Center 2009: 5). However, the population in New York City increased by almost a million from 7.3 million in 1990 to 8.2 in 2006 (NYU Furman Center 2007: 39). The real estate boom could not keep up with the demand, which pushed up the house prices: from 1974 to 2006, home prices increased by 250 percent, with half of the growth rate resulting from the boom between 1996 and 2006, when housing prices increased by 124 percent (NYU Furman Center 2008: 6).

This economic and real estate growth in New York City had negative effects on the housing market, especially in the low-income housing sector. Income increases couldn't keep up with the inflated housing costs. From 1975 to 1999, average rent increased by 33 percent, while the average income of renters in New York City only went up by 3 percent (Rose, Lander, and Feng 2004: 5). By 2005, about 1.8 million were officially designated poor in New York. Poverty in the city was at 22 percent – about twice the national average and much higher than it was in 1975 (Moody 2007: 288). Over the period of 1990–2006, the vacancy rate was constantly below 5 percent and mostly affected lower rent units – a clear indication of a distressed housing market (NYU Furman Center 2007: 39; Rose et al. 2004: 5). The lack of affordable housing was further marked by growing waiting lists for subsidized housing and record-high homelessness rates (Rose et al. 2004: 5).

The financial meltdown of 2007 briefly halted growth in the housing market in both cities. However, house prices in both cities rose once again and rapidly reached pre-credit crunch levels. In London, for example, house prices returned to pre-credit crunch levels by 2010. Between 2009 and 2016, they increased by almost 100 percent (Sayce et al. 2017: 5). In 2017, residential development in London was at its highest since 1977 (GLA 2018a: 13). In New York City, house prices have increased by about 51 percent between 2009 and 2017. Meanwhile, by 2017, residential building permits returned to the level they were before the subprime mortgage crisis of 2007 (NYU Furman Center 2018: 34).

Although house prices briefly fell, this did not translate to more affordable housing. In New York City, the unemployment rate grew from 8.4 percent in 2005 to 11.2 percent in 2010. In just one year (2009–10), the poverty rate increased by 1.4 percentage points while median household income declined. As of 2010, the median household income was $50,130, compared to $52,334 in 2009. While incomes have fallen and unemployment has grown, rents between 2005 and 2010 have increased on average by 7.7 percent for all renters, and by as much as 11.2 percent for those signing new rental contracts during this period (NYU Furman Center 2011: 48ff).

Meanwhile in London, "affordable housing" delivery through Section 106 dropped after the credit crunch by about 60 percent between 2007 and 2010 (Department for Levelling Up, Housing and Communities (DLUHC) 2021). In 2012, the number of households on the housing waiting list peaked at more than 380,000 households, compared to about 331,000 households just before the credit crunch in 2006 (Ministry of Housing, Communities and Local Government (MHCLG) 2021). Consequently, the need for affordable housing was not abated but rather increased during that period.

The dramatic increase in housing prices is thus seen to have arisen in connection with both the real estate boom and the national government's inadequate response to extreme and uneven economic growth. The deregulation and privatization policies of the Reagan and Thatcher administrations, which were later carried forward by their successors and adopted by local authorities through the mid- to late-2000s, thus can be seen to have stimulated the uneven urban development visible today in both New York and London. Against this backdrop, local authorities in both cities who saw IHPs as a tool to profit from the real estate boom, expanded the program in the mid- and late-2000s.

Inclusionary Housing's Push Toward the Marketplace

In this second phase, inclusionary housing became one of the key policy agendas for the delivery of "affordable housing" in both cities. At the same time, it was used to further encourage private-sector housing construction.

New York City: Inclusionary Housing as a Developer's Choice

Facing a severe affordable housing shortage by the early 2000s, mainly due to the privatization of *in rem* housing, a decline of the protected rental segment, and a growth in the unprotected private rental segment, the newly elected Republican Mayor Michael Bloomberg launched a housing plan called New Housing Marketplace Plan in 2002. The goal was to finance the construction and preservation of 65,000 "affordable housing" units within the next five years. A hallmark of his administration, Bloomberg's Plan marked the start of the largest investment in the city's housing stock since Ed Koch's Ten-Year Housing Plan (New York City Department of Housing, Preservation and Development (NYC HPD) 2002: 3). Spurred by the real estate boom of the pre-2007 crash and the growing affordability crisis that low- and middle-income households faced, Bloomberg adjusted his housing plan three times: in 2004, he increased the plan's goal to 68,000 units, and in 2006, he further expanded it to finance the creation and preservation of 165,000 "affordable housing" units, thus "making it the largest municipal housing effort in the nation's history" (ibid.: 5). In 2010, when the nation was sliding into an economic recession after the foreclosure crisis of 2008 and credit for construction came to a halt, Bloomberg added another million to the city's investment in the plan, raising the total public budget allocation to $8,5 billion, compared to $5,1 under the Koch administration (NYC HPD 2002: 6).

As the name of the plan already suggests, Bloomberg's plan to increase "affordable housing" depended very much on what he called "innovative government policy" (ibid: 5), that is, the active engagement in strong public-private partnerships. Thus, the plan emphasized: "(1) finding new land for workforce housing; (2) creating incentives to develop housing for new populations; (3) harnessing the private market to create 'affordable housing'; and (4) preserving government-assisted housing" (ibid.: 6).

Consistent with Bloomberg's growth plan was his so-called "zoning blitz" (Angotti 2016a: 32), when through almost 140 separate zoning proceedings about 40 percent of the land in the city was rezoned. According to a study done by the NYU Furman Center in 2010, the rezoning reflected "a wide range of goals: advancing the City's economic development agenda; accommodating expected population growth [...] and responding to the varied needs and preferences of the City's diverse neighborhoods" (NYU Furman Center 2010: 1). Interestingly, the majority of these rezonings were downzonings that had the aim of preserving existing neighborhoods (Angotti 2016a: 32), in contrast to upzoning that primarily aims at increasing the area's capacity for development. The mentioned study looked at the impact of 76 rezonings that took place before the credit crunch of 2008 and found that, on the one hand, "[u]pzoned lots were more likely to be in areas that have a higher share of Black and Hispanic residents than the City median" (NYU Furman Center 2010: 10), while on the other hand, "[d]ownzoned lots were more likely to be located in tracts with a higher share of non-Hispanic white residents than the City median" (ibid.: 9). In other words, while these rezonings primarily protected affluent white neighborhoods through downzoning, they opened up primarily of color neighborhoods to development through upzoning (or no change in zoning regulations when the surrounding neighborhoods were protected through downzoning).

In large response to growing pressure from campaigns by community-based organizations (Angotti and Morse 2016: 69) to ensure that these upzonings did not have an adverse impact on the affected neighborhoods by increasing local housing prices and rent burdens of local residents, the Bloomberg Administration in 2005 expanded New York City's Inclusionary Zoning ordinance by creating a voluntary inclusionary housing system called the *Specified Designated Growth Areas (Designated Areas) Inclusionary Housing Program* (IHP).

This new "branch of the Inclusionary Housing Program" (ANHD 2015: 9) was an expansion of Koch's 1987 Inclusionary Zoning Program in two respects: first, it expanded the program across all boroughs, where developers now had the option of a density bonus that included medium-density residential development in areas designated as inclusionary housing zones. The areas generally had a density of three- to nine-FAR. The allowable increase in FAR for a density bonus was determined at a maximum of 33 percent, in exchange for the construction or preservation of 20 percent of the total units as affordable (on or off-site). Said differently, a developer received a density bonus of 1.25 square feet for every square foot of "affordable housing" built or preserved, which amounted to a maximum density bonus of 33 percent if 20 percent of the units were set aside as permanently affordable (ANHD 2015: 9). This stands in contrast to the 1987 IHP that only provided a density bonus in R10-areas where developers were able to increase their allowable FAR to 12.0 in exchange for permanently "affordable housing" units at or below 80 percent of the AMI (Table 1.1).

Second, in contrast to the R10-IH program, the new program allowed developers to combine the density bonus with public subsidies. In order to keep the city attractive for development and in order to make the program attractive for developers – in response to many developers initially choosing not to participate in the program due to its voluntary nature – the city provided developers with a range of subsidies, such as the 421a tax exemption, tax-exempt bond financing, or the federal program Low-Income Housing Tax Credits (LIHTC), in exchange for the provision of approximately 20 percent "affordable housing" units. In that way, the developers were able to "double-dip" – receive a density bonus and access to public subsidies.

Even though this so-called "*Designated Areas*" IHP adopted under the Bloomberg administration was generally considered to be a "significant neighborhood victory and policy step forward for the city" (Dulchin, Gates, and Williams 2013: 5), it has received much criticism, in particular for generating far too few affordable housing units and for distributing them too unevenly within the city.

A 2013 report by the Office of Council Member Brad Lander that reviewed the effectiveness of Bloomberg's inclusionary zoning program found that the program had generated only 2,769 "affordable housing" units since its inception in 2005 (Ullman, Freedman-Schnapp, and Lander 2013: 1). Furthermore, the loss of rent-regulated apartments due to demolition in those areas, which the report estimated at about 1,000 rent-regulated units, reduced "the net 'affordable housing' generated in those areas by 36% to around 1,700" (ibid.: 17). This is similar to the number of affordable units created with Koch's R10-IH program, which created only 1,753 affordable units in the 25 years from 1987 to 2013 (ANHD 2015: 10).

Table 1.1 Evolution of Inclusionary Housing Based on the Mayor's Housing Plans in New York City

	R10-Inclusionary Housing Program*	Inclusionary Housing Program (IHP) Designated Areas	Mandatory Inclusionary Housing (MIH)
	1987	2005	2016
	Ten Year Plan	New Housing Marketplace	Housing New York
	Mayors: Edward Koch	Mayor: Michael Bloomberg	Mayor: Bill de Blasio
	Democrat	Republican/independent	Democrat
	1978–98 (+ Dinkins, Giuliani)	2002–13	2014–21
Affordable housing target	150,000	165,000	200,000**
Preservation	N/A	N/A	120,000
New construction	N/A	N/A	80,000
IH target	N/A	10,000	12,000
Voluntary/mandatory	Voluntary	Voluntary	Mandatory
IH percentage	Max. 5%	20%	20–30% (depending on the option)***
AMI target	>80 % AMI (at or below)	>80 % AMI (at or below)	40 AMI–115 AMI (on average, depending on the option)***
Affordability Duration	Permanently	Permanently	Permanently
Density bonus	20%	Up to 33%	Yes
Off-site allowance	Yes	Yes	Yes
In-lieu fee	Yes	Yes	Yes
Can be combined with housing subsidies	No	Yes	Yes
Area of application	Manhattan (areas with R10 density)	Specific areas citywide	Citywide in case of upzoning
Total unit production (changes underway)	1,753	2,769	4,000 (as of 2022)

* Remains applicable today.
** In 2017, the target was upped to 300,000 housing units (120,000 new and 180,000 preserved) by 2026.
*** For more information see Table 1.3.
Source: Data compiled by author, based on Mayor's Housing Plans and HPD data.

In a report done by the ANHD, a non-profit neighborhood housing group, the authors Benjamin Dulchin, Moses Gates, and Barika Williams further argued that the voluntary inclusionary zoning program has "not produced nearly as many units as the city needs, or as it should be gaining in return for the value granted to the developer through the rezoning" (Dulchin et al. 2013: 5). According to them, the units generated by this program between 2005 and 2011 were less than 2 percent of the total units developed under the Bloomberg administration's rezoning and "is a far cry from the 10,000 units of 'affordable housing' the city was projecting would be generated from IHP" (ibid.: 6).

Furthermore, the upzonings created through a density bonus in areas such as Williamsburg/Greenpoint along the waterfront enormously increased the value of the rezoned land for the developer or landowner due to the land's higher possible income by selling or renting the newly developed residential units. Since a higher-density property generally has a larger number of tenants or owners on the same lot, it presents a greater potential income for the owner in rents and for the developer in sales. These increased land values have made it harder for long-time residents to afford to rent or buy an apartment in their community, leading to new-build gentrification and displacement of neighborhood residents. In the long run, it contributed to a further deepening instead of a relieving of the affordable housing crisis, since it "fueled an upward spiral in the cost of local real estate" (ibid.: 5).

The voluntary IHP, thus, signified a continuation and greater expansion as well as a diversion of Koch's IHP. While one continuing factor was the dependency on the private market for the provision of "affordable housing," it expanded Koch's R10-IH to a citywide program that could be combined with public subsidies, thus making it more attractive for real estate development. In doing so, the voluntary IHP was part of "the Bloomberg way" (Brash 2011: 130) that saw the government primarily as a corporation whose fundamental aim was economic and urban development.

London: Johnson's Shift Toward the Middle Class

Boris Johnson became the first Conservative Mayor of London after he was elected in 2008. In 2010, he presented the first statutory London Housing Strategy (LHS), a result of the new power and responsibility that was given to the Mayor by the GLA Act of 2007. The act had further given him, as Mayor, a new leading role in housing and strengthened powers over planning. It provided the mayor with the power to influence the borough's Local Development Schemes to ensure that they reflect London's strategic priorities. In terms of development control, Johnson had considerable powers to intervene in planning agreements being worked out at the borough level.

While the London Plan sets the overall parameters of the spatial development strategy for Greater London, the LHS lays out the mayor's proposal and policies for promoting the improvement of housing conditions and meeting the housing needs based on the availability of public sector investment. It further outlines how housing targets set in the London Plan can be best delivered. Having been elected in the year of the fiscal and economic meltdown, Johnson set out his LHS against the backdrop of that event and in the context of London's severe housing crisis. According to

Johnson, the drop in house prices and sales had not changed London's position as a global city and a motor of the national economy. However, the city's economic success had "come at a cost for many of those seeking a home here, resulting in problems of affordability, homelessness, and overcrowding" (GLA 2010: 13).

Considering London's housing market conditions and housing needs, Johnson based his "affordable housing" target on the draft of the new London Plan that was published a year later in 2011 and set out a London wide "affordable housing" target of 50,000 new homes in the four years from 2008 to 2012, delivering at least 13,200 affordable dwellings each year (ibid.: 15). The draft London Plan abolished Livingstone's "affordable housing" planning target of 50 percent in favor of the private market, reducing the percentage of the affordable homes target from 50 percent to 40 percent. Johnson further reduced the percentage of social rented housing to be delivered from 70 percent in the 2004 Plan to 60 percent in the 2010 Strategy. At the same time, he increased the provision of intermediate housing to 40 percent, since one of his LHS's main goals was to help homeowners to become first-time buyers (ibid.: 17). For the same reason, he expanded the target population for intermediate "affordable housing" from annual households earning between £15,000 and £40,000 as determined in the 2004 Plan to a target population that had a household earning between £18,100 and £61,400 a year (and with a new upper limit of £74,000 for family-sized homes with three or more bedrooms) (ibid.: 21). The scholars Nathan Marom and Naomi Carmon, who analyzed New York's and London's housing plans in the context of neoliberal urban governance from the 1980s to 2012, point out that in doing so, Johnson "directs the supposedly 'affordable housing' in the category of intermediate housing to households well above the median income in London" (Marom and Carmon 2015: 998), which was about £36,000 in 2009 (GLA 2015). In the years from 2004/2005 to 2011/2012, the percentage of new affordable homes has risen in London but, so it seems, has been mainly achieved through increasing the delivery of intermediate homes. According to a report done by the London Tenants Federation in 2011, called *The Affordable Housing Con,* one of the key findings of the analysis of Livingstone's and Johnson's housing policies can be read as follows:

> The strategy applied in terms of 'affordable housing' seems to have been to meet the needs of what is deemed the 'squeezed middle-(class)' at the expense of working-class households that have income levels below the median.
> (London Tenants Federation 2011: 6)

In terms of planning agreements, Johnson's 2010 Housing Strategy was similar to Ken Livingstone's approach to planning. They both encouraged local authorities to meet local needs and deliver more "affordable housing" through their negotiations of Section 106 agreements. Reflecting the role of planning within the production of "affordable housing," Johnson stated that "up to two-thirds of 'affordable housing' over recent years has been delivered with some Section 106 contribution (GLA 2010: 47).

In 2014, Johnson published a revised version of his LHS in which he set even more ambitious targets for the promotion of new and "affordable housing." Reflecting on his previous affordable house-building achievements and goals over the two terms as Mayor, Johnson stated that "[a]ffordable house-building is on track to deliver 100,000 homes by 2016, a record in the history of City Hall" (GLA 2014: 2) and announced "to double house-building and build 42,000 new homes a year, every year, for the next twenty years. That's a level of house-building unseen in our great city since the 1930s" (ibid.: 2). He further stated that of these, 15,000 homes should be affordable (ibid.: 4).

A significant change between his 2010 and 2014 strategies was reflected in their different definition of "affordable housing." In the 2014 strategy, Johnson accepted the differentiation specified by the central government in 2012 between three types of "affordable housing" (social rent, affordable rent, and intermediate rent), as opposed to just two types: social and intermediate rent. He differentiated between low-cost homeownership (intermediate housing) and affordable rent, compromising equal shares of "capped" rent and "discounted" rent. While the "capped" rent – also known as social rented housing – targeted those households most in need, the "discounted" rent was to be no more than 80 percent of the local market rent (GLA 2014: 18), so as to prioritize key worker households. In his new strategy, Johnson, however, formally kept the affordable tenure mix ratio of 40 percent intermediate housing and 60 percent social rent. Thus, by introducing the new affordable rent tenure as part of the social rent, Johnson further reduced social rented housing from formerly 60 percent (or 70 percent during the Livingstone administration) to 30 percent, impacting those most in need. He further raised the annual household income limit for intermediate housing from £61,400 to £66,000 (or £80,000 for families buying a three-bedroom or larger apartment) (Table 1.2).

The "affordable housing" percentage that should be implemented in relation to the private market units varies within London and is determined on the local level in the borough's Local Plan. The more affluent borough, the City of Westminster, for example, seeks to exceed 30 percent units of all housing delivery to be affordable (Westminster City Council 2013), while boroughs like Camden or Tower Hamlets seek to exceed 50 percent "affordable housing" (Camden Council 2010; Tower Hamlets Council 2010). The actual delivery of these "affordable housing" goals is very different from the set target and varies widely within London, as we will see in more detail in Chapter 3.

In sum, the changes within the housing strategies in the decade between Livingstone's London Plan in 2004 to Johnson's LHS in 2014 reflect a shift within the definition of "affordable housing," which "realign[ed] 'affordable housing' closer to market prices and median income" (Marom and Carmon 2015: 998). In other words, social housing was meant to be gradually replaced by far more expensive housing with flexible tenancies rather than secure lifetime tenancies (Hodkinson and Robinson 2013: 70).

In addition, Boris Johnson approved the redevelopment of large-scale housing estates as mixed-income communities such as the Heygate Estate in Southwark in order to, as he described it, "unlock the economic potential of this strategically important area of south-east London and create thousands of new homes" (Mayor of London 2013). As I will discuss in more detail in Chapter 2, rather than creating

Table 1.2 Evolution of Inclusionary Housing Based on the Mayor's Housing Plans in London

	London Plan 2004 Ken Livingstone Labour Party 2004–8	LHS 2010 Boris Johnson Conservative 2008–12	LHS 2014 Boris Johnson Conservative 2012–16	LHS 2018 Sadiq Khan Labour Party Since 2016
Annual housing target (per year)	30,000	50,000	40,000	65,000
Private market	50%	60%	60%	50%
Affordable housing	50%	40%	40%	50%
IH percentage			35%	35–50%
Social rent	70%	60%	30%	50%*
Affordable rent (<80% local market rate)	/	/	30%	/
Intermediate rent	30%	40%	40%	50%**
Annual household income band	£15,000–£40,000	£18,000–£61,400	£18,000–£66,000	London Living Rent: <£60.000, shared ownership: £90,000
(Income limit for family-sized units with three or more bedrooms		£74,000	£80,000	

* This includes Social Rent and London Affordable Rent.
** This includes London Living Rent and London Shared Ownership.
Source: Data compiled by author, based on London Plan (Greater London Authority 2004), London Housing Strategy (Greater London Authority 2010, 2014, and 2018b).

more affordable housing, the redevelopment of the estate primarily added market-rate housing, which, in turn, created further development pressure on the surrounding low-income area.

This shift is paralleled with the national austerity policy that followed the election of David Cameron's coalition government in 2010. The massive cuts in public spending at both national and local levels greatly impacted funding of social housing and facilitated the shift to the marketplace in the production of "affordable housing." In particular, in London, the austerity measures taken had a great impact on the provision of "affordable housing" through Section 106 agreements.

As a governmental response to the weak position of the local authorities and the criticism concerning the lack of transparency and accountability of S106 agreements, some new initiatives were introduced: The Planning Act 2008 implemented the Community Infrastructure Levy (CIL), a locally fixed tariff on development to provide broader local infrastructure if the local planning authority has decided to set a charge in its area. It usually takes a relative form, depending on the size of the development (Austin, Gurran, and Whitehead 2014: 467; Morrison and Burgess

2014: 429). Together, S106 planning obligations and CIL make up the system of developer contributions that are used to secure funding for local infrastructure and to mediate the site-specific effects on the local community (Lord et al. 2018: 6). According to the scholars Tony Crook and Sarah Monk (2011), on the one hand, the new planning tool was promising since it is easier and less time-consuming for local authorities to collect a fixed charge from developers than to negotiate "affordable housing" units. On the other hand, they expressed as a key concern that the potential decrease of S106 agreements might decrease the developer's contribution to new "affordable housing" (Crook and Monk 2011: 1014). Crook and Whitehead (2019) show that about ten years after its implementation CIL has been mainly used by local authorities in high-demand areas, in particular in London, rather than in low-income ones. According to them, this is "in part because the fixed charge can reduce the development value 'left over' for 'affordable housing,' which continues to be a priority for many authorities" (Crook and Whitehead 2019: 372).

The immediate aftermath of the financial crisis of 2008 also brought about fundamental institutional change. The newly elected Coalition Government in 2010 shifted planning from regional to local tiers and deregulated the planning system in a way that facilitated the involvement of the private and not-for-profit sectors. This is clearly seen in the 2012 National Planning Policy Framework (NPPF), which is seen to be one of the most significant reformulations of planning policy and practices since the Town and Planning Act of 1947, which laid the foundation for the collection of planning gain (Colenutt 2020: 92; Hodkinson and Robbins 2013). In terms of inclusionary housing policy, the changes made in the 2012 NPPF[10] fundamentally also altered the provision of "affordable housing" through Section 106 agreements in favor of the developer and economic development.

The property lobby used the recession as a window of opportunity to pressure the Coalition government to change the rules with regard to planning obligations. As developers saw their profits dwindling in light of the credit crunch, they argued that planning obligations should be lowered if they could demonstrate that planning obligations would make the development project "unviable" and, thus, not deliverable. In line with the government's growth and decentralization agenda, the coalition government satisfied the developers' demands by introducing "viability" in the 2012 NPPF as an assessment factor in planning decisions. Prior to its introduction in the 2012 NPPF, the concept of viability, which determines whether a proposed development is financially viable, barely existed in planning policy. The viability clause in the 2012 NPPF was legitimized as a temporary measure to help developers through the recession. In other words, the introduction of the concept of viability into the plan-making and decision-taking phase represented a huge win for developers by allowing them to dispute previous planning obligations on the grounds that said obligations threatened the financial viability of the proposed development. The crucial paragraph 173 of the 2012 NPPF states:

> Pursuing sustainable development requires careful attention to viability and costs in plan-making and decision-taking. Plans should be deliverable. Therefore, the sites and the scale of development identified in the plan should

not be subject to such a scale of obligations and policy burdens that their ability to be developed viably is threatened. To ensure viability, the costs of any requirements likely to be applied to development, such as requirements for affordable housing standards, infrastructure contributions or other requirements should, when taking account of the normal cost of development and mitigation, provide competitive returns to a willing landowner and willing developer to enable the development to be deliverable.

(MHCLG 2012: §137)

This paragraph radically reformulated planning practices and affected town planning in England more broadly. Bob Colenutt (2020: 93) identified four main aspects that point to the far-reaching impact of paragraph 173: first, it equates "sustainable" development with commercial development by defining sustainable solely in terms of financial viability. Second, the viability and deliverability of a development proposal are primarily determined on the grounds of whether the development scheme is financially viable, and not, for example, socially or environmentally so. The third factor relates to the position of the local authority. It directly states that local authorities should not place any "obligations and policy burdens" on developers that would threaten a development scheme to go ahead. That places local authorities in a difficult position during the decision-making since developers generally perceive planning obligations such as the provision of "affordable housing" as a burden. Fourth, the position of the local authority is further weakened by the "competitive return" clause, leaving it up to the developer to define how much their profits should be and depending on this profit whether a development scheme is "financially viable," hence deliverable.

This introduction of "viability" in the 2012 NPPF can thus be seen as further deregulation of the planning system and housing policies in favor of economic growth and private interests, in particular those of developers.

In short, in this second phase of inclusionary housing, both mayors expanded their respective programs, thereby encouraging real estate development and stimulating urban regeneration. In London, Boris Johnson shifted the definition of "affordable housing" closer to market prices and median income. New York's Mayor Michael Bloomberg expanded the program from exclusively Manhattan to "designated areas" in all five boroughs and combined it with public subsidies to make it more attractive for real estate developers. These shifts in favor of developers reflect the austerity measures taken by the national governments in favor of economic growth and private interests, especially in England with the introduction of the "viability" clause into planning and decision-making. Moreover, in both cities, the mayors tried to stimulate the IHPs through policy-led regeneration plans in desirable locations. While Bloomberg initiated large-scale rezonings in, for example, Williamsburg/Greenpoint, Johnson pushed the redevelopment of large-scale housing estates as mixed-income communities. In both cases, their policies have led to gentrification of large areas with an "upgrading effect" on the social composition of the area.

Third Phase of Inclusionary Housing

The Deepening of the Housing Affordability Crisis in New York City
and London in the Aftermath of the Economic Recession

In the aftermath of the economic recession of 2008, the affordable housing crisis further deepened in both cities. Neither in London nor in New York City did income keep pace with rising rent prices, thus further fueling each city's prevailing affordability crises, especially among low-income and moderate-income households: while the median household income in NYC more or less stagnated at around $56,000 between 2000 and 2015, the median rent increased by about 30 percent in the same period. Low-income households suffered the most: the number of severely rent-burdened low-income households increased by about 8 percent, making up almost half of all the rent-burdened households in 2015 (NYU Furman Center 2016: 36). In London, private rents increased by 24 percent between 2010 and 2017, while median income increased by only 3 percent (Copley 2019). Even though the number of households on the council housing waiting list decreased by about 39 percent from its highest point in 2012 to about 232,000 in 2018, the demand for affordable housing remained high: in particular in low-income urban areas such as in the inner London boroughs of Tower Hamlets, Hackney, Lambeth, or Newham, the number of people on waiting lists remained high (MHCLG 2021).

At the same time, temporary housing and rough sleeping[11] were seen to increase drastically in both cities. In New York City, more than 60,000 people, including almost 25,500 children, were homeless by 2015: more than double the number in 2001 (Coalition for the Homeless 2021). In London, rough sleeping more than doubled between 2009 and 2017. Between 2017 and 2018, there were more than 55,440 households living in temporary accommodation, representing an increase of about 42 percent since 2009–10 (MHCLG 2018).

The continuous dismantling of public housing and subsidized rental stock only exacerbated the ongoing housing affordability crisis in both cities. In New York City, as a result of the neoliberalization of the protected rental market, the rental housing segment shifted primarily from protected to unprotected. Public housing was continuously defunded at the federal level and New York State programs such as rent control or the Mitchell-Lama were discontinued. In addition, due to deregulation and the time-delimited nature of some programs, thousands of units were taken out of the protected housing stock in the last two decades. For example, "affordable housing" requirements for developments that were built under the Mitchell-Lama program expire after 30 years, or, if landlords paid off their mortgage on the building, in as little as 20 years. If the units were built before 1974, they enter rent stabilization. Rent-stabilized units last until the rent reaches $2,000 and the tenant moves out. If a tenant moves out, landlords can increase the rent by 20 percent. They can further add some renovation costs to the rent. Landlords have therefore frequently pressured and harassed tenants to move out to transfer their units out of the protected rental segment. This translated into a loss of low-income units: between 1991 and 2011, about 110,000 rent-stabilized or rent-controlled units were lost in this way, which translates to a decline of about 24 percent. In comparison, the private rental market[12] grew at the same time by about 54 percent (NYU Furman Center 2014: 3).

The national government's self-imposed austerity measures in England had further weakened local authorities. With fewer resources, local authorities (again) had to develop and redefine policy-making and housing strategies. As it was for local governments in low-income urban areas, the austerity measures created especially challenging dynamics for many inner London boroughs, whose housing budgets and funding for social housing were already greatly weakened by the neoliberalization of housing policies in the 1990s.

Above all, viability assessments usually led to a drop in "affordable housing" requirements or other planning obligations (Colenutt 2020; Edwards 2016: 232, Layard 2019: 94; Minton 2017: 35). Particularly in London, developers frequently used their right to renegotiate planning obligations after the credit crunch, citing financial viability problems in order to reduce the number of "affordable housing" (Morrison and Burgess 2014), while at the same time earning huge profits (Colenutt 2020: 96). Anna Minton further shows how real estate consultant agencies like Savills even advertised on their website how they were able to decrease the number of "affordable housing" to be delivered as a result of their viability assessment in various development schemes (Minton 2017: 35).

As viability assessments are not usually accessible to them, community groups, local activist organizations, and occasionally local authorities have tried to challenge viability assessments. Developers have been very resistant to disclose viability assessments to the public or even to the respective local councilors involved in the decision-making process, arguing that it would expose their company practices to competitors. Local collectives such as the 35% Campaign in Southwark[13] or Concrete Action[14] are fighting for more transparency in planning processes. The 35% Campaign, for example, demands Southwark Council meet the minimum policy requirement of 35% "affordable housing" in all new residential developments while arguing that viability assessments should be made public. In the case of the redevelopment of the Heygate Estate in the London Borough of Southwark, the group was able to obtain the viability assessment via a Freedom of Information request and subsequently made it public. The assessment revealed that Savills, which was commissioned by the developer Land Lease to produce the assessment, included 25 percent profit for the developer. Accordingly, the "affordable housing" percentage was set at only 25 percent rather than at 35 percent required by Southwark policy. The 35% Campaign revealed in this case how viability means profitability for the developer (Elephant Amenity Network 2015). Some local councils such as Islington, Southwark, Lambeth, and Tower Hamlets have also been concerned about the use of viability assessments by developers and have produced policy guidance to disclose viability assessments in the public interest.

Despite these concerns, "affordable housing" delivery through Section 106 requirements has increased drastically from about 400 units in 2010 to about 3,000 units in 2017 (DLUHC 2021). The overall "affordable housing" delivery has, however, decreased in London by about 37 percent between 2009 and 2017 (Sayce et al. 2017: 5). Thus, this shows how Boris Johnson prioritized "affordable housing" delivered via Section 106 agreements over other "affordable housing" programs. Since Section 106 contributions are tied to the market, they have inevitably fallen during the recession, but they have also increased with the new real estate boom, despite the introduction of financial viability assessments. However, the increase in Section 106 contributions has scarcely addressed the housing affordability problems in London.

Consequently, by the mid-2010s the housing affordability crisis was much worse in both cities than in the 2000s. In London, Johnson's emphasis on the provision of housing for the middle-class rather than low-income households most in need of social housing support led to calls for deeper affordability targets within Section 106 agreements. In New York City, growing unaffordability helped Bill de Blasio into office, with a campaign that aimed at ending inequality in the city. De Blasio proposed a massive housing plan, including a strategy to make inclusionary housing mandatory for developers. In the following, I will examine the extent to which each mayor's approach to inclusionary housing has meant a shift in the public-private governance arrangements and low-income housing development toward the interests of those in need.

Inclusionary Housing Hailed as Solution to the Housing Affordability Problems

At a time when the demand for affordable housing was growing, inclusionary housing was suddenly touted by many politicians as the "progressive," common-sense solution to the prevailing housing affordability crisis. Even though this third phase is characterized by government commitment to creating more "affordable housing," these commitments would primarily benefit developers and landlords.

New York City: Inclusionary Housing as "Progressive" Strategy

Bill de Blasio took office in 2014 with the promise of making "the tale of two cities" – one poor and one rich – the tale of *ONE* city. At the kickoff event for his campaign, he stated that in too many ways New York "has become a tale of two cities, a place where City Hall has too often catered to the interests of the elite rather than the needs of everyday New Yorkers" (quoted in Walker (2013)). The ambitious housing program that he launched shortly after he took office was supposed to be a key initiative in his fight against inequality in New York. City officials praised the housing plan "as the most ambitious in the city and nation's history [that] aims to build and preserve 200,000 units of 'affordable housing' over the next 10 years" (Velsey and Colvin 2014). De Blasio's $41 billion plan (Goldman 2014) proposed to finance the preservation of 120,000 housing units and the creation of 80,000 new units of "affordable housing." While about $8.2 billion had to be made available by the city in addition to some federal and state contributions, the majority of the funding – $30 billion – was planned to come from the private sector (Viteritti 2017: 204).

To preserve low-income housing, the de Blasio administration not only strengthened tenants' rights and restricted corporate landlords' aggressive behavior toward tenants, but it also introduced new and revised programs that helped to finance the rehabilitation of properties in distress and to protect "affordable housing" at risk of being lost to the private market. De Blasio, for example, used the federal Rental Assistance Demonstration (RAD)[15] program to transfer a majority of public housing developments to private management to facilitate the long-needed funds for repairs – a move that was appreciated by some tenants and housing advocates but also criticized by others for privatizing public housing (Kadi et al. 2021: 359).

In terms of creating new "affordable housing," the de Blasio administration primarily incentivized the production of new private housing. One strategy to meet the ambitious housing goals set by the administration was to make inclusionary housing mandatory in areas rezoned by the city to allow increased housing density. The main goals of this program were the production of "affordable housing" through the marketplace and at the same time the fostering of socio-economic diversity. The city estimated that the program would produce at least 12,000 of the 80,000 "affordable housing" units the city hoped to provide.

On March 22, 2016, the New York City Council ultimately adopted two rezoning resolutions – Mandatory Inclusionary Housing (MIH), and Zoning for Quality and Affordability (ZQA) – as text amendments to the 1961 Zoning Resolution. Under the MIH program, "affordable housing" would be permanent and mandatory – not voluntary as under Bloomberg – in areas that have been upzoned as part of a city neighborhood plan or where developers are seeking residential rezoning for their development projects. In addition to that, the ZQA program's goal would be to change these newly rezoned areas in a way that the zoning serves the neighborhoods' and the communities' quality of life.

The final vote by the City Council, however, preceded a long and wide-ranging debate about the program's effectiveness. The overwhelming approval of 42 to 5 council members in favor of the MIH proposal[16] surprised many involved in the process since four out of five borough presidents as well as 50 of 59 community boards formally rejected the MIH proposal.[17] Critics and opponents of MIH can be mainly divided into two groups: those who feared that MIH would slow down housing development by making it too expensive for developers to build, and those for whom MIH did not address the magnitude of the affordability crisis enough. Unsurprisingly, the first group was mainly developers and investors concerned that cross-subsidizing "affordable housing" would make their development projects less profitable and even unfeasible. Some were also skeptical about placing "affordable housing" directly inside their market-rate buildings since it could result in lower private rental or selling prices. Others feared that their development project would not be feasible without incentives like the 421a tax exemption that expired in January 2016, and it wasn't clear at that point whether it would be extended by the New York State Legislature in Albany.[18]

According to a report done by the NYU Furman Center (2015), the MIH program is only likely to succeed without further subsidies by the city in neighborhoods with high rents, especially in combination with a density bonus. In neighborhoods with lower rent markets, MIH is not likely to encourage developers to produce more "affordable housing" units, not even with a density bonus, unless it is additionally subsidized by the city. The report further highlights the importance of the 421-a tax exemption to the success of the city's MIH policy by pointing out its potential to cross-subsidize "affordable housing" units. Otherwise, the report concludes, "developers will require much higher rents in order to go forward with rental developments, even if fully market rate" (NYU Furman Center 2015: 15).

The affordability's levels as well as the number of affordable units to be provided by the developers were the main points of contention for the second group, who argued that MIH did not go far enough in addressing the housing needs of most New Yorkers. Many housing advocates, unions, and neighborhood-based organizations protested vehemently against the mayor's housing plan. For example, Barika Williams, Deputy Director for the neighborhood-based ANHD, asked in her testimony before the NYC Council Subcommittee on Zoning and Franchises to revise the administration's proposal and to "add additional options with deeper affordability levels to meet the full range of incomes and neighborhoods across the City" (Williams 2016). She called for a deep affordability option of 30% "affordable housing" units within one development at an average of 30 percent of the AMI (ibid.), arguing that the current proposal "misses the core of the housing crisis and even the core of NYC's population" (ibid.).

One, if not the, leading coalition opposing the proposed citywide mandatory inclusionary zoning plan was a group of tenant associations, community organizations, faith groups, and housing advocates called Real Affordability for All (RAFA) which came together shortly after de Blasio's housing plan was announced to advocate for more low-income housing. RAFA stated in a report that "there is a total gap of 532,752 units for households earning 50 percent AMI or below" (RAFA 2015: 3). Similar to ANHD, RAFA argued that "affordable housing" created under MIH would benefit moderate- and middle-income households more than low-income communities, adding that rather than limiting it, the policy would likely accelerate gentrification and displacement of the current low-income residents (ibid.: 5). In the report, RAFA urged the de Blasio administration to base affordability standards on median neighborhood income, rather than the AMI which was $86,300 for a family of four in 2015 (ibid.: 7–8). Using this neighborhood calculation, they further pressured the administration to make at least 50 percent of the new apartments affordable for people at or below the median income of the respective neighborhood (ibid.: 7).

About ten days before the upcoming vote in the New York City Council, on March 13, 2016, RAFA, however, reversed its position and spoke out in support of de Blasio's MIH plan after the mayor agreed to conduct a study of the neighborhoods lined up for rezoning (Whitford 2016). The impact this late, and for many surprising, endorsement had on the final vote in the City Council is hard to estimate, but it surely helped to make way for a sweeping new housing policy that the mayor himself labeled as "the nation's most progressive housing law" (Office of the Mayor 2016). The Nation called it a "landmark housing deal" (The Nation 2016), and the New York Times announced it as the "new rent rules to blunt gentrification" (Goodman 2016).

The final version of the MIH program that was ultimately adopted imposed either one of two basic options (Table 1.3): the first option requires that 25 percent of the units must be set aside for "affordable housing" and for residents with income averaging 60 percent AMI which, as of 2018, was $56,340 per year for a family of three. If developers choose the second option, they had to set aside 30 percent "affordable housing" units for residents with income averaging 80 percent AMI which, as of 2018, was $75,120 per year for a family of three. The city could further add a so-called deep affordability option where 20 percent of the total residential units must be for residents with incomes averaging 40 percent AMI or a so-called workforce option where 30 percent of the total residential units must be for residents with incomes averaging 115 percent, but no units could go to residents with incomes above 135 percent AMI (Table 1.3). None of these last two options allow the use of direct subsidies, even though the deep affordability option can be used with a subsidy when more "affordable housing" is provided (New York City Department of City Planning (NYC DCP) 2016).

Another important difference from previous housing programs is that the threshold for the percentage of AMI is calculated on average rather than at or below a certain percentage. This means that while MIH offers deeper affordable options than previous programs, it also allows for affordable housing for higher-income groups.

Since MIH is only triggered in cases of residential upzoning, de Blasio also announced his intention to rezone 15 neighborhoods throughout New York City so as to create the conditions under which MIH would apply. Since one concern among critics of MIH is that areas designated for upzoning trigger a rise in land value that encourages speculation and gives landlords an incentive to increase their rent or sale prices, the involved communities were afraid that they would face higher rent burdens and substantial gentrification and displacement. In fact, in Brooklyn's neighborhood East New York – the first neighborhood that had been rezoned under the de Blasio administration – the average land price rose by 63 percent in the

Table 1.3 Levels of Affordability Required under Mandatory Inclusionary Housing

Options	Affordable Housing set-aside	Area Median Income (AMI)	Maximum annual income (example for a family of three)*
(1)	**25%**	**60% (on average)**	**$56,340 (on average)**
	with 10% required at	40%	$37,560
(2)	**30%**	**80% (on average)**	**$75,120 (on average)**
(3)	**20%**	**40% (on average)**	**$37,560 (on average)**
Deep affordability option			
(4)	**30%**	**115% (on average)**	**$107,985 (on average)**
		but not above 135%	**$127,065**
Workforce option	with 5% required at	70%	$65,730
	with 5% required at	90%	$84,510

* Based on the 2018 NYC Area AMI.
Source: Data from NYC Housing Preservation and Development (HPD).

rezoning area, whereas it only increased by 26 percent within the community district during the two years between the rezoning's announcement and its formal approval (Savitch-Lew 2016). The RAFA report also found that based on the existing income levels, the new housing created through the upzoning would be too expensive for most residents, especially those of color in East New York (RAFA 2015: 5).

Although more will be said about the particular socio-spatial effects of MIH and rezoning in the chapters to come, at this point, it is important to note that even though it has been clearly shown that the de Blasio administration adopted a stronger commitment in creating more "affordable housing" than Bloomberg and MIH represents a major expansion of his predecessor's voluntary program, it does not constitute a revision of the prior system. Tom Angotti even argues that MIH is a continuation of Bloomberg's discriminatory housing policy that is not "race neutral" (Angotti 2016a: 33) but is likely to result in substantial gentrification and displacement of communities of color.[19] That indicates that "many of the same critiques of Bloomberg's conservative housing program can be applied to the new progressive version of inclusionary zoning" (Stein 2018: 6).

According to the geographer Samuel Stein, there are three main points that suggest that de Blasio's and Bloomberg's approaches are not so dissimilar as many are led to believe: first, though MIH is a citywide program, the housing created through MIH depends on the scale of the rezoning of the designated area. Second, even though the levels of AMI reach lower than under Bloomberg, they also go far higher, allowing 115 percent on average for "affordable housing" to be built. And third, in both programs, the AMI levels do not address the city's full housing needs (ibid.). According to a report published by the Community Service Society in 2021, 75 percent of the affordable housing units created through MIH projects "were targeted toward people making more than the neighborhood average" (Stein 2021: 19). In short, though de Blasio has strengthened the city's role in setting stricter "rules of the game," about two-thirds of the housing created are market-rate, which practically means luxury condominiums or expensive private-market rentals, and as such the creation of "affordable housing" continues to be a "by-product of luxury housing production" (Stabrowski 2015: 1133).

London: Inclusionary Housing as "Good Growth"

Sadiq Khan, a member of the Labor Party, won the election in 2016 and became London's first elected Muslim mayor. One of his biggest challenges as a new mayor was to tackle London's ongoing housing crisis. Just a few months after his election win, Khan published a policy document called *A City for All Londoners* (2016) that laid out his ambition as Mayor, discussing topics like growth, housing, economy, environment, transport, and public space. In terms of growth and housing, he stated that he planned to "develop the city according to the principles of 'good growth,' with a target of 50 percent of new housing built across the city being affordable" (GLA 2016: 23). With respect to his growth agenda, Khan argued that [b]uilding enough housing is an important part of economic development – and, […] economic development will also help us to build more homes" (GLA 2016: 41). Thus, in his 2018 LHS, Khan raised the overall target of new homes from 42,000 homes per year to 65,000 homes per year (GLA 2018a: 49).

In order to meet his housing targets, he has worked closely with London business groups and others to lobby the national government. In total, he secured £4.82 billion from the central government to invest in his "affordable housing" strategy (Mayor of London 2016). According to Khan, using the planning system is crucial to securing more affordable homes per development and to ensuring what he calls "good growth" (GLA 2016: 25) principles that include affordable homes with good design and quality that meet the needs of all Londoners. One key pillar of this new approach is the introduction of a new threshold for "affordable housing" that "works by providing a Fast-Track Route through the planning system for developers that provide at least 35 percent affordable homes without public subsidy" (GLA 2018b: 112). Financial incentives can then be used to increase the proportion of "affordable housing" to 50 percent or more and help applicants get planning permission within two years (ibid.). The mayor further offers developers financial incentives to ensure that the minimum proportion of 35 percent of affordable housing in new development schemes is met.

One of the promises on which Khan built his election campaign was to make "affordable new homes" genuinely affordable, adapting the word "genuinely" to the overall definition of "affordable housing" (Sadiq Khan 2016: 8). He further introduced new types of "affordable housing" that slightly differ from the types defined in Johnson's LHSs. Khan promoted three types of "affordable housing": social rent – including a new tenure called London Affordable Rent – the new tenure London Living Rent and shared ownership, also known as intermediate housing. What has been formerly known as affordable rented housing has now been split into two new types of "affordable housing": London Affordable Rent and London Living Rent. The newly introduced London Affordable Rent is part of social rent and aimed at low-income households, with rent caps based on social rent levels. As an example, the LHS cited the rent price for a two-bedroom London Affordable Rent home that would "therefore have a rent of £153 a week in 2017/18, around 45 percent of the median private rent for the same-sized home" (GLA 2018b: 104). In contrast, the newly introduced tenure London Living Rent is aimed at middle-income Londoners and is designed to support tenants to save for a deposit to buy a home. The limit of the household income was set at £60,000 and the rent is supposed to be 80 percent or less of market rent (ibid.: 105). Landlords of London Living Rent tenants are supposed to help their tenants to homeownership within ten years by allowing them to buy a share of their rented apartment. Khan further raised the annual household income limit for intermediate housing to £90,000 (ibid.: 108) (Table 1.2). Khan has, however, been criticized for the introduction of this new tenure type that continues to define affordable rented housing as affordable at 80 percent of market-rate rents which is unaffordable for a lot of Londoners in many areas of the city (Apps 2020).

The essential difference between Khan's approach to housing policy and that of Boris Johnson is that he has taken a more interventionist approach and demonstrated a greater drive in promoting the creation of "affordable housing" across the spectrum of needs. Nevertheless, the changes in the definition of "affordable housing" types over the course of the three administrations have led to a prioritization of the middle class. The introduction of affordable rent type by the Johnson administration or the Living Rent type introduced by Sadiq Khan has masked the decline in social-rented housing. During Johnson's second term, the three types of "affordable housing" (social rent, affordable rent, and intermediate housing) were evenly distributed, each accounting for about one-third of the total "affordable housing" provided. However, the number of social rent units fell from 5,326 units in 2004/05 to 1,150 units in 2016/17, marking an 80% decline over the years. Although the figures for the provision of "affordable housing" have increased slightly during the first years of the Khan administration, the creation of social rent units through Section 106 agreements has declined (DLUHC 2021). In general, it is notable that his housing plan to provide "affordable housing" through Section 106 includes very few changes that would radically alter the housing approach established by the previous two mayors.

Despite his vision of "genuine" "affordable housing," Khan's definition of "affordable housing" continues to focus on intermediate housing rather than housing that is actually affordable to lower-income households and similarly defines social mix in terms of housing tenures mix rather than communities that actually socially mix.

Khan's rather pragmatic approach to "affordable housing" is mirrored on the national scale. Due to growing concern in England and primarily in London about the viability clause in the NPPF, paragraph 173 of the 2012 NPPF was finally removed in 2018. But instead of removing viability assessments from the policy framework altogether, it was only reformulated in the 2018 NPPF:

> Where up-to-date policies have set out the contributions expected from development, planning applications that comply with them should be assumed to be viable. It is up to the applicant to demonstrate whether particular circumstances justify the need for a viability assessment at the application stage. The weight to be given to a viability assessment is a matter for the decision-maker, having regard to all the circumstances in the case, including whether the plan and the viability evidence underpinning it is up to date, and any change in site circumstances since the plan was brought into force. All viability assessments, including any undertaken at the plan-making stage, should reflect the recommended approach in national planning guidance, including standardized inputs, and should be made publicly available.
>
> (DLUHC 2018: §58)

Developers are now expected to comply with local plans and meet the required planning obligations, including "affordable housing" targets. However, developers are still able to use viability assessment to decrease the "affordable housing" requirements. According to the urban scholar Bob Colenutt, this revision, therefore, "looks very much like the paragraph 173 system in another form with a bit more discretion to the local authority" (Colenutt 2020: 96).

These changes to the planning policies in relation to the provision of "afford-able housing" underscore the market-centered approach and the pro-development agenda of the national governments since 2012, which is also reflected in the development plans of the city and local governments. Priority has been placed on economic development rather than on the encouragement of "affordable housing" provision by allowing developers to fast-track challenges against Section 106 planning obligations. This shifts the power balance between local authorities and developers with the effect that developers are the primary beneficiaries of the policy changes.

To conclude, while both cities have expanded their IHPs and introduced deeper affordability options, the new programs do not constitute a revision of the previous systems in favor of lower-income groups. Instead, they continue to primarily support luxury real estate development, which in turn drives up property values and rents, and subsequently spurs gentrification and displacement.

Continuity Despite Change

In her book *Fear City* (2017*)*, Kim Phillips-Fein wrote about New York City: "today as in the 1970s, austerity remains a political choice" (Phillips-Fein 2017: 25). At the time, the austerity measures taken in New York City in 1975 or in England in 2010 may have seemed an inevitable governmental response to the fiscal crisis that similarly seemed inevitable. However, what followed in New York City was the imposition of a neoliberal agenda based on cuts in welfare and public expenditures, the privatization of governmental services, and the devolution of governmental risks and responsibilities to the local scale while at the same time opening up new spaces for the involvement of the private and not-for-profit sectors. In England, the self-imposed austerity measures of the Coalition government strengthened neoliberal restructuring strategies (Peck 2012), especially in London, which had been affected particularly badly by austerity measures.

Similar things can be said about the IHPs in New York City and London. Beset by budget cuts, believing there to be "no alternative but to follow the path to austerity" (Peck 2012: 15), local authorities in both cities have increasingly turned to market-based housing programs, such as inclusionary housing, and in doing so have played a huge role in crafting and coordinating inclusionary housing policies that reflect "austerity urbanism" (Peck 2012, 2014). Inclusionary housing highlights the changing public-private relationships within the context of urban austerity. In this way, it can be classified as an inherently neoliberal program in which the local government's role is conceptualized as furthering the interests of the developers and local elites rather than primarily addressing the housing needs of residents.

In this chapter, I introduced a periodization of inclusionary housing to demonstrate the parallel evolution of inclusionary housing approaches enacted in both cities. Seen in a historical context, the three phases of inclusionary housing demonstrate an expansion of the use of inclusionary housing in times of real estate booms and increasing housing affordability problems. In both cities, the local administrations have justified the use of inclusionary housing as a way for the public to benefit from the real estate boom by promoting the creation of "affordable housing" through the marketplace. However, in doing so, the local administrations have primarily boosted real estate values and promoted real-estate-led development. This has translated into a push toward the marketplace and an overwhelming reliance on the private market to deliver "affordable housing." This is primarily evident in the shift from the first to the second phase of inclusionary housing. While the shift from the second to the third phase of inclusionary housing may entail some aspects toward lower-income households, it does not constitute a revision of the prior systems in favor of lower-income groups but continues to support luxury real estate development, and subsequently advances processes of gentrification and displacement.

This periodization facilitates the study of current as well as historical approaches to inclusionary housing within the broader context of urban austerity politics. Like this, in spite of the recent and at times laudable changes made to them, the most recent programs in both cities can be clearly seen to continue to embrace the very market-based policy approach to affordability housing that created the ongoing affordability problem in the first place.

Studies on post-neoliberal housing policy have reached similar conclusions, pointing to the difficulties of deviating from the chosen neoliberal paths (i.a. Kadi et al. 2021; Schipper 2021). In the conclusion of their paper on the question of whether recent housing reforms in Berlin, Vienna, and New York City can be characterized as post-neoliberal, Kadi et al. briefly discuss four structural factors that safeguard the dominance of the neoliberal paradigm and, thus, hinder a post-neoliberal transformation: according to them, many housing finance or reform decisions are made at higher levels than local government, limiting the ability of local authorities to act. Moreover, neoliberal governance arrangements are deeply inscribed into local policy practices, and the real estate sector exerts great influence on local policy-making and planning-decisions, while the global financial investors pour massive amounts of capital into real estate development as a competitive return strategy (Kadi et al. 2021: 368).

In London and New York City, the history of inclusionary housing reflects the overwhelming continuity of these neoliberal paradigms of public-private governance relationships, in which top-down, and oftentimes commercially driven planning and policymaking decisions have been largely maintained, despite some significant changes. Although both the de Blasio and Khan administrations have done more than their predecessors to produce more "affordable housing" units and to make said units actually more affordable to lower-income households, the "affordable housing" crisis remains as acute as before: rents keep rising and displacement pressures on low-income neighborhoods are only intensifying. In a word, "affordable housing" continues to be primarily geared to middle-income rather than low-income households. Hence, the production of "affordable housing" through inclusionary housing constitutes a form of what I call *gentrification through the back door*.

Although at the time of writing, there is not enough evidence to provide conclusive proof that inclusionary housing policies have worsened the affordability situation in low-income areas, it is clear they have done little to counteract it. So little in fact that in Chapter 2, I will explore if, and in what ways, inclusionary housing has been exploited by both cities to induce rather than prevent gentrification in low-income areas.

Notes

1 Broadly speaking, post-neoliberalism represents a shift away from neoliberal policy practices. In relation to housing, Kadi et al. (2021), for example, argue that post-neoliberal housing policies must address three interrelated dimensions, such as decommodification, affordability, and democratization.

2 Like all American cities, New York City depends heavily on tax revenues generated within its own boundaries. With the flight of many white middle-class residents to the suburbs in response to severe economic and political troubles in the city in the 1970s, New York City was drained of tax revenue, and entire neighborhoods were left devastated by abandonment and arson (NYU Furman Center 2006). Amplified by this urban crisis, the nationwide economic stagnation morphed into a severe fiscal crisis in New York City.

3 Even though Scotland and Wales have similar legislation for the provision of affordable housing through the planning system, this act only refers to England.

4 London reorganized its overall structure three times since the mid-1960s. First, in 1965, the London County Council (LCC) which was only in charge of the inner boroughs was replaced by the Greater London Council (GLC). In 1986, the GLC was abolished by the Local Government Act of 1985 that transferred its functions to central government and the 32 new London borough councils. After the dissolution of the GLC, London had little influence over housing policy. In 2000, the Greater London Authority (GLA) was established as the new regional governance body of Greater London and the City of London, consisting of two political branches: the directly elected Mayor of London and the separately elected London Assembly.

5 In real estate, in rem action is a lawsuit that may be brought against the property of debtors to collect amounts owed or to foreclose mortgages. Under the Koch administration, for example, this was done so that properties could be preserved and better used for affordable housing.

6 Since the city did not plan on building or operating new housing itself, the plan involved a wide range of nonprofit and for-profit actors to provide and operate the housing. Some of the programs relied exclusively on money provided by the city, but most of the programs depended critically on federal loan programs such as the Federal Low-Income Housing Tax Credit or support from state or local financial institutions. The state-funded 421-a program, for example, became a crucial tax exemption program for Koch's housing plan because it aimed at giving property tax breaks to developers of residential buildings.

7 Residential areas designated as R10 areas in New York City are the densest residential areas and have the largest and tallest residential buildings in the city.

8 Project-Based Section 8 housing is a government-funded program that provides affordable housing by giving rental assistance to private owners of multifamily housing. The program makes up the difference between the market rate and what low-income renters can afford if they pay 30 percent of their household income for rent. The program was renewed in 1997. For more information, see https://www.hud.gov/hudprograms/rs8pbra.

9 Mitchell-Lama was a New York State-funded program that started in 1955. Under the program, developers received subsidies if they agreed to certain affordability requirements for their apartments. Coverage typically ends after 30 years, but after 20 years, landlords can opt out of the program by paying off the mortgage. If the building was built before 1974, it falls under rent stabilization; otherwise, landlords are free to charge market rents. For more information, see https://www1.nyc.gov/site/hpd/services-and-information/mitchell-lama-program.page (last accessed: 06/12/2022).

10 The NPPF sets out the national government's planning policies that have to be applied by lower government tiers.
11 Temporary housing and rough sleeping are two forms of homelessness. Rough sleeping refers to people sleeping on the streets, while someone can be homeless even if they are staying in temporary accommodation overnight.
12 It includes market-rate as well as other subsidized housing units.
13 For more information, see https://www.35percent.org/ (last accessed: 06/12/2022).
14 For more information, see https://concreteaction.github.io/ (last accessed: 06/12/2022).
15 The Rental Assistance Demonstration (RAD), launched in 2012, is a program of the U.S. Department of Housing and Urban Development (HUD) that provides tools to generate funding to preserve and improve public housing properties.
16 ZQA was approved by 40 to 6 with one abstention by the City Council.
17 In total, 55 of 59 community boards rejected ZQA. See here for more details: www.citylandnyc.org/wp-content/uploads/sites/14/2015/12/MIH-ZQA-CB-Tracker-Final-ALL-VOTES-IN.pdf (last accessed: 06/12/2022).
18 The program was extended and renamed the Affordable Housing New York Program in 2017.
19 In the individual chapters, I only touch on the important topic of race discrimination as it appears in the practice of inclusionary housing, mainly by pointing to the displacement of low-income communities of color. Due to the limited scope of the research, I have not conducted a systematic study of the systemic role of race, and gender discrimination in inclusionary housing practices. However, further research on this topic is urgently needed.

References

Aalbers, Manuel B. 2019. "Introduction to the Forum: From Third to Fifth-Wave Gentrification." *Tijdschrift Voor Economische En Sociale Geografie* 110 (1): 1–11. https://doi.org/10.1111/tesg.12332.
Angotti, Tom. 2016a. "Land Use Zoning Matters." In *Zoned Out! Race, Displacement, and City Planning in New York City*, edited by Tom Angotti and Sylvia Morse, 18–45. New York: UR.
———. 2016b. "Alternatives: Community-Based Planning and Housing in the Public Domain." In *Zoned Out! Race, Displacement, and City Planning in New York City*, edited by Tom Angotti and Sylvia Morse, 142–86. New York: UR.
Angotti, Tom, and Morse Sylvia. 2016. "Racialized Land Use and Housing Policies." In *Zoned Out! Race, Displacement, and City Planning in New York City*, edited by Tom Angotti and Sylvia Morse, 46–71. New York: UR.
Apps, Peter. 2020. "The End of Section 106 Could Prove a Transformative Moment for Affordable Housing." *Inside Housing*, August 5. https://www.insidehousing.co.uk/comment/comment/the-end-of-section-106-could-prove-a-transformative-moment-for-affordable-housing-67414.
Association for Neighborhood and Housing Development (ANHD). 2015. "NYC Inclusionary Zoning: A District by District Analysis of What Was Lost and Gained and What Remains." Association for Neighborhood and Housing Development. https://anhd.org/wp-content/uploads/2015/07/ANHD-Inclusionary-Zoning-Rpt-7-15.pdf.
Austin, Patricia M., Nicole Gurran, and Christine M. E. Whitehead. 2014. "Planning and Affordable Housing in Australia, New Zealand and England: Common Culture; Different Mechanisms." *Journal of Housing and the Built Environment* 29 (3): 455–72.
Braconi, Frank. 1999. "In Re in Rem: Innovation and Expediency in New York's Housing Policy." In *Housing and Community Development in New York City: Facing the Future*, M. H. Scill. Albany, NY: State University of New York Press.
Brash, Julian. 2011. *Bloomberg's New York: Class and Governance in the Luxury City*. Athens: University of Georgia Press.

Camden Council. 2010. *Camden Core Strategy 2010–2025*. https://www.camden.gov. uk/ccm/navigation/environment/planning-and-built-environment/planning-policy/ local-development-framework–ldf-/core-strategy/.

Coalition For The Homeless. 2021. "Basic Facts About Homelessness: New York City." Coalition For The Homeless. https://www.coalitionforthehomeless.org/basic-facts-about-homelessness-new-york-city/.

Colenutt, Bob. 2020. *The Property Lobby: The Hidden Reality Behind the Housing Crisis*. Policy Press.

Copley, Tom. 2019. *Homelessness: The Visible Effect of Austerity*. London Assembly Labour.

Crook, Antony (D. H.) 1996. "Affordable Housing and Planning Gain, Linkage Fees and the Rational Nexus: Using the Land Use Planning System in England and the USA to Deliver Housing Subsidies." *International Planning Studies* 1 (1): 49–71. https://doi.org/ 10.1080/13563479608721643.

Crook, Antony, and Sarah Monk. 2011. "Planning Gains, Providing Homes." *Housing Studies* 26 (7–8): 997–1018. https://doi.org/10.1080/02673037.2011.619423.

Crook, Antony, and C. Whitehead. 2019. "Capturing Development Value, Principles and Practice: Why Is It so Difficult?" *Town Planning Review*. https://doi.org/10.3828/tpr.2019.25.

Cullingworth, Barry, and Vincent Nadin. 2006. *Town and Country Planning in the UK*. London: Routledge.

Davidson, Mark, and Kevin Ward. 2018. "Introduction." In *Cities Under Austerity: Restructuring the US Metropolis*, edited by Mark Davidson and Kevin Ward, 1–26. SUNY Press.

Department for Levelling Up, Housing and Communities (DLUHC). 2018. *National Planning Policy Framework*. https://www.gov.uk/guidance/national-planning-policy-framework/4-decision-making#para57.

———. 2021. "Live Tables on Affordable Housing Supply." Department for Levelling Up, Housing and Communities. https://assets.publishing.service.gov.uk/government/uploads/ system/uploads/attachment_data/file/1034089/Live_Table_1011.xlsx.

Dulchin, Benjamin, Moses Gates, and Barika Williams. 2013. "Housing Policy for a Strong and Equitable City." Association for Neighborhood and Housing Development. https:// www.gc.cuny.edu/CUNY_GC/media/CUNY-Graduate-Center/PDF/Centers/Center%20 for%20Urban%20Research/Resources/21cforall_housing.pdf.

Edwards, Michael. 2016. "The Housing Crisis and London." *City* 20 (2): 222–37. https:// doi.org/10.1080/13604813.2016.1145947.

Elephant Amenity Network. 2015. "Heygate Viability Assessment Finally Revealed." *35% Campaign* (blog). https://www.35percent.org/posts/2015-06-25-heygate-viability-assessment-finally-revealed/.

Fainstein, Susan. 1994. *The City Builders: Property Development in New York and London*. Oxford, New York: Blackwell.

Goldman, Henry. 2014. "De Blasio Unveils $41 Billion Plan for Affordable Housing." *Bloomberg.Com*, May 5, 2014. https://www.bloomberg.com/news/articles/2014-05-05/ de-blasio-unveils-41-billion-plan-for-affordable-housing.

Goodman, J. David. 2016. "New York Passes Rent Rules to Blunt Gentrification." *The New York Times*, March 22. https://www.nytimes.com/2016/03/23/nyregion/new-york-council-passes-zoning-changes-de-blasio-sought.html.

Gordon, Ian, and Michael Harloe. 1992. "A Dual to New York? London in the 1980s." In *Dual City: Restructuring New York: Restructuring of New York*, edited by John H. Mollenkopf and Manuel Castells. New York, NY: Russell Sage Foundation.

Greater London Authority (GLA). 2004. *The London Plan: Spatial Development Strategy for Greater London*. London: Greater London Authority. https://www.london. gov.uk//what-we-do/planning/london-plan/past-versions-and-alterations-london-plan/ london-plan-2004.

———. 2009. "Housing in London: The Evidence Base for the London Housing Strategy." Greater London Authority. http://static.london.gov.uk/mayor/housing/strategy/docs/housing-in-london2009.pdf.

————. 2010. "The London Housing Strategy." Greater London Authority. https://www.london.gov.uk/sites/default/files/uploads/Housing_Strategy_Final_Feb10.pdf.

————. 2014. "The London Housing Strategy." Greater London Authority. https://www.london.gov.uk/what-we-do/housing-and-land/housing-and-land-publications/mayors-london-housing-strategy-june-2014.

————. 2016. "A City for All Londoners." Greater London Authority. https://www.london.gov.uk/sites/default/files/city_for_all_londoners_nov_2016.pdf.

————. 2018a. "Housing in London – The Evidence Base for the Mayor's Housing Strategy." Greater London Authority. https://data.london.gov.uk/dataset/housing-london.

————. 2018b. "The London Housing Strategy." Greater London Authority. https://www.london.gov.uk/sites/default/files/2018_lhs_london_housing_strategy.pdf.

————. 2020. "London's Population." London Datastore. https://data.london.gov.uk/dataset/londons-population.

Hackworth, Jason, and Neil Smith. 2001. "The Changing State of Gentrification." *Tijdschrift Voor Economische En Sociale Geografie* 92 (4): 464–477. https://doi.org/10.1111/1467-9663.00172.

Harvey, David. 2005. *A Brief History of Neoliberalism*. Oxford: Oxford University Press.

Hodkinson, Stuart, and Glyn Robbins. 2013. "The Return of Class War Conservatism? Housing under the UK Coalition Government." *Critical Social Policy* 33 (1): 57–77.

Hodkinson, Stuart, Paul Watt, and Gerry Mooney. 2013. "Introduction: Neoliberal Housing Policy – Time for a Critical Re-Appraisal." *Critical Social Policy* 33 (1): 3–16.

Horwitz, Will, and David Robinson. 2015. *Changing London: A Rough Guide for the Next London Mayor*. London Publishing Partnership.

Jacobs, Keith. 2019. *Neoliberal Housing Policy: An International Perspective*. New York; London: Routledge.

Kadi, Justin, and Richard Ronald. 2016. "Undermining Housing Affordability for New York's Low-Income Households: The Role of Policy Reform and Rental Sector Restructuring." *Critical Social Policy* 36 (2): 265–88.

Kadi, Justin, Lisa Vollmer, and Samuel Stein. 2021. "Post-Neoliberal Housing Policy? Disentangling Recent Reforms in New York, Berlin and Vienna." *European Urban and Regional Studies* 28 (4): 353–74.

Koch, Edward. 1985. "The State of the City: Housing Initiatives." Office of the Mayor. https://chpcny.org/assets/Koch-1985-SOC-housing-plan.pdf.

Layard, Antonia. 2019. "Planning by Numbers: Affordable Housing and Viability in England." In *Planning and Knowledge: How New Forms of Technocracy Are Shaping Contemporary Cities*, edited by Mike Raco and Federico Savini. Bristol: Policy Press, 213–24. https://policy.bristoluniversitypress.co.uk/planning-and-knowledge.

Lees, Loretta, Tom Slater, and Elvin Wyly. 2008. *Gentrification*. NY: Routledge.

London Tenants Federation. 2011. "The Affordable Housing Con." London Tenants Federation. http://www.londontenants.org/publications/other/theafordablehousingconf.pdf.

Lord, Alex, Richard Dunning, Bertie Dockerill, Gemma Burgess, Adrian Carro, Tony Crook, Craig Watkins, and Cristine Whitehead. 2018. "The Incidence, Value and Delivery of Planning Obligations and Community Infrastructure Levy in England in 2016–17." Ministry of Housing, Communities and Local Government.

Mallach, Alan, and Nico Calavita, eds. 2010. "United States: From Radical Innovation to Mainstream Housing Policy." In *Inclusionary Housing in International Perspective: Affordable Housing, Social Inclusion, and Land Value Recapture*, Nico Calavita and Alan Mallach. Cambridge, Mass: Lincoln Institute of Land Policy, 15–78.

Marcus, Norman Esq. 1992. "New York City Zoning – 1961–1991: Turning Back the Clock – But With An Up-To-The-Minute Social Agenda." *Fordham Urban Law Journal* 19 (3): 707.

Marom, Nathan, and Naomi Carmon. 2015. "Affordable Housing Plans in London and New York: Between Marketplace and Social Mix." *Housing Studies* 30 (7): 993–1015. https://www.tandfonline.com/doi/abs/10.1080/02673037.2014.1000832?journalCode=chos20.

Marsden, Joel. 2015. "House Prices in London – an Economic Analysis of London's Housing Market." Greater London Authority. https://www.london.gov.uk/sites/default/files/house-prices-in-london.pdf.

Mayor of London. 2013. "Mayor Approves £1.5bn Regeneration of Elephant and Castle." London City Hall. March 8, 2013. https://www.london.gov.uk//press-releases-4998.

———. 2016. "Homes for Londoners: Affordable Homes Programme 2016–2023." London City Hall. November 22. https://www.london.gov.uk//what-we-do/housing-and-land/homes-londoners-affordable-homes-programmes/homes-londoners-affordable-homes-programme-2016-2023.

———. 2021. "Mayor Announces 'Right to Buy-Back' to Boost Supply of Council Homes." London City Hall, July 13. https://www.london.gov.uk//press-releases/mayoral/right-to-buy-back-to-boost-council-home-supply.

Ministry of Housing, Communities and Local Government (MHCLG). 2012. *National Planning Policy Framework*. https://www.gov.je/SiteCollectionDocuments/Government%20and%20administration/IPR1-ATT5%20-%20extract%20from%20NPPF%202013.12.10.pdf.

———. 2018. "Live Tables on Homelessness." Government UK. https://www.gov.uk/government/statistical-data-sets/live-tables-on-homelessness.

———. 2021. "Households on Local Authority Waiting List, Borough." London Datastore. https://data.london.gov.uk/dataset/households-local-authority-waiting-list-borough.

Minton, Anna. 2017. *Big Capital: Who Is London For?* UK: Penguin.

Moody, Kim. 2007. *From Welfare State to Real Estate: Regime Change in New York City, 1974 to the Present*. New York: The New Press.

Morrison, Nicky, and Gemma Burgess. 2014. "Inclusionary Housing Policy in England: The Impact of the Downturn on the Delivery of Affordable Housing Through Section 106." *Journal of Housing and the Built Environment* 29 (3): 423–38.

Mulliner, Emma, and Vida Maliene. 2013. "Austerity and Reform to Affordable Housing Policy." *Journal of Housing and the Built Environment* 28 (2): 397–407. https://doi.org/10.1007/s10901-012-9305-6.

New York City Department of City Planning (NYC DCP). 2016. "Mandatory Inclusionary Housing." New York City Department of City Planning. https://www1.nyc.gov/site/planning/plans/mih/mandatory-inclusionary-housing.page.

New York City Department of Housing, Preservation and Development (NYC HPD). 2002. "The New Housing Marketplace Plan 2003–2014." New York City Department of Housing, Preservation and Development.

———. 2017. "The New York City Housing and Vacancy Survey." New York City Department of Housing Preservation and Development.

Newman, Kathe. 2018. "Urban Governance and Inclusionary Housing in New York City." In *Cities Under Austerity: Restructuring the US Metropolis*, edited by David Davidson and Kevin Ward. Albany: SUNY Press, 127–42. https://www.amazon.com/Cities-under-Austerity-Restructuring-Metropolis-ebook/dp/B079M955KQ/ref=sr_1_2?keywords=austerity+cities&qid=1559857008&s=books&sr=1-2.

NYU Furman Center. 2006. *Housing Policy in New York City: A Brief History*. NYU Furman Center. https://furmancenter.org/research/publication/housing-policy-in-new-york-city-a-brief-history.

———. 2007. "State of New York City's Housing & Neighborhoods – 2007 Report." NYU Furman Center. https://furmancenter.org/research/sonychan/2007-report.

———. 2008. "State of New York City's Housing & Neighborhoods – 2008 Report." NYU Furman Center. https://furmancenter.org/research/sonychan/2008-report.

———. 2009. "State of New York City's Housing & Neighborhoods – 2009 Report." NYU Furman Center. https://furmancenter.org/research/sonychan/2009-report.

———. 2010. "Policy Brief: How Have Recent Rezonings Affected the City's Ability to Grow?" NYU Furman Center. https://furmancenter.org/files/publications/Rezonings_Furman_Center_Policy_Brief_March_2010.pdf.

————. 2011. "State of New York City's Housing & Neighborhoods." NYU Furman Center. https://furmancenter.org/research/sonychan/2011-report.

————. 2014. "Profile of Rent-Stabilized Units and Tenants in New York City." NYU Furman Center. https://furmancenter.org/research/publication/profile-of-rent-stabilized-units-and-tenants-in-new-york-city.

————. 2015. "Creating Affordable Housing Out of Thin Air: The Economics of Mandatory Inclusionary Zoning in New York City." New York City: NYU Furman Center. http://furmancenter.org/files/NYUFurmanCenter_CreatingAffHousing_March2015.pdf.

————. 2016. "State of New York City's Housing & Neighborhoods – 2016 Report." NYU Furman Center. https://furmancenter.org/research/sonychan/2016-report.

————. 2018. "State of New York City's Housing & Neighborhoods – 2018 Report." NYU Furman Center. https://furmancenter.org/research/sonychan/2018-report.

Office of the Mayor 2016. "Statement from Mayor de Blasio on Progress under NYC's New Mandatory Inclusionary Housing Law," December 16. https://www1.nyc.gov/office-of-the-mayor/news/954-16/statement-mayor-de-blasio-progress-under-nyc-s-new-mandatory-inclusionary-housing-law.

Pawson, Hal, David Mullins, with Tony Gilmour. 2010. *After Council Housing: Britain's New Social Landlords*. Basingstoke: Palgrave.

Peck, Jamie. 2012. "Austerity Urbanism. American Cities Under Extreme Economy." *City* 16 (6): 626–55. https://doi.org/10.1093/cjres/rst018.

————. 2014. "Pushing Austerity: State Failure, Municipal Bankruptcy and the Crises of Fiscal Federalism in the USA." *Cambridge Journal of Regions, Economy and Society* 7 (1): 17–44. https://doi.org/10.1093/cjres/rst018.

Phillips-Fein, Kim. 2017. *Fear City: New York's Fiscal Crisis and the Rise of Austerity Politics*. New York: Henry Holt.

Real Affordability for All (RAFA). 2015. "Real Affordable Communities: Mayor Bill de Blasio and the Future of New York City." Real Affordability for All. http://alignny.org/wp-content/uploads/2016/09/Real-Affordable-Communities-Final-Report-for-September-21-2015-1.pdf.

Rinn, Moritz. 2018. "Ein Urbanismus Der Ungleichheit: ‚Neue Soziale Stadtpolitik' in Hamburg Als Strategie Der Verbürgerlichung." *Sub\urban. zeitschrift für kritische stadtforschung* 6 (1): 9–28. https://doi.org/10.36900/suburban.v6i1.332.

Rose, Kalima, Brad Lander, and Karoleen Feng. 2004. "Increasing Housing Opportunity in New York City. The Case for Inclusionary Zoning." Policy Link and Pratt Institute Center for Community and Environmental Development. https://www.policylink.org/sites/default/files/NEWYORK-INCLUSIONARYZONING_FINAL.PDF.

Sadiq, Khan. 2016. "Sadiq Khan for London: A Manifesto for All Londoners." http://london.laboursites.org/wp-content/uploads/sites/5/2018/02/x160668_Sadiq_Khan_Manifesto.pdf.

Sassen, Saskia. 2001. *The Global City: New York, London, Tokyo*. Princeton, NJ: Princeton University Press.

Savitch-Lew, Abigail. 2016. "Some Suspect East New York Rezoning Has Triggered Speculation - City Limits." *City Limits*, March 1. https://citylimits.org/2016/03/10/some-suspect-east-new-york-rezoning-has-triggered-speculation/.

Sayce, S., N. Crosby, P. Garside, Rob Harris, and A. Parsa. 2017. "Viability and the Planning System: The Relationship between Economic Viability Testing, Land Values and Affordable Housing in London." Tower Hamlets Council. https://www.towerhamlets.gov.uk/Documents/London_Viability/Research_Viability_and_the_Planning_System_Research_January_2017.pdf.

Schipper, Sebastian. 2015. "Towards a 'Post-Neoliberal' Mode of Housing Regulation? The Israeli Social Protest of Summer 2011." *International Journal of Urban and Regional Research* 39 (6): 1137–54. https://doi.org/10.1111/1468-2427.12318.

————. 2021. "Der Staat Als Adressat Städtischer Sozialer Bewegungen. Wohnungspolitische Kämpfe Und Postneoliberale Konstellationen." *Zeitschrift Für Wirtschaftsgeographie* 65 (April): aop. https://doi.org/10.1515/zfw-2020-0027.

Schwartz, Alex. 1999. "New York City and Subsidized Housing: Impacts and Lessons of the City's $5 Billion Capital Budget Housing Plan." *Housing Policy Debate* 10 (4): 839–77.

Soffer, Jonathan. 2010. *Ed Koch and the Rebuilding of New York City.* New York: Columbia University Press. https://doi.org/10.7312/soff15032.

Stabrowski, Filip. 2015. "Inclusionary Zoning and Exclusionary Development: The Politics of 'Affordable Housing' in North Brooklyn." *International Journal of Urban and Regional Research* 39 (6): 1120–36. https://doi.org/10.1111/1468-2427.12297.

Stein, Samuel. 2018. "Progress for Whom, Toward What? Progressive Politics and New York City's Mandatory Inclusionary Housing." *Journal of Urban Affairs* 40 (6): 770–81. https://doi.org/10.1080/07352166.2017.1403854.

Stein, Samuel. 2021. "Assessing de Blasio's Housing Legacy: Why Hasn't the "Most Ambitious Affordable Housing Program" Produced a More Affordable City?" Community Service Society (Jan.). https://www.cssny.org/publications/entry/assessing-de-blasios-housing-legacy.

The Nation. 2016. "The Landmark Housing Deal That Could Help Quell New York's Affordability Crisis," *The Nation*, March 18. https://www.thenation.com/article/archive/the-landmark-housing-deal-that-could-help-quell-new-yorks-affordability-crisis/.

Tower Hamlets Council. 2010. *Local plan.* Tower Hamlets Council. http://www.towerhamlets.gov.uk/lgsl/451-500/494_planning_guidance/local_plan.aspx.

Toy, Vivian S. 2008. "A Downturn Begins." *The New York Times*, November 7. https://www.nytimes.com/2008/11/09/realestate/09cov.html.

Ullman, Seth, Michael Freedman-Schnapp, and Brad Lander. 2013. "Inclusionary Zoning in New York City: The Performance of New York City's Designated Areas Inclusionary Housing Program Since Its Launch in 2005." Office of Council Member Brad Lander. https://www.scribd.com/doc/160544058/Inclusionary-Zoning-in-New-York-City-The-performance-of-New-York-City-s-Designated-Areas-Inclusionary-Housing-Program-since-its-launch-in-2005.

Velsey, Kim, and Jill Colvin. 2014. "De Blasio Unveils 'Most Ambitious' Affordable Housing Plan in Nation." *The Observer*, May 5. http://observer.com/2014/05/de-blasio-unveils-most-ambitious-affordable-housing-plan/.

Viteritti, Joseph P. 2017. *The Pragmatist: Bill de Blasio's Quest to Save the Soul of New York.* New York, NY: Oxford University Press Inc.

Vogelpohl, Anne, and Tino Buchholz. 2017. "Breaking With Neoliberalization by Restricting the Housing Market: Novel Urban Policies and the Case of Hamburg." *International Journal of Urban and Regional Research* 41 (2) 266–81. https://doi.org/10.1111/1468-2427.12490.

Walker, Hunter. 2013. "Bill de Blasio Tells 'A Tale of Two Cities' at His Mayoral Campaign Kickoff." *The Observer*, January. https://observer.com/2013/01/bill-de-blasio-tells-a-tale-of-two-cities-at-his-mayoral-campaign-kickoff/.

Ward, Stephen V. 2004. *Planning and Urban Change.* London; Thousand Oaks, Calif: SAGE Publications Ltd.

Westminster City Council. 2013. "Westminster City Plan." Westminster City Council. http://transact.westminster.gov.uk/docstores/publications_store/Westminster's%20City%20Plan%20Adopted%20November%202013%20FINAL%20VERSION.pdf.

Whitehead, Christine. 2007. "Planning Policies and Affordable Housing: England as a Successful Case Study?" Housing Studies 22 (1)." *Housing Studies* 22 (1): 25–44.

Whitford, Emma. 2016. "De Blasio's Toughest Affordable Housing Critics Reverse Their Position: Gothamist." *Gothamist*, March 14. http://gothamist.com/2016/03/14/vocal_critics_of_mayors_affordable.php.

Williams, Barika. 2016. "Testimony of Barika X. Williams Before the New York City Council Subcommittee on Zoning and Franchises Regarding the Proposed 'Mandatory Inclusionary Housing' Text Amendment." Association for Neighborhood and Housing Development, February 9. https://anhd.org/report/testimony-barika-x-williams-anhd-staff-new-york-city-council-subcommittee-zoning-and.

2 Creating Value for Profit Rather Than "Affordable Housing"

Neighborhood Regeneration Under the Pretext of Inclusionary Housing

It is Thursday afternoon, 5pm, on March 23rd, 2017. People start to gather in the biggest room at Bolney Meadow Community Centre, 31 Bolney Street, in Lambeth, London. Before entering the building, everybody is asked to sign in. Security agents check every bag for possible weapons. Banners are not allowed either. Policemen are standing at the entrance to the conference room. In the room, the atmosphere feels tense, the air seems to be filled with hope and expectations of the people streaming in. A small group outside hands out flyers for Saturday's *March for Council Housing, Not for Luxury Flats* event. Today is the day of the final decision: the day when Lambeth Cabinet decides on the proposal to demolish and rebuild Central Hill Estate.

(Fieldnotes 2017/03/23[1])

Central Hill estate is a low-rise estate with more than 450 homes in the south London borough of Lambeth. Built during the 1960s and early 1970s, it is a well-designed estate, where all residents have access to views over London, green public spaces, and good-quality apartments with plenty of daylight – a landmark of post-war architecture sited on a valuable piece of land today (Architects for Social Housing (ASH) 2018a). Despite residents and local community groups urging Lambeth Council to consider refurbishing the estate, the Cabinet pushed through – without a formal vote – plans to proceed with the estate's demolition.

Lambeth is one of the most densely populated boroughs in the country. It is one of the most deprived boroughs in London and adjacent to the inner East London boroughs of Islington, Tower Hamlets, and Newham. As of 2016, it is ranked as having the highest number of households on the social housing waiting list of all boroughs in London (Ministry of Housing, Communities and Local Government 2019). Regardless of the lack of social housing, Central Hill is but one of six council estates that are threatened to be demolished by Lambeth Council. By demolishing the Central Hill estate, the council argues that it is "investing in better neighborhoods and building the homes we need to better house the people of Lambeth" (Lambeth Cabinet 2017). Although the council justifies the demolition of nearly 450 council homes by planning to construct new "affordable housing" units via Section 106 agreements with the site's developer, of the 1,500 properties slated

DOI: 10.4324/9781003468479-3

to be built only a small fraction will actually be affordable to the people currently living on the estate (ASH 2018a: 6).

About a year later, in August 2018, the New York City Council approved in a 43-1 vote a sweeping rezoning proposal in Inwood, Manhattan. The plan encompassed the land-use changes of 59 blocks in this neighborhood located at the northern tip of Manhattan – an area that has often been referred to as "Manhattan's Last Affordable Neighborhood" (Mays and Robertson 2018). The city promised to invest $200 million in the neighborhood to preserve and create "affordable housing," parks, and open spaces, as well as provide educational opportunities and support for small businesses (New York City Economic Development Corporation (NYCEDC) 2017). The goal of the plan is to preserve 2,500 affordable homes and to create about 1,600 units of "affordable housing" on public sites through the Mandatory Inclusionary Housing program.

The rezoning plan was approved, however, amid strong protest from the community, as I could observe during my fieldwork. The main point of contention was that the plan for "affordable housing" was largely not affordable to the current residents. For a long time, Inwood has been home to working-class communities and immigrants, predominantly hailing from the Dominican Republic. But in recent years, the neighborhood has become the latest frontier of an ongoing gentrification process sweeping across the north of Manhattan. The area has increasingly attracted more affluent people, most of them non-Hispanic white households, which has led to skyrocketing rents and the displacement of mainly low-income Dominicans (Hernández, Sezgin, and Marrara 2018).

The upzoning would allow for buildings between 18 and 30 stories tall that would include up to 75 percent market-rate housing in a neighborhood that is primarily comprised of mid-rise, walk-up tenement buildings. The protesting community saw the rezoning plan as the opening of Inwood to more luxury development that would initiate an unprecedented process of gentrification and likely displace many of Inwood's long-term, working-class, and immigrant residents.

These two examples present two different ways in which entrepreneurial neighborhood regeneration efforts affect local communities at risk. By pointing to public benefits such as "affordable housing" to legitimize their neighborhood revitalization efforts in spite of fierce local opposition, the local governments in both cities demonstrate how they cater to the interests of real estate over that of the communities they are meant to serve.

In New York City, the de Blasio administration targeted areas where it saw potential for urban regeneration and for real estate development, where Inwood is but one of 15 neighborhoods slated by the administration for rezoning. As outlined in Chapter 1, MIH was one of the pillars of de Blasio's housing plan. Since MIH is triggered whenever an upzoning occurs, the Inwood rezoning aimed at creating value to be recaptured in the form of "affordable housing" from future development schemes within that specific area. The de Blasio administration's argument, thus, is that the upzoning is essential to encourage developers to build more "affordable housing." But by allowing greater density and height within a specific area than the existing zoning would allow, the city also provided the incentives for widespread new residential development, which in turn is likely to result in gentrification and substantial displacement of the surrounding community.

In London, neighborhood regeneration in form of demolition and redevelopment, as planned with the Central Hill estate, is nothing new. The list of public housing estates that were demolished or are planned to be demolished in London alone is very long. Indeed, the two prime examples of British estate renewal are just a stone's throw away from Central Hill estate: the Aylesbury estate in Southwark, London – one of the largest housing estates in Europe, with about 2,700 dwellings and at its peak approximately 7,500 residents – is in the process of being demolished. The Heygate Estate – at its time home to about 3,000 people – was demolished in 2014 and is in an ongoing regeneration process to make way for new mixed-income developments. By demolishing these large housing estates, local authorities have generally argued that they are investing in more socially mixed and "sustainable" neighborhoods and are creating new "affordable housing" – regardless of whether this involves massive displacement of local communities who often have no way of accessing any of the new affordable housing units. What is new, however, is that rather than looking for private developers to redevelop Central Hill estate, Lambeth Council set up a council-owned company to do the work. Lambeth Council, thus, no longer acts as merely the enabler of urban development but has become a developer itself.

At first glance, these two examples may look like a strengthening of local authorities' position in the context of austerity-imposed restrictions. On closer inspection, however, this shift to a more interventionist role does not represent a departure from entrepreneurial governance. Through a detailed analysis of these two cases in Lambeth and Inwood, I will discuss how city and local governments use inclusionary housing to pursue entrepreneurial urban regeneration strategies.

I begin by first addressing urban regeneration in the context of urban entrepreneurialism and financialization in London and New York City. I then link inclusionary housing practice of value creation to urban regeneration in both cities. Afterward, I analyze each of the above-presented cases in more detail and draw my conclusions by juxtaposing these two governmental practices of inclusionary housing.

Urban Regeneration in the Context of Urban Entrepreneurialism and Financialization of Housing in London and New York City

As I have outlined in the Introduction, with the exception of some recent studies primarily focused on New York City (Stabrowski 2015; Stein 2016), inclusionary housing has rarely been analyzed in relation to urban regeneration efforts.

The role of the state in neighborhood regeneration has, however, been the subject of intensive academic debate and criticism (i.a. Angotti and Morse 2016a; Davidson and Lees 2005; Imrie et al. 2009). Policy-led regeneration has often been associated with state-led gentrification and urban entrepreneurialism (i.a. Bridge, Butler, and Lees 2012; Davidson 2018; Watt and Smets 2017). From the 1970s, urban governance sought to promote economic growth and urban regeneration through state initiatives, facilitating private investment. In particular, in London, policy-led regeneration in the form of demolition and redevelopment of social housing estates as mixed-income developments has often been classified as a state-led gentrification strategy that results in substantial displacement of low-income households (i.a. Glucksberg 2017; Watt 2009a, 2013, 2021).

Similarly, though not as extensively, scholars researching gentrification and displacement have criticized city-initiated rezoning strategies in New York City (Angotti and Morse 2016b) or in the US more widely (Trounstine 2018) as having an upgrading effect on the surrounding area's social composition. In particular, the substantial and citywide rezonings that the Bloomberg administration (2002–14) undertook have been criticized for being part of Bloomberg's "growth machine" politics that has accelerated gentrification and displacement processes and repro-duced historic patterns of racial discrimination (Angotti 2016a; Davis 2021). Like-wise, de Blasio's recent rezoning initiatives have been criticized (Stein 2018, 2019) for fueling speculation and driving up land and property values.

In the context of austerity politics imposed on local authorities after the financial crisis of 2008 and the massive investment of capital into real estate, one of the ways in which local authorities saw potential to promote economic development and to make-up for the loss of financial revenues from higher governmental tiers was to intensify their engagement in urban regeneration. Although austerity has in some ways strengthened community involvement in land-use planning initiatives, espe-cially in England, scholars have found that their involvement in urban regeneration schemes is rather limited, and private developers as well as local authorities are the ones driving urban regeneration (Deas and Doyle 2013; Panton and Walter 2018; Watt 2018, 2021).

In this context, urban researchers have identified a trend toward financializa-tion of local government that is especially visible in the way local governments participate in real estate development (Aalbers 2019; Beswick and Penny 2018; Christophers 2017; Wainwright and Manville 2017). In the context of fiscal re-trenchment, local authorities have been looking for ways and opportunities to generate revenue mechanisms in order to become less reliant on national govern-ment spending, and, thus, embraced methods and practices of the financial sector, and have looked at how "affordable housing" can be financialized (Aalbers 2019; Wainwright and Manville 2017). Focusing on the role of the UK state in financial-izing its land, Christophers (2017) highlights the crucial role the state plays in enabling the financialization of its public land. According to him, the state has not treated its council housing estates as financial assets per se but has financialized them indirectly by selling the land to private actors who treat it as such.

However, Beswick and Penny (2018), who have explored local authorities' re-cent interventionist approaches to the austerity-induced measures in London, argue that in their attempts to assume a more regulatory role, local authorities in London adopted a new mode of urban entrepreneurialism that they call "financialized mu-nicipal entrepreneurialism" (Beswick and Penny 2018: 2). According to them, one of the new entrepreneurial ways for local governments to cope with the austerity measures imposed on them is the use of special purpose vehicles (SPV), which have been increasingly established in London and the UK more broadly (Barnes 2016). In recent years, over half of London's 32 local authorities – including Lambeth Council – have set up or are in the process of setting up such SPVs (Beswick and Penny 2018: 11). Beswick and Penny define those SPVs as follows:

> [c]ouncil-owned SPVs are opening up smooth governance space, outside of a number of financial regulatory constraints imposed from above, enabling councils to act commercially and speculatively by building private homes to sell and rent by providing an enhanced role for financial capital in the housing of London's low-income population.
>
> (Beswick/Penny 2018: 2)

The establishment of these council-owned SPVs signals a clear retreat from earlier forms of entrepreneurial governance, where local authorities are again acting as developers instead of merely facilitating the private sector to act as a provider for "affordable" homes. In the demolition of existing public housing estates and their replacement with tenure-mixed developments, a strategic goal of the SPVs, Beswick and Penny argue, is, "creating ambiguous public/private tenancies that function as both homes and the basis for liquid financial assets" (ibid.: 2). This approach enables local councils to generate their own income revenues and to intervene more directly in the financialization and regeneration of their local housing estates.

Similar to Christophers, in New York City, Fields (2017) argues that the state has indirectly financialized its rental housing stock, which she calls the most recent "frontier of financialization" (Fields 2017: 589), through the continuous dismantling of rent regulations and opening up of the public rental stock to private investors. On the basis of Field's and Christopher's observations, I argue that the rezoning of low-income areas traditionally zoned for manufacturing as part of public-private partnerships in New York City can also be seen in the context of financialization. Comparable to the local SPVs in London, the public-private NYCEDC alongside the Department of City Planning (DCP) has led to various rezonings, among which the Inwood rezoning described above. While the DCP is responsible for land use review and changes on the zoning map, the Economic Development Corporation is a public-private corporation whose stated mission is to realize "economic growth."[2] In practice, the corporation is often "responsible for long-range planning" (Angotti 2010: 14) or as the historian Oltman describes it, it is the "mayor's instrument for negotiating tax breaks, city land deals, and infrastructure benefits to developers" (Oltman 2018). Oltman further states that as a semi-private agency, NYCEDC, is "subject to limited government oversight" and funds itself "by profits from the project it brokers" (Oltman 2018). Moreover, its proximity to the financial and real estate industry becomes even more obvious through the fact that its president, James Patchett, as well as its executive vice president, Lindsay S. Greene, have both worked in banking and private equity at Goldman Sachs.[3]

Following the abovementioned recent studies on urban entrepreneurialism and financialization of land and housing, I explore in this chapter the nexus of inclusionary housing, urban regeneration, and financialization of land and housing in London and New York City. I argue that the redevelopment of the Central Hill estate in London and the rezoning of Inwood in New York City can both be seen in the context of the financialization of land and non-market housing. I will show how inclusionary housing opens a pathway – or figuratively speaking a "back door" – to state-led gentrification and urban regeneration. In the name of inclusionary housing policies, the city in conjunction with various other governmental as well as private actors has, thus, pursued an investment strategy using inclusionary housing approaches which in turn has led to the reinforcement of existing neighborhood-level inequalities across London and New York City.

In this way, I seek to expand the discussion of inclusionary housing by situating it in more recent debates on urban regeneration and municipal financialization of land. At the same time, I contribute to the debates on financialized governance and urban regeneration by providing empirical evidence of how city and local governments have used inclusionary housing as a powerful tool to encourage real estate development rather than "affordable housing." For this purpose, I make further use of the work of the urban planning scholar Minjee Kim (2020) who distinguishes between the "creation of value" and the "capturing of value" with land use regulations efforts. I use Kim's approach to "value creation" for my analysis of neighborhood regeneration through inclusionary housing. I illustrate how by leveraging their land use regulations to create the value to be captured for public benefit from future real estate development, both cities in fact engage in financializing their land and housing.

Creating Value Out of Thin Air?

The capturing of value for public benefits such as "affordable housing" is not new and widely discussed in the literature (i.a. Calavita and Mallach 2010; Fainstein 2012; Helbrecht and Weber-Newht 2018; Mallach 1984; Mill 1949). Similar to the policy concepts of "social mixing" or "diversity," land value capture is also widely seen as a positive policy idea that allows the public to profit from real estate development. As described in the Introduction, the underlying idea is that governmental activities may increase the property value and as such create benefits for the existing or future property owner. Since this increment is the result of government decisions or public investments in infrastructure rather than the landowner's own effort, they are "unearned" and, therefore, should be recaptured for public benefit.

Kim (2020) analyzes how city authorities in the five major US cities of Boston, Chicago, San Francisco, Seattle, and New York City use their land use regulation powers to reclaim value for the public benefit and divide the process of value capture into two distinct components: "value creation" and "value recapture."[4] According to Kim, local governments "create value" through upzoning in the form of density and height bonus programs. The higher density and height allowances increase the value of the future development which in turn allows local governments to recapture this increased value in the form of "affordable housing."

While upzoning is a necessity for all MIH development projects in New York City, I will use Kim's approach of "value creation" to show how the state-induced regeneration effort in Inwood is supposed to work as an incentive for future real estate development from which value could then be recaptured via the mandatory inclusionary housing program. I will further apply Kim's approach to the demolition and redevelopment of public housing estates in London

A report by the NYU Furman Center exploring the economics of mandatory inclusionary housing in New York City, titled *Creating Affordable Housing Out of Thin Air* (2015), alludes to the economic potential of mandatory inclusionary housing to require the provision of "affordable housing" units without public subsidies or – in a more figurative sense – "out of thin air" (NYU Furman Center 2015).

The rezoning and neighborhood regeneration efforts in New York City and London mentioned at the beginning of this chapter also seem to follow this notion of creating value "out of thin air." A case in point in London is the recommendation of a famous report, titled *City Villages: More Homes, Better Communities*, issued by the Institute for Public Policy Research (Adonis and Davies 2015). In the report, Andrew Adonis, Tony Blair's former policy chief, states that the estimated 3,500 housing estates in London are "the greatest source of publicly owned land suitable for new housing features" (Adonis and Davies 2015: 9). By recategorizing these housing estates as "brownfield land," local authorities could "pioneer the creation of many hundreds of new city villages London-wide" (ibid.). In urban planning terms, "brownfield land" usually describes an area of land that has previously been used for industry, potentially contaminated, but upon which new buildings could now be constructed. As such, by applying the term to London's housing estates, the generally low-income residents of these estates are potentially seen as "another kind of industrial waste" (Elmer and Dening 2016: 273) that can be "thrown out."

Both city governments followed the general claim that one can simply build itself out of the housing crisis (see Chapter 1). The "value" created for the provision of "affordable housing" is, however, not created out of "nothing" but facilitated through massive displacement of low-income households in London and the initiation of a state-led gentrification process in New York City.

As house prices increase dramatically and the demand for (affordable) housing outstrips supply, both cities have increasingly disinvested in their local housing stock. The contrast between the existing land use regulations and the local housing stock and real estate development potential has consequently created a huge "rent gap" (Smith 1979). A rent gap describes the difference between the current rent and the potentially achievable rent that could be charged by a landlord (ibid.).

With respect to London and the redevelopment of housing estates, Paul Watt calls this phenomenon a "state-induced rent gap" (Watt 2009b: 235). Effectively created by the state's continuous disinvestment from public housing since the 1980s, the value of the land an estate sits on is associated with higher development potential. This "massive capital accumulation potential" (ibid.) has sparked the interest of local governments as much as of real estate investors and developers. With most of inner London now gentrified, public housing estates have become the "final gentrification frontier" (Lees 2014: 150). Local governments have, thus, increasingly legitimized the demolition of large, partly run-down council estates as the best solution to free up this development potential and create much-needed "affordable housing" as well as "sustainable," "healthy," and "vibrant" communities. At the same time, they have contributed to the maximization of profit for private development companies, through engaging in public-private partnerships. As mentioned earlier, an extensive body of critical literature exists about the demolition of council estates and their "regeneration" as mixed communities being a prime example of the neoliberalization of housing policy that results in gentrification and displacement (i.a. Hodkinson and Robbins 2013; Watt and Smets 2017).

The decision by the councils of London boroughs to demolish their housing estates is, thus, a decision to exploit the "manufactured" rent gap. The value created from this "state-induced rent gap" can be primarily seen in the form of real estate capital. In other words, demolition opens up massive accumulation potential for private capital. This potential is seen when looking at the number of new dwellings that will be created. To provide examples of this, the community interest company ASH compared in one of their reports the number of demolitions and the number of homes to be built in some of the most famous estate regeneration schemes. In all of the studied regeneration schemes, the number of dwellings is more than double and in some cases such as Central Hill more than triple the housing units replaced (ASH 2018b: 6).

In addition, a report by the London Assembly Housing Committee (2015) found that most units created have been or will be market-rate housing. The report also found that in the 50 housing estates that were subject to redevelopment between 2004 and 2014, the number of new homes almost doubled to about 68,000 due primarily to the huge number of new market-rate housing (cited in Watt and Minton 2016: 2012). Local authorities used these high numbers of potential dwellings to be created – including "affordable housing" – to provide greater legitimacy to their regeneration efforts.

The provision of "affordable housing" is, however, negotiation-based and a case-by-case decision process. Even though each borough has its own "affordable housing" targets, these are rarely reached in planning agreements, as I show in more detail in the Chapter 3. Thus, the loss of existing social housing, even after new "affordable housing" units are created through Section 106 planning agreements, has been immense. The loss has to be compared against the gain of "affordable housing" units. In the cited report, the net loss of social rent housing was about 8,300 units (ibid.). On the website Estate Watch – initiated by the campaign group Just Space and the London Tenants Federation – it has been estimated that 161 housing estates have been demolished and 131,000 people displaced since 1997.[5]

A prime example of a state-induced rent gap is the redevelopment of the Heygate Estate into the Elephant and Caste development. It is one of the most cited redevelopment schemes as it "symbolizes all that's gone wrong with regeneration at London's unique council-built estates" (ibid.). According to the community-based Elephant Amenity Network's 35% Campaign engaged in anti-regeneration in Southwark, of the approximately 2,689 new dwellings that replace the 1,214 homes of the Heygate Estate, only 541 will be "affordable housing," of which only 92 will be social rent (Elephant Amenity Network 2019). In other words, only about 20 percent of the newly-created units will be "affordable housing," and less than 5 percent of all the new dwellings will be social rent. This shows how the added density as well as the change in housing tenure significantly increase the accumulation potential of private capital rather than the provision of "affordable housing." In 2013, the 35% Campaign investigated the displacement of the Heygate estate's tenants. They found that "only 45 Heygate tenants have actually been rehoused in new homes" (Elephant Amenity Network 2013) and that only around 216 out of 1,034 Heygate secure tenants have actually remained in the area. The rest has moved to the fringes of the borough and beyond (Elephant Amenity Network 2013; Flynn 2016).[6]

While local authorities in London saw in the demolition of often low-density housing estates the potential for the creation of new "affordable housing," the New York City administration targeted wide-ranging areas for rezoning, where it saw potential to exploit the so-called "rent gap." In both cases, inclusionary housing functioned as a means to initiate neighborhood regeneration. In New York City, the foundation for this was laid by the Bloomberg administration through its adoption of the *"Designated Areas" Inclusionary Housing Program*. Except for Staten Island, the program created designated areas in more than 24 sites across all boroughs in New York City, which were mapped in medium- and high-density neighborhoods where the city saw potential for upzoning to create new housing opportunities.

A report by the Office of Council Member Brad Lander reviewing the effectiveness of NY's inclusionary zoning program from its start in 2005 up to 2013 reveals that the program was effective in producing "affordable housing" units in only two neighborhoods: on Manhattan's West Side and in Greenpoint-Williamsburg (North Brooklyn) (Ullman, Freedman-Schnapp, and Lander 2013). However, in both areas, the generated "affordable housing" units were part of major luxury development projects, which "averaged almost 500 total units per development" (ibid.: 12). Moreover, in both "designated areas," most developers agreed to deals that involved the construction of 20 percent "affordable housing," which made them eligible for major subsidies such as a density bonus, a 421-a tax exemption for 20 years and other financing incentives like the federal Low-Income Housing Tax Credit (LIHTC) (ibid.). Put differently, the city effectively subsidized the creation of market-rate housing.

In, particular, the waterfront developments in the Greenpoint-Williamsburg district in North Brooklyn have been sharply criticized (i.a. DePaolo and Morse 2016; Stabrowski 2015; Susser 2012), not only for the level of public subsidies granted to the developers but also for the suspension of the two community-based neighborhood plans. In 2005, the New York City Council approved a comprehensive rezoning plan of nearly 200 blocks that authorized the transformation of Greenpoint's and Williamsburg's low-density manufacturing areas along the waterfront and elsewhere in the neighborhood into a space consisting of mainly upscale, mixed-use residential towers. The city claimed that the rezoning plans would result in 3,548 new "affordable housing" units. However, in the decade after the rezoning, "affordable housing" has been slow to materialize – only 16 percent of the more than 9,000 units built in total are "affordable," and of those, only 13 percent are permanently affordable, according to a report done by the Office of Council Member Antonio Reynoso (2016: 2).

The biggest impact of the rezoning has been the "massive displacement of industry, residents and the small, locally owned businesses," the scholars and activists Philip DePaolo and Sylvia Morse point out (DePaolo and Morse 2016: 74). According to them, the Latino population of Williamsburg in particular was "zoned out" (ibid.: 72): the Hispanic/Latino population declined in this area by 27 percent between 2000 and 2013, while the white population grew by 44 percent over the same period (ibid.: 87). From 2000 to 2016, the median rent in the Greenpoint-Williamsburg district increased by approximately 53 percent, which is higher than the increase in median rent in Brooklyn (25 percent) or even Manhattan (30 percent) in the same period (NYC Furman Center 2016). Like this, Greenpoint-Williamsburg transformed from being one of the most affordable neighborhoods to one of the top ten most expensive neighborhoods in New York City (ibid.). The activist and scholar Philip Stabrowski observed that even though Greenpoint-Williamsburg has been seen as a success compared to other "designated areas" where the inclusionary housing program was used, "it has utterly failed to stem the tide of rising rent levels" (Stabrowski 2015: 1126). Instead, it encouraged real estate and corporate investment that has led to massive displacement of the local community.

Following in the footsteps of the Bloomberg administration, the de Blasio administration has targeted 15 areas for rezoning to advance the new mandatory inclusionary housing program. By 2020, just before the outbreak of the global COVID-19 pandemic, the city had approved six rezonings: East New York in Brooklyn, Downtown Far Rockaway in Queens, Jerome Avenue in the South Bronx, East Harlem and Inwood in Manhattan and Bay Street in Staten Island.[7] The proposed rezoning in Flushing Queens, southern Boulevard in the Bronx and Bushwick in Brooklyn were defeated or withdrawn. Other areas – among them Chinatown in Manhattan, Long Island City in Queens, and Gowanus in Brooklyn – were anticipated or in the process of being rezoned.[8] Most of these targeted neighborhoods are predominantly low-income communities and communities of color, and most of them had voted overwhelmingly for Bill de Blasio in the mayoral election (New York Times 2013). Furthermore, they have generally been neighborhoods considered by the city government as underutilized manufacturing areas and waterfronts. Most of the targeted neighborhoods have not experienced major rezonings since the 1961 Zoning Resolution, which divided the city into commercial, residential, and manufacturing areas. The Inwood rezoning plan reflects this approach by the city. The area targeted for primarily residential rezoning is currently zoned for manufacturing and one- to two-story commercial buildings and businesses that have barely any other place left to go in the city. The de Blasio administration justified its rezoning strategy by arguing that in those areas falling under its rezoning strategy gentrification is already a reality and that in targeting these neighborhoods rezoning will reduce rather than enable future displacement (Shaw 2018: 218).

By rezoning certain places as MIH areas, the city created new special purpose districts to "promote the development of 'affordable housing' [and to] encourage economic development that benefits the local community."[9] Through upzoning, the city administration created additional value through the zoning changes. Any developer who wanted to build in that area in the future had to comply with MIH requirements. All this created the conditions for the city to "reclaim value" from future developments in the form of "affordable housing." But at the same time, the city provided the opportunity for developers to create far more market-rate than "affordable housing," and, thus, opened the area to land speculation and private development. In other words, the city government provided the incentive for developers to close the state-induced rent gap. It is very doubtful that the "affordable housing" reclaimed through the MIH regulation can counterbalance the accelerated displacement generated by the wave of new development that will very likely follow in the rezoned area.

I will now take a closer look at the social housing regeneration process of Central Hill in Lambeth, London, and the rezoning process in Inwood, New York City. The aim here is not to directly compare both processes since they differ immensely due to their distinct national and local contexts but to illustrate how city and local governments in both cities engaged in the financialization of land and housing through urban regeneration and inclusionary housing. Further, since each housing estate's regeneration and MIH-related rezoning process are essentially unique and the level of community involvement varies, both are occasionally set in relation to other ongoing neighborhood regeneration processes in each city.

I chose the two cases not only because I was able to track parts of these planning processes through participant observation but, more importantly, because each represents London's and New York's engagement in urban regeneration under the pretext of inclusionary housing practices more broadly. In New York City, the Inwood rezoning process is an illustrative example of the de Blasio administration's tendency to strategically target areas with lower-income communities of color for new development, accelerating a process of gradual gentrification already underway and displacement of longtime residents and small businesses (Angotti 2016a: 32). In London, Central Hill is a case in point for the regeneration of council housing estates that could be refurbished but instead are used by the state as financial assets to pursue a profit-making regeneration strategy.

In terms of my sources and methods, my results are mostly obtained from a close analysis of policy documents, reports, and secondary sources produced by councils, activist groups, the press, and other scholars. This is primarily due to the lengthy nature of these neighborhood regeneration processes, where following the entire process during my various phases of field research was neither practical nor possible. Nevertheless, I add to these sources my own observations of discussions between community activists and local planners and politicians at one planning meeting for the Central Hill regeneration and various local community meetings, rallies, and planning meetings for the Inwood rezoning. My findings suggest that inclusionary housing is used in both cites to – directly or indirectly – financialize land and housing through urban regeneration rather than actually address the housing affordability crisis.

The State as Developer: The Redevelopment of Central Hill Estate in London

In the middle of the Central Hill's redevelopment process, Lambeth Council withdrew from its initial plan to enable the transformation of a publicly owned council housing estate into a space open for capital investment and urban development. Instead, Lambeth Council appointed the council-owned company Homes for Lambeth (HfL) as the rebuilding entity of the housing estate. In the following, I illustrate how this new approach does not actually signify a shift away from opening council estates to capital investment and urban development, even if it constitutes a shift from the council merely being the enabler of private housing development to being (once again) the developer itself.

In 2017, the Labor-controlled Lambeth Council justified its decision to demolish and rebuild Central Hill estate as "the best option for improving the quality of council tenants' homes" and for enabling "hundreds of additional homes to be built to help ease the housing crisis" (Lambeth Cabinet 2017). This is in line with Lambeth's local housing policy that states that the council will "take full advantage of opportunities to deliver sustainable new housing, and in particular maximize the delivery of 'affordable housing,' including through estate renewal and regeneration strategies" (Lambeth Cabinet 2015: 44).

Before this decision, Lambeth Council had organized an officially managed participatory consultation process over the course of two years that included workshops with residents, public meetings, and handing out flyers to residents informing them about the redevelopment of their homes. Nevertheless, despite vehement protests from activist groups and residents, Lambeth Council concluded that rebuilding is "the only practical way to improve living conditions for people living on the estate" (Lambeth Cabinet 2017). The Cabinet legitimized its decision by referring to the estate's inherent fundamental design issues as well as the poor living conditions. According to the report, "[m]any families on the Central Hill estate are living in very poor-quality homes, many facing problems with damp, mold, cold bridging and noise transference, while the design of the overall estate creates serious accessibility problems for older and mobility-disabled residents" (Lambeth Cabinet 2017). This argumentation by the Lambeth Cabinet has been pursued by local authorities (both Conservative and Labour-controlled) and housing associations across the city as a way to legitimize demolishing local housing estates (Watt 2018: 121; Watt 2021).

According to The Guardian, residents of the estate maintain that the "defects in the fabric are the result of poor maintenance by the council" (Moore 2016). The decision to demolish Central Hill, thus, means instead of getting these long overdue repairs, most residents will be forced out of their homes – as have so many residents before them on other estates doomed to the same fate. In spite of what local councils say, for many residents of Central Hill, the estate is not an ensemble of "underused" and "run-down" buildings or an asset that sits on a lucrative piece of land with high development potential. For them, it is a place where they "have lived for decades, raised families, made friends, formed attachments to people and place" (Moore 2016). In short, most residents formed a sense of identity and community that is attached to the place. In the literature, the loss of this sense of community due to the demolition of housing estates has been identified as almost as severe as the displacement itself (Hodkinson and Essen 2015).

Shortly after Lambeth Council informed the residents about the redevelopment plans in December 2014, a group of residents came together and started the Save Central Hill Community campaign to save their homes from potential demolition. They called upon ASH, a collective of architects, urban designers, engineers, planers, and artists whose self-proclaimed goal is "to respond architecturally to London's housing 'crisis.'" In the course of the following year, ASH developed an alternative regeneration plan for the Central Hill estate that involved a substantial community consultation process. In May 2016, ASH presented an alternative proposal to Lambeth Council's demolition centered-approach to Central Hill. They maintained that "without demolishing a single home or evicting a single resident, we can increase the housing capacity on these estates by between 40 and 50 per cent" (ASH 2018a: 4). They further argued that if around half of the newly build homes would be sold or rented on the private market, it would be possible to raise the necessary funds to do the long overdue repairs on the existing estate (ibid.). ASH's report was praised and endorsed by many urban scholars as well as architects, urban designers, and community and housing rights organizations as "excellent work" (Rendell), "an important document" (McKenzie), and as "a great help" (Edwards) for other community groups fighting the demolition of their estates. Urban scholar Paul Watt further pointed out that "the report provides a detailed architectural, financial and environmental critique of the current dominant policy practice of estate-regeneration as demolition" (Architects for Social Housing 2018a.).[10]

Even though ASH was able to present their plan to the Resident Engagement Panel (REP), which acts as a body for Lambeth Council that engages with residents affected by estate regeneration programs, the proposal was not taken into closer consideration by Lambeth Council. In June 2016, just a month after ASH's presentation to the REP, Lambeth Council Capital Program Manager Fiona Cliffe denounced the proposal as "not feasible to be developed" (Cliffe 2016). In a short report, Cliffe explored the deliverability of the ASH proposal on Central Hill and concluded that it will not "generate any surplus money to fund the refurbishment of the existing homes" (Cliffe 2016).

Consequently, in March 2017, Lambeth Council decided to demolish the Central Hill estate (Figure 2.1). A year later, the council made public that it had chosen the construction company Mace "to manage the demolition and rebuilding of Central Hill estate" (Jessel 2019). Mace is a global consultancy and construction company headquartered in London that was involved in major development projects such as the London Eye and the Shard. Based on its annual report from 2017, it had a total annual revenue of about £2 billion (Mace Group 2017:10).

However, about a year later, in April 2019, the newly elected Lambeth Council[11] decided to redevelop the estate not with Mace but with its newly established SPV, HfL, a 100 percent council-owned development company. In doing so, it believed that "significant costs [could] be saved by managing the work in-house, as well as giving more control on key decisions" (Jessel 2019). The council had set

Figure 2.1 (a) Lambeth Cabinet meeting on the decision to demolish Central Hill Estate, Bolney Meadow Community Center, 31 Bolney Street, Lambeth, London, March 23, 2017. (b) Protesters at the Lambeth cabinet meeting.

Source: © Yuca Meubrink

up Lambeth for Homes in 2015 "to undertake housing and commercial developments and to reinvest the development surpluses generated […] for the benefit of Lambeth's residents, rather than seeing them go to private developers" (Lambeth Cabinet 2015: 2). Effectively, this allows Lambeth Council to "act as a property developer" (ibid.: 13). In 2019, just a few weeks before announcing its decision to hand the redevelopment of Central Hill to HfL, Lambeth Council was able to secure housing association status for HfL (Simpson 2019). This meant that HfL became registered with the Regulator of Social Housing and can now manage the affordable housing delivered by the council or buy affordable housing created through Section 106 agreements. In order to avoid a public-private partnership with private developers such as Mace or other Housing Associations, as Lambeth Council has previously done, HfL took control of the decision-making process for the redevelopment of the council's own housing estates.

Despite the council's claims that HfL will be able "to build the homes we need to house the people of Lambeth where the private market is failing" (Lambeth Cabinet 2015:1), community groups and residents have continued to fight the demolition of their housing estates all across Lambeth. All of the six council estates selected for regeneration in Lambeth – Cressingham Gardens, Knights Walk, Westbury, Fenwick, South Lambeth, and Central Hill – will be redeveloped by HfL.[12] One of the most active communities in fighting the demolition of their homes by HfL has been the residents of Cressingham Gardens Estate. Since 2012, they have consistently organized an estate-based community struggle through the "Save Cressingham Gardens" campaign, using a wide range of tactics from leafletting, demonstrations, holding workshops and open houses to lobby the council and imposing on the council two legal challenges via Judicial Review (one successful) as well as drawing up an alternative People's Plan in 2016 (Watt 2018: 122). Nevertheless, the council has stuck to its strategy of demolition rather than refurbishment.

The establishment of HfL points to an ambiguous form of housing delivery that Beswick and Penny argue has a "janus-faced" characteristic (Beswick and Penny 2018: 19): in contrast to the housing delivered through the marketplace, the affordable housing produced by a company entirely owned by the council possesses a public quality. One could, therefore, hope that by using HfL instead of a private developer the council would invest in building more homes for its low-income residents, with deeper affordability levels and greater rent stability than the current private market offers.

On the other hand, the council's approach is a partial privatization of "affordable housing" since HfL is a SPV that has a certain autonomy from state regulations. The "affordable housing" produced is, for example, not subject to state regulation as the rents can be defined by the SPV at its discretion, and it can be transferred to market-rate housing when tenants change (ibid.: 17). In addition, HfL enables the council to build private homes for sale and to access new sources of funding, including from private institutional investors. It can, thus, act commercially and speculatively like any private developers, which would otherwise not be possible due to restrictions on the council's housing budget (ibid.: 10). In this way, Lambeth Council uses its own housing estates and the land they are built on as financial assets to pursue "a profit-making, self-financing regeneration strategy" (ibid.: 10).

Despite continuing protest from local community groups as well as residents of Central Hill, in 2020, Lambeth Council was moving forward with the redevelopment of Central Hill by pushing ahead the demolition of the first building on the estate, Truslove House (Inside Croyden 2020). In 2023, Lambeth Council, however, surprisingly halted its plans to demolish the Central Hill estate, along with Cressingham Gardens and Fenwick estates, and is instead reconsidering plans for redevelopment (Heren 2023). This decision came after an independent report, chaired by independent peer Lord Bob Kerslake, found a series of problems with how HfL has operated and recommended a "fundamental rethink of the council's approach to these [...] estates" and a greater commitment "to undertake resident ballots and genuine engagement with residents" (Kerslake 2022). While this is a great testament to the endurance and the commitment of these communities that have continued to campaign for refurbishment rather than demolition, it remains to be seen which of the two contrasting "janus-faced" characteristics of the provision of "affordable housing" prevail in the coming years.

The State as Enabler: Rezoning Inwood in New York City

In 2018, the Inwood neighborhood rezoning was ready to enter the seven-month public review process called Uniform Land Use Review Procedure (ULURP). Similar to the redevelopment of the Central Hill estate, it was led primarily by a semi-public agency: the NYCEDC. The rezoning aimed at strengthening the city's negotiation power through MIH since it offers the city the possibility to recapture value from real estate development projects. In the following, I demonstrate how by delegating the power to semi-private institutions and by targeting primarily low-income neighborhoods for rezonings, the city has actually facilitated the financialization of land by changing its land use regulation in favor of the real estate industry rather than the people they are entrusted to serve and protect. I show this by pointing to the tensions between city officials and the local community fighting the city's rezoning plans.

Through the designation of a large part of the Inwood neighborhood as a new Special Inwood District, the city has created an area with specific standards that channels residential and economic development into Inwood. Inwood is located at the northern tip of Manhattan and has for a long time been home to working-class communities and new immigrants, most recently Dominican immigrants. The area to be rezoned was previously zoned as a mix of medium residential- and commercial-use buildings and low-density manufacturing and industrial buildings. This zoning reflects a plan laid down in 1961, left almost entirely unchanged since. The Inwood zoning district was established to modify the existing zoning and its underlying requirements to allow more changes "to the use, bulk, ground floor design, parking, and enclosures" (City Planning Commission (CPC) 2018: 20) of the area – in short, to allow greater development, including a portion of mandated income-targeted housing.

Although the city made various efforts to engage in a broad neighborhood planning process that involved discussion with various local residents, community groups, non-profit organizations, local businesses, and elected officials, the rezoning ultimately paid little attention to the local community's views and concerns. Over the course of about three years prior to the start of the ULURP in 2018, the NYCEDC held several public events and workshops, organized stakeholder working groups, and conducted surveys in an attempt to engage diverse sectors of the local community. The Inwood NYC Action Plan of 2017, for example, states that Inwood rezoning had taken shape through dialogue with over 2,300 residents, local nonprofits, businesses, and elected officials (NYCEDC 2017: 10). Many community groups and locals participating, however, had a different vision of the rezoning process and for their neighborhood. Most saw themselves as protectors of Inwood. Despite recent gentrification pressures, many locals have described Inwood as a walkable, laid-back, family friendly community (Vanasco 2018) comprising mid-rise walk-up tenements and multi-family residential buildings with ground-floor commercial uses.

For many residents, Inwood would be irrevocably changed by the so-called Inwood Action Plan laid out by the NYCEDC and the plan would "ruin its character, creating luxury towers along the commercial corridor and the waterfront" (ibid.). In their view, the plan represents a "trojan horse" (Krisel 2018) for displacement and gentrification, as it would not protect the large number of Inwood residents living in rent-stabilized housing from displacement, particularly those on preferential rent.[13]

During that time, local community groups held many protests and rallies and organized individual communal information events to protest the city's action plan. They attended the public events and workshops organized by NYCEDC and gave their testimonies in the public hearings of the ULURP process to protest the city's action plan.

I attended one of the Public Open House meetings in July 2016, at the Manhattan Bible Church in Inwood, where a draft of the rezoning proposal was presented to the public. At the entrance, I met a core member of the Northern Manhattan not For Sale (NMN4S) coalition,[14] one of the leading organizations in the fight against the Inwood rezoning. She was already on her way out, frustrated with the way the draft was presented to the public – it didn't allow any general discussions, she complained. Upon entering, I knew what she meant. I saw in the large auditorium, the Inwood NYC Neighborhood Plan goals and timeline presented on billboards (Figure 2.2).

Figure 2.2 NYCEDC's Public Open House meeting at the Manhattan Bible Church, Inwood, July 2016, where a draft of the rezoning proposal was presented to the public.

Source: © Yuca Meubrink

In addition, there were four breakout rooms devoted to four topics: "affordable housing," land use and zoning, neighborhood infrastructure, and placemaking, as well as community and economic development. All of them were full of poster presentations or maps of the area to be rezoned that briefly explained the potential rezoning as well as several flyers to take home. When I entered the room titled "land use and zoning," a group of people had gathered around a table that displayed the area to be rezoned (Figure 2.3). Two women in particular – one turned out to be a member of the local Community Board and the other a member of a local activist

Figure 2.3 (a), (b) Local community members discussing the city's rezoning plans at the NYCEDC's Public Open House meetings in Inwood, July 2016.

Source: © Yuca Meubrink

group – were engaged in an intense debate with one of NYCEDC's representatives. They were debating the proposed zoning changes. As the NYCEDC employee was visibly overwhelmed by the questions, a co-worker stepped in and put an end to the discussion, telling the two women to stop asking questions since they were not, in his view, the voice of the community (Fieldnote 2016/28/07). Experiences like this, where the questions and concerns of residents weren't taken seriously, are sadly all too common. As I also observed some of the rezoning processes of East New York in Brooklyn, East Harlem in Manhattan, or parts of Jerome Avenue in the Bronx, I repeatedly experienced what Tom Angotti has called "planning charades" that may "result in giant wish lists that are then followed by a rezoning cooked up in advance by the Department of City Planning" (Angotti 2016b: 144).

As the rezoning application was working its way through the ULURP in 2018, various local community and business groups formed a coalition named *Uptown United* which released the Uptown United Platform as a reaction to NYCEDC's proposed rezoning. The 16-page document entailed an alternative zoning proposal, a set of recommendations including demands for 100 percent "affordable housing" on upzoned land, greater preservation of the character of the neighborhood, the protection of small local businesses and addressing of infrastructural, environmental, and social justice concerns before any increase in density (Uptown United Platform 2018). The local Community Board unanimously adopted the rezoning application with recommendations that incorporated many of the demands raised by the Uptown United Platform (Savitch-Lew 2018). In April 2018, Borough President Gale Brewer adopted NYCEDC's plan but also recommended a set of changes to the rezoning plan. Her recommendations were more fragmented and did not go as far as the recommendations made by the Community Board. The CPC then approved the plan as proposed, ignoring the advisory recommendations by the local Community Board as well as those made by the Borough President (CPC 2018).

Just a week before the Subcommittee on Zoning and Franchise was scheduled to vote on the proposal, a review and report of the Inwood zoning proposal was released by three professors at the City University New York (Rickenbacker, Krinsky, and Schaller 2018). The rezoning review was requested by the local New York City Council Member Ydanis Rodriguez. According to one of the three professors, John Krinsky, who assessed the rezoning plan's effects on "affordable housing" in the neighborhood, Inwood may already be in the process of gentrification, but it is still a largely affordable neighborhood (Krinsky 2018: 15). More than 60 percent of the neighborhood still has rent-regulated housing. However, since about 30 percent of renters pay preferential rent, which can be increased to the allowable rent on a new lease, the affordability of the neighborhood is very much threatened (Krinsky 2018: 18). As the report states, about one-quarter of the Inwood population had an income below $20,000 in 2016 and nearly half of the low-income households were severely rent-burdened (Krinsky 2018: 19). With respect to MIH and the income bands of the future "affordable housing" units, which he finds "inadequate" for the neighborhood, Krinsky argues that "the idea that displacement and gentrification could be addressed by MIH quotas – at almost whatever level – is, in this context, not simply fantastical but hallucinatory" (Krinsky 2018: 26). He concludes his review by stating that "[a]pproving a rezoning without a thorough study of displacement dynamics focused especially on landlord behavior seems both premature and frankly, negligent" (Krinsky 2018: 28). However, the report did not find its way into the ULURP negotiations.

After closed-door negotiations between the Subcommittee of Zoning and Franchise and the local Council Member Ydanis Rodriguez, the committee approved a modified plan that included more "affordable housing" at lower AMI and left out of the rezoning a much-debated commercial area known as the "Commercial U" (Kully 2018). Even though this was a partial success for the Inwood community, many residents continued to oppose the modified rezoning plan approved by the City Council in August 2018 (Mays 2018).

Following the rezoning of Inwood, local community activists filed a lawsuit on behalf of the community coalition Northern Manhattan Not for Sale against the City of New York to challenge the land use changes. They questioned the environmental review of the rezoning proposal and claimed that it did not properly evaluate the racial and socio-economic impacts of the rezoning on longtime residents. In 2019, the Supreme Court of New York County sided with the local community group and annulled the Inwood rezoning on the grounds that the city failed to conduct a proper environmental review (Kully 2019). However, in 2020, the Appeals Court unanimously reversed the lower court's decision, stating that "[t]he City Council acted properly, and consistently [...] in approving the rezoning."[15]

Like that of Inwood, many neighborhood rezonings under the de Blasio administration have been top-down. Among them are the rezonings of East New York (Brooklyn), Jerome Avenue (the Bronx), and East Harlem (Manhattan), all of which are predominately low-income communities of color. Moreover, what almost all neighborhood rezonings under the de Blasio administration share is that they have been vehemently contested and faced significant opposition from the local community. In a word, with the Inwood rezoning, the city government in tandem with NYCEDC facilitated the financialization of land through its land use regulations.

Comparing New York City and London

This chapter has so far discussed examples of how London's and New York City's municipalities have in recent years treated low-income communities as strategic investment opportunities. They illustrate the nexus between inclusionary housing, urban regeneration, and financialization of land and housing. In response to austerity-imposed policies, local authorities have shown a more interventionist approach to housing, implementing entrepreneurial ways to create more "affordable housing." In both cases presented here, the underlying assumption shared by both local authorities is that regeneration is necessary because of a lack of new affordable housing development. That might make sense on a general citywide level since both cities find it increasingly difficult to match the demand for affordable housing, intensified by economic constraints, a growing influx of people, and dramatically rising house prices. But targeting neighborhoods that are especially vulnerable to displacement pressures and imposing top-down regeneration plans on them does not reflect the progressive aims those local authorities in both cities claim to be guided by. Instead, it presents a form of state-led new-build gentrification, signaling to potential developers where to invest and, thus, laying the groundwork for future displacement of low-income communities.

Moreover, in both cases, the local authorities claim that addressing the housing affordability crisis requires making changes to designated neighborhoods that allow greater density. However, the way these changes were enacted greatly differed. For example, rather than merely enabling urban development, Lambeth Council in London has become a developer to meet its housing targets. In contrast to the government's mass production schemes of social housing estates in the heyday of the Keynesian welfare state, the council has acted as a private speculative developer whose "core operating logics and practices have been borrowed from the private and financial sector" (Beswick and Penny 2018: 14). In New York City, the de Blasio administration continued to act as an enabler of urban development, limiting itself to strategic oversight of private development and to creating the best conditions for MIH to work. But despite the fact that inclusionary housing has been made mandatory in upzoned areas, the city cannot guarantee a specific number of "affordable housing" units nor their affordability as they are all subject to individual case-by-case planning processes – as we will see in more detail in Chapter 3. Nor can the city make promises of additional affordable units above the 25 percent or 30 percent options, because it cannot require developers on private land to take public subsidies for additional "affordable housing."

In contrast to London's, New York City government's role in the financialization of land and housing has been more "indirect," as Christophers (2017: 2) would describe it. While the financialization itself has been left to developers, hence the private sector, the city government provides the conditions for the real estate industry to pursue their profitable investment strategies. Reclaiming some of the increased value in the form of "affordable housing" is a very small sum in comparison to the speculative value of the development unleashed through rezoning. On the contrary, it will most likely reinforce already existing inequalities within targeted neighborhoods across the city.

These differences, however, do not seem to matter much for the outcome of recent neighborhood regeneration schemes. Despite official promises by governmental actors and agencies, the "affordable housing" reclaimed through the regeneration schemes will for the most part not be able to counterbalance the loss of social and "affordable housing" through the demolition of housing estates in Lambeth or the massive gentrification and displacement pressures that will likely be triggered through the upzoning in Inwood.

In what way this form of creation of value through neighborhood regeneration in the name of inclusionary housing has served as an opportunity for the public sector to reclaim value in the form of "affordable housing" from future urban development projects remains to be seen. But given the urban-growth as well as gentrification-oriented approaches to neighborhood redevelopment by each city's local governments, it is unlikely that there will be a turning away from former entrepreneurial neighborhood regeneration efforts, as exemplified in this chapter by the Greenpoint-Williamsburg rezoning in New York City under the Bloomberg administration and the demolition of the Heygate Estate under the Johnson administration. How and how much "affordable housing" city and local governments have recaptured from private real estate developments will be part of the Chapter 3.

Fieldnotes

Meubrink, Yuca. Participant observation of NYCEDC's Public Open House meeting related to the rezoning in Inwwod, Manhattan Bible Church, Inwood, Manhattan, New York City, July 28, 2016.

Meubrink, Yuca. Participant observation of Lambeth Cabinet meeting, Bolney Meadow Community Centre, 31 Bolney Street, in Lambeth, London., March 23, 2017.

Notes

1 This ethnographic field note has been slightly edited for publication.
2 For more information, see https://edc.nyc/meet-nycedc (last accessed: June 12, 2022).
3 For more information on NYCEDC's leadership, see https://edc.nyc/people (last accessed: June 12, 2022).
4 One could also broaden the debate by including David Harvey's discussion on use value and exchange value in his work *The Limits to Capital* (1982). However, I focus on Kim's distinction of "value creation" and "value capture" as it is directly related to inclusionary housing.
5 For further information, see https://estatewatch.london/research/ (last accessed: December 28, 2020).
6 For more information, see the displacement map of the Heygate Estate Tenants: https://www.35percent.org/posts/2013-06-08-the-heygate-diaspora/ (last accessed: June 12, 2022).
7 For more information, see NYC's official Rezoning Commitments Tracker: https://www1.nyc.gov/site/operations/performance/neighborhood-rezoning-commitments-tracker.page (last accessed: June 12, 2022).
8 In the afterword, I will go into more detail about the rezoning of the Gowanus neighborhood, which was approved by the New York City Council in 2021.
9 For reference and more information on special purpose districts, see https://www1.nyc.gov/site/planning/zoning/districts-tools/special-purpose-districts-manhattan.page (last accessed: December 28, 2020).
10 For references and more information, see the endorsements on ASH's website: https://architectsforsocialhousing.co.uk/2018/04/10/central-hill-a-case-study-in-estate-regeneration/ (last accessed: December 21, 2020).
11 In the 2018 election, the Labour Party maintained its control of the council, though its majority was reduced by two seats. With the Conservatives winning only one seat, the Green Party became the official opposition for the first time since the establishment of the council.
12 For more information on the status of each of these six estates, see Homes for Lambeth's website: https://engage.homesforlambeth.co.uk/ (last accessed: June 12, 2022).
13 In New York City, preferential rent is a legal concept that allows landlords to charge lower rents than the legal rent on rent-stabilized apartments. For more information, see https://www.metcouncilonhousing.org/help-answers/preferential-rents-2/ (last accessed: January 27, 2021).

14   The Northern Manhattan Not for Sale coalition is a broad coalition of various local community and action groups, such as the Met Council on Housing, Inwood Preservation, Uptown for Bernie, Moving Forward Unidos, and others.
15   Matter of Northern Manhattan Is Not for Sale v City of New York 2020 NY, Slip Op 04235, decided on July 23, 2020, Appellate Division, First Department. For more information see: https://law.justia.com/cases/new-york/appellate-division-first-department/2020/11742-161578-18.html (last accessed on December 30, 2020).

References

Aalbers, Manuel B. 2019. "Introduction to the Forum: From Third to Fifth-Wave Gentrification." *Tijdschrift Voor Economische En Sociale Geografie* 110 (1): 1–11.
Adonis, Andrew, and Bill Davies. 2015. City Villages: More Homes, Better Communities. 5–20. Institute for Public Policy Research. http://www.ippr.org/publications/cityvillages-more-homes-better-communities.
Angotti, Tom. 2010. "Land Use and the New York City Charter." submitted to the New York City Charter Commission. http://www.hunter.cuny.edu/ccpd/repository/files/charterreport-angotti-2.pdf.
———. 2016a. "Land Use Zoning Matters." In *Zoned Out! Race, Displacement, and City Planning in New York City*, edited by Tom Angotti and Sylvia Morse, 18–45. New York: UR.
———. 2016b. "Alternatives: Community-Based Planning and Housing in the Public Domain." In *Zoned Out! Race, Displacement, and City Planning in New York City*, edited by Tom Angotti and Sylvia Morse, 142–65. New York: UR.
Angotti, Tom, and Sylvia Morse, eds. 2016a. *Zoned Out! Race, Displacement, and City Planning in New York City*. New York: UR.
———. 2016b. "Racialized Land Use and Housing Policies." In *Zoned Out! Race, Displacement, and City Planning in New York City*, edited by Tom Angotti and Sylvia Morse, 46–71. New York: UR.
Architects for Social Housing (ASH). 2018a. "Central Hill: A Case Study in Estate Regeneration." Architects for Social Housing. https://architectsforsocialhousing.co.uk/2018/04/10/central-hill-a-case-study-in-estate-regeneration/.
———. 2018b. "The Costs of Estate Regeneration." Architects for Social Housing. https://architectsforsocialhousing.co.uk/2018/09/07/the-costs-of-estate-regeneration/.
Barnes, Sophie. 2016. "More than a Third of Councils Set up Housing Companies." *Inside Housing*, December 9. https://www.insidehousing.co.uk/news/news/more-than-a-third-of-councils-set-up-housing-companies-48870.
Beswick, Joe, and Joe Penny. 2018. "Demolishing the Present to Sell off the Future? The Emergence of 'Financialized Municipal Entrepreneurialism' in London." *International Journal of Urban and Regional Research* 42 (4): 612–32. https://doi.org/10.1111/1468-2427.12612.
Bridge, Gary, Tim Butler, and Loretta Lees. 2012. *Mixed Communities: Gentrification by Stealth?*. Bristol: POLICY PR.
Calavita, Nico, and Alan Mallach, eds. 2010. *Inclusionary Housing in International Perspective: Affordable Housing, Social Inclusion, and Land Value Recapture*. Cambridge, MA: Lincoln Institute of Land Policy.
Christophers, Brett. 2017. "The State and Financialization of Public Land in the United Kingdom." *Antipode* 49 (1): 62–85. https://doi.org/10.1111/anti.12267.
City Planning Commission (CPC). 2018. *Inwood Rezoning – City Planning Commission Report. C 180204(A) ZMM*. New York City: City Planning Commission.
Cliffe, Fiona. 2016. "Deliverability of the ASH Proposal on Central Hill." Architects for Social Housing. https://architectsforsocialhousing.co.uk/2016/09/21/deliverability-of-the-ash-proposal-on-central-hill-ash-response-to-lambeth-labour-council/.

Davidson, Mark. 2018. "New-Build Gentrification." In *Handbook of Gentrification Studies*, Loretta Lees and Martin Phillips, 247–61. Cheltenham; Northampton, MA: Edward Elgar Publishing. https://doi.org/10.1068/a3739.

Davis, Jenna. 2021. "How Do Upzonings Impact Neighborhood Demographic Change? Examining the Link between Land Use Policy and Gentrification in New York City." *Land Use Policy* 103 (April). https://doi.org/10.1016/j.landusepol.2021.105347.

Deas, Iain, and Jennifer Doyle. 2013. "Building Community Capacity Under 'Austerity Urbanism': Stimulating, Supporting and Maintaining Resident Engagement in Neighbourhood Regeneration in Manchester." *Journal of Urban Regeneration and Renewal* 6 (January): 365–80.

DePaolo, Philip, and Sylvia Morse. 2016. "Williamsburg: Zoning Out Latinos." In *Zoned Out! Race, Displacement, and City Planning in New York City*, edited by Tom Angotti and Sylvia Morse, 72–94. New York: UR. https://www.urpub.org/books/zonedout.

Elephant Amenity Network. 2013. "The Heygate Diaspora." *35% Campaign* (blog). June 8. https://www.35percent.org/posts/2013-06-08-the-heygate-diaspora/.

———. 2019. "Elephant Park MP5 – the Final Chapter." *35% Campaign* (blog). 2019. https://www.35percent.org/posts/2019-08-05-elephant-park-final-phase-affordable-housing/.

Elmer, Simon, and Geraldine Dening. 2016. "The London Clearances." *City* 20 (2): 271–77. https://doi.org/10.1080/13604813.2016.1143684.

Fainstein, Susan. 2012. "Land Value Capture and Justice." *Value Capture and Land Policies*, 21–40.

Fields, Desiree. 2017. "Unwilling Subjects of Financialization." *International Journal of Urban and Regional Research* 41 (4): 588–603. https://doi.org/10.1111/1468-2427.12519.

Flynn, Jerry. 2016. "Complete Control." *City* 20 (2): 278–86. https://doi.org/10.1080/13604813.2016.1143685.

Glucksberg, Luna. 2017. "'The Blue Bit, That Was My Bedroom': Rubble, Displacement and Regeneration in Inner-City London." In *Social Housing and Urban Renewal. A Cross-National Perspective*, Paul Watt and Peer Smets. UK: Emerald Publishing, 69–104.

Harvey, David. 1982. *The Limits to Capital*. Chicago: University of Chicago Press.

Helbrecht, Ilse, and Francesca Weber-Newth. 2018. "Recovering the Politics of Planning." *City* 22 (1): 116–29.

Heren, Kit. 2023. "PRP's Plan to Demolish Central Hill Estate Paused by Council." *Architects Journal*, March 3. https://www.architectsjournal.co.uk/news/prps-contentious-demolition-of-central-hill-estate-paused-by-council?tkn=1.

Hernández, Ramona, Utku Sezgin, and Sarah Marrara. 2018. "When a Neighborhood Becomes a Revolving Door for Dominicans: Rising Housing Costs in Washington Heights/Inwood and the Declining Presence of Dominicans." CUNY Dominican Studies Institute. https://academicworks.cuny.edu/cgi/viewcontent.cgi?article=1025&context=dsi_pubs.

Hodkinson, Stuart, and Chris Essen. 2015. "Grounding Accumulation by Dispossession in Everyday Life: The Unjust Geographies of Urban Regeneration under the Private Finance Initiative." *International Journal of Law in the Built Environment* 7 (April): 72–91. https://doi.org/10.1108/IJLBE-01-2014-0007.

Hodkinson, Stuart, and Glyn Robbins. 2013. "The Return of Class War Conservatism? Housing under the UK Coalition Government." *Critical Social Policy* 33 (1): 57–77.

Imrie, Rob, Loretta Lees, and Mike Raco, eds. 2009. *Regenerating London: Governance, Sustainability and Community in a Global City*. Milton Park, Abingdon, Oxon ; New York, NY: Routledge.

Inside Croydon. 2020. "Activists Set up Camp to Fight against Central Hill Demolition." *Inside Croydon*, December 7. https://insidecroydon.com/2020/12/07/activists-set-up-camp-to-fight-against-central-hill-demolition/.

Jessel, Ella. 2019. "Central Hill: Lambeth to Bring Controversial Overhaul Back in-House." *The Architects' Journal*, April 17. http://www.architectsjournal.co.uk/news/central-hill-lambeth-to-bring-controversial-overhaul-back-in-house.

Kerslake, Bob. 2022. "Kerslake review of affordable housing in Lambeth." *Lambeth Council.* https://moderngov.lambeth.gov.uk/documents/s142089/Kerslake%20Review%20into% 20Affordable%20Housing%20in%20Lambeth.pdf.

Kim, Minjee. 2020. "Upzoning and Value Capture: How U.S. Local Governments Use Land Use Regulation Power to Create and Capture Value from Real Estate Developments." *Land Use Policy* 95 (June): 104624.

Krinsky, John. 2018. "Recommendations for Assessing Risks of and Responses to Residential Displacement." In *Inwood Rezoning Proposal: Review and Report*, edited by Shawn Rickenbacker, John Krinsky and Susanna Schaller, 15–29. New York City: CUNY.

Krisel, Brendan. 2018. "Inwood Rezoning Foes Implore Council to Vote Down Plan." *NY Patch*, July 10. https://patch.com/new-york/washington-heights-inwood/inwood-rezoning-foes-implore-council-vote-down-plan.

Kully, Sadef Ali. 2018. "Inwood Rezoning Sees Major Amendment, Passes First Council Votes." *City Limits*, August 2. https://citylimits.org/2018/08/02/inwood-rezoning-sees-major-amendment-passes-first-council-vote/.

———. 2019. "Judge Annuls Inwood Rezoning, Citing Flaws in City's Review." *City Limits*, December 20. https://citylimits.org/2019/12/20/judge-annuls-inwood-rezoning-citing-flaws-in-citys-review/.

Lambeth Cabinet. 2015. "Homes for Lambeth: A Special Purpose Vehicle for Lambeth." Lambeth Cabinet. https://moderngov.lambeth.gov.uk/documents/s77350/Homes%20 for%20Lambeth%20an%20SPV%20for%20Lambeth.pdf.

———. 2017. "Investing in Better Neighbourhoods and Building the Homes We Need to House the People of Lambeth – Central Hill." Lambeth Cabinet. https://moderngov. lambeth.gov.uk/documents/s77350/Homes%20for%20Lambeth%20an%20SPV%20 for%20Lambeth.pdf.

Lees, Loretta. 2014. "The Death of Sustainable Communities in London?" In *Sustainable London? The Future of a Global City*, edited by Rob Imrie and Loretta Lees, 149–71. Bristol: Policy Press.

London Assembly Housing Committee. 2015. *Knock It Down or Do It Up? The Challenge of Estate Regeneration.* London: Greater London Authority.

Mace Group. 2017. Annual Report 2017. Mace Group.

Mallach, Alan. 1984. *Inclusionary Housing Programs: Policies and Practices.* New Brunswick, N.J.: Rutgers University Center for Urban.

Mays, Jeffery C. 2018. "City Council Approves Inwood Rezoning, Despite Resident Protests." *The New York Times*, August 8. https://www.nytimes.com/2018/08/08/nyregion/ inwood-rezoning-manhattan-affordable-housing.html.

Mays, Jeffery C., and Aaron Robertson. 2018. "Fighting Over the Future of Inwood, Manhattan's Last Affordable Neighborhood." *The New York Times*, August 7. https://www. nytimes.com/2018/08/07/nyregion/inwood-rezoning-nyc-manhattan.html.

Mill, John Stuart. 1949. "The Unearned Increment." Fabian Tract No. 30. Fabian Municipal Program No. 1. http://webbs.library.lse.ac.uk/50/1/FabianTracts30.pdf.

Ministry of Housing, Communities and Local Government (MHCLG). 2019. "Affordable Housing Supply Statistics (AHS) 2019-20. Live Tables - 1011S, 1011C." Government UK. https://www.gov.uk/government/statistical-data-sets/live-tables-on-affordable-housing-supply#live-tables.

Moore, Rowan. 2016. "Housing Estates: If They Aren't Broken…." *The Guardian*, January 31. http://www.theguardian.com/artanddesign/2016/jan/31/council-estates-if-they-arent-broken-lambeth-council-central-hill-estate-social-housing-affordable.

New York City Economic Development Corporation (NYCEDC). 2017. "Inwood NYC Planning Initiative." 2017. New York City Economic Development Corporation. https:// edc.nyc/project/inwood-nyc-planning-initiative.

NYU Furman Center. 2015. *Creating Affordable Housing Out of Thin Air: The Economics of Mandatory Inclusionary Zoning in New York City.* New York City: NYU Furman Center. http://furmancenter.org/files/NYUFurmanCenter_CreatingAffHousing_March2015.pdf.

————. 2016. "State of New York City's Housing & Neighborhoods – 2016 Report." NYU Furman Center. https://furmancenter.org/research/sonychan/2016-report.

Office of Council Member Antonio Reynoso. 2016. "Councilmember Reynoso Lessons from Williamsburg and Bushwick." Office of Council Member Antonio Reynoso. https://www.documentcloud.org/documents/3179084-Councilmember-Reynoso-Lessons-From-Williamsburg.html.

Oltman, Adele. 2018. "Zoning for the 1%." *Dissent Magazine*, November 3. https://www.dissentmagazine.org/online_articles/inwood-rezoning-bill-de-blasio-mih.

Panton, Mark, and Geoff Walters. 2018. "'It's Just a Trojan Horse for Gentrification': Austerity and Stadium-Led Regeneration." *International Journal of Sport Policy and Politics* 10 (1): 163–83. https://doi.org/10.1080/19406940.2017.1398768.

Rickenbacker, Shawn, John Krinsky, and Susanna Schaller. 2018. *Inwood Rezoning Proposal: Review and Report*. New York City: CUNY. https://www.researchgate.net/publication/329451451_Inwood_Rezoning_Proposal_Review_and_Report?enrichId=rgreq-430b0cd90db9b04ea51f373f4a2436e4-XXX&enrichSource=Y292ZXJQY-WdlOzMyOTQ1MTQ1MTtBUzo3MDA4ODIyNzg3MDMxMDI1AMTU0N-DExNDc2NTgyMA%3D%3D&el=1_x_3&_esc=publicationCoverPdf.

Savitch-Lew, Abigail. 2018. "On Inwood Rezoning, Community Board Committee Adopts Many Residents' Demands." *City Limits*. https://citylimits.org/2018/03/16/on-inwood-rezoning-community-board-committee-adopts-many-residents-demands/.

Shaw, Randy. 2018. *Generation Priced Out: Who Gets to Live in the New Urban America*. Oakland, California: University of California Press.

Simpson, Jack. 2019. "Lambeth Council-Owned Company Secures Housing Association Status." *Inside Housing*, March 25. https://www.insidehousing.co.uk/news/news/lambeth-council-owned-company-secures-housing-association-status-60740.

Smith, Neil. 1979. "Toward a Theory of Gentrification a Back to the City Movement by Capital, Not People." *Journal of the American Planning Association* 45 (4): 538–48. https://doi.org/10.1080/01944367908977002.

Stabrowski, Filip. 2015. "Inclusionary Zoning and Exclusionary Development: The Politics of 'Affordable Housing' in North Brooklyn." *International Journal of Urban and Regional Research* 39 (6): 1120–36. https://doi.org/10.1111/1468-2427.12297

Stein, Samuel. 2016. "Chinatown: Unprotected and Undone." In *Zoned Out! Race, Displacement, and City Planning in New York City*, edited by Tom Angotti and Sylvia Morse. New York: UR: 122–41. https://www.urpub.org/books/zonedout.

————. 2018. "Progress for Whom, toward What? Progressive Politics and New York City's Mandatory Inclusionary Housing." *Journal of Urban Affairs* 40 (6): 770–81. https://doi.org/10.1080/07352166.2017.1403854.

————. 2019. *Capital City: Gentrification and the Real Estate State*. London; Brooklyn, NY: Verso.

Susser, Ida. 2012. *Norman Street: Poverty and Politics in an Urban Neighborhood*. Oxford University Press. http://www.oxfordscholarship.com/view/10.1093/acprof:oso/9780195367317.001.0001/acprof-9780195367317.

The New York Times. 2013. "New York City Mayor - 2013 Election Results." *The New York Times*, November 6. https://www.nytimes.com/projects/elections/2013/general/nyc-mayor/map.html.

Trounstine, Jessica. 2018. *Segregation by Design: Local Politics and Inequality in American Cities*. New York: Cambridge University Press.

Ullman, Seth, Michael Freedman-Schnapp, and Brad Lander. 2013. "Inclusionary Zoning in New York City: The Performance of New York City's Designated Areas Inclusionary Housing Program Since Its Launch in 2005." Office of Council Member Brad Lander. https://www.scribd.com/doc/160544058/Inclusionary-Zoning-in-New-York-City-The-performance-of-New-York-City-s-Designated-Areas-Inclusionary-Housing-Program-since-its-launch-in-2005.

Uptown United Platform. 2018. "Uptown United Platform." Uptown United. https://www.documentcloud.org/documents/4384164-Uptown-United-Platform-Feb-21.html.

Vanasco, Jennifer. 2018. "Inwood Residents & Small Business Owners Fear Rezoning Plan Will Open Gentrification Floodgates." *Gothamist*, July 10. https://gothamist.com/news/inwood-residents-small-business-owners-fear-rezoning-plan-will-open-gentrification-floodgates.

Wainwright, Thomas, and Graham Manville. 2017. Financialization and the third sector: Innovation in social housing bond markets. *Environment and Planning A*, 49 (4): 819–38. doi:10.1177/0308518X16684140.

Watt, Paul. 2009a. "Social Housing and Regeneration in London." In *Regenerating London. Governance, Sustainability and Community in a Global City*, edited by Rob Imrie, Loretta Lees, and Mike Raco. London: Routledge: 226–48.

———. 2009b. "Housing Stock Transfers, Regeneration and State-Led Gentrification in London." *Urban Policy and Research* 27 (3): 229–42.

———. 2013. "'It's Not for Us." *City* 17 (1): 99–118.

———. 2017. "Social Housing and Urban Renewal: An Introduction." In *Social Housing and Urban Renewal. A Cross-National Perspective*, edited by Paul Watt and Peer Smets, 1–36. UK: Emerald Publishing.

———. 2018. "'Social Housing Not Social Cleansing': Contemporary Housing Struggles in London." In *Rent and Its Discontents. A Century of Housing Struggle*, edited by Neil Grey, 117–35. London: Rowman & Littlefield.

———. 2021. *Estate Regeneration and Its Discontents: Public Housing, Place and Inequality in London*. Bristol: Policy Press.

Watt, Paul, and Anna Minton. 2016. "London's Housing Crisis and Its Activisms." *City* 20 (2): 204–21. https://doi.org/10.1080/13604813.2016.1151707.

Watt, Paul, and Peer Smets. 2017. *Social Housing and Urban Renewal: A Cross-National Perspective*. Bingley: Emerald Publishing Limited.

3 Reclaiming What, Where, and for Whom?

How the Provision of a "Public Good" Contributes to New-Build Gentrification

Despite the generally more discretionary nature of the British planning system, the scope and scale of developer contributions in both cities are greatly determined by what is negotiated with the city and local governments. In this chapter, I discuss how city and local governments use their regulatory power to "capture value" from real estate development for the public benefit. My aim here is, however, not only to provide a more nuanced understanding of how inclusionary housing operates in and through the planning process in both cities but to highlight the recurrent features and repeating patterns of how "value" is recaptured in both cities through "affordable housing."

Through a detailed consideration of the negotiation process and local community participation efforts in four application cases in each city, I demonstrate how governmental actors have accepted different planning obligations. Despite contextual differences and particularities, I show how these planning obligations vary less between the two cities than between neighborhoods.

In Chapter 2, I showed that local authorities have primarily directed urban development into low-income neighborhoods. My results in this chapter additionally suggest that city and local governments have been more engaged in implementing "affordable housing" requirements in low-income neighborhoods than in affluent ones. These disparate approaches of city and local governments to the different neighborhoods show again how inclusionary housing enhances gentrification and displacement processes and reinforces neighborhood inequalities.

The Role of Local Governments in the Uneven Spatial Distribution of Inclusionary Housing Developments

As mentioned in the Introduction, the literature does not provide a clear picture of the spatial impact of inclusionary housing. Overall, there are only a few studies that focus explicitly on the spatial impact of inclusionary housing, and almost none that focus on the role of city and local governments in the matter.

Nonetheless, more recent literature studying inclusionary housing in London or New York City has stressed that inclusionary housing is sited primarily in low-income neighborhoods of color (Angotti 2016; Li and Guo 2020; Stein 2018).

DOI: 10.4324/9781003468479-4

Angotti (2016) and Stein (2018), who focused explicitly on New York City, have argued that inclusionary housing tends to be placed in low-income neighborhoods of color. Both authors have primarily looked at neighborhoods targeted for rezoning by the de Blasio administration to trigger MIH but have not looked at the distributional outcome of inclusionary housing programs (IHPs) in specific developments. At the time of writing, there have only been a few reports or publicly available datasets that tracked affordable housing production under MIH (Kober 2020; Stein 2021: 19, NYC Office of the Mayor 2021). The number of homes created through the Mandatory Inclusionary Housing (MIH) Program varies widely, which may be related to the timing of the surveys.[1] In 2021, the Office of the Mayor itself, for example, stated that more than 4,000 affordable housing units have been created through MIH (NYC Office of the Mayor 2021). According to a report published by the Manhattan Institute, a Conservative think tank, the author Eric Kober notes that only 2,065 "affordable housing" units have been created between the implementation of MIH in March 2016 and 2020 (Kober 2020: 9). The report further states that most MIH units created are deeply subsidized, 100 percent "affordable housing" developments and concentrated in low-income areas. That means that MIH has so far primarily been used by "affordable housing" providers who are already dedicated to the creation of "affordable housing" and have received heavy public subsidies. Only in rare cases do such developments include market-rate units or have been placed in affluent neighborhoods (Kober 2020).

Li and Guo (2020) noted the lack of empirical studies on the spatial distribution of inclusionary housing developments, particularly in the British context. In their study, they examined the potential effects of inclusionary housing implemented in London (and Lisbon) since the early 2000s. Using quantitative methods, they found that "affordable housing" units created through Section 106 agreements are more likely to be placed in low-income neighborhoods with higher poverty rates and racial minorities (Li and Guo 2020: 987). They further highlighted that developments in more affluent neighborhoods are less likely to include "affordable housing" on-site or when they do, they provide a smaller percentage of "affordable housing" (ibid.: 988).

Though these more recent studies paint a clearer picture of the unequal spatial distribution of inclusionary housing in both cities, the question of how inclusionary housing is dispersed within different neighborhood contexts, and how this relates to the role of local government, lacks empirical evidence.

Further, although it is clear that local governments play a pivotal role in the uneven distribution of inclusionary housing developments, the actual role of city and local government, and the occasional tensions between them when it comes to the provision of "affordable housing," remains little discussed. Li and Guo (2020) examined whether local policies or more precisely the political make-up of local councils play a role in the spatial dispersal of inclusionary housing development. They concluded that even though Labor councils tend to be able to place more "affordable housing" in new developments, the make-up of local councils does not alone explain the "strong association" (Li and Guo 2020: 987) between the low-income neighborhoods and on-site inclusion of "affordable housing."

Other scholars who have focused more on the role of local authorities in the context of austerity than the spatial distribution of inclusionary housing have come to the conclusion that local authorities have adopted entrepreneurial and pro-growth strategies with regard to urban development (i.a. Fuller 2018, Fuller and West 2017; Lowndes and Gardner 2016; Panton and Walters 2018). Lowndes and Gardner (2016), who focused on the impact of austerity policies on local authorities, for example, argued that local governments have been confronted with "a situation of super-austerity, in which new cuts come on top of previous ones" (Lowndes and Gardner 2016: 2). According to them, local authorities have focused on economic development and major strategic services at the expense of other local day-to-day services, including social care and housing.

Examining the discursive logic used by local authorities and planners to justify the adoption of pro-growth strategies involving the promotion of urban development and place-based interventions, Fuller and West (2017) claim that local authorities' lack of resources and capacity due to austerity policies has translated into a focus "on key areas, sites and projects that will 'deliver growth'" (Fuller and West 2017: 2100). In the context of austerity governance, Panton and Walters (2018) discuss the planning process of the redevelopment of the Tottenham Hotspur FC in the London Borough of Haringey. They argue that Haringey Council has taken a pragmatic rather than an entrepreneurial approach:

> The fact that the football club had been successful on viability grounds in reducing an original 2011 Section 106 requirement for 50% of 200 units on the site of the old ground to be 'affordable housing' to 585 units at full market value by December 2015 provided evidence that Haringey Council were taking a pragmatic approach: by that it means that the threat of the football club leaving the area or not being able to pursue the stadium development due to financial concerns, together with a changed institutional context linked to an austerity budget from central government, resulted in the council making additional concessions to enable the scheme to go ahead.
>
> (Panton and Walter 2018: 173)

In contrast to Panton and Walter, one could also argue that Haringey's Council had in fact adopted an entrepreneurial approach to urban development, defined in terms of the council adopting an urban growth strategy by allowing the scheme to go ahead without any provisions for much-needed "affordable housing." Using examples from different neighborhoods in both cities, I will show how local governments have ultimately adopted entrepreneurial strategies despite the differing socio-economic composition of different neighborhoods.

Cases Studied in Each City

Through primarily qualitative data, I examine four development proposals in each city from 2014 to 2020, looking primarily at similarities and significant differences in land value capture through developer-contributed forms of "affordable housing." In each planning case, I examine the way inclusionary housing has been negotiated and contested, the amount captured from the decisions being made as well as who benefited from the "affordable housing." As I mentioned above, there are considerable differences between London and New York City when inclusionary housing is triggered. This also impacts how often inclusionary housing is applied in each city and ultimately how much "affordable housing" can be captured in total from urban development.

In New York City, the creation of "affordable housing" through MIH has been very little in the four years since the policy's implementation. In 2020, only "38 developments have committed to the provision of 2,065 MIH units" (Kober 2020: 9). Of these 38 MIH developments, only two have been completed, while another two do not yet have planning permission. By 2021, however, more than 70 MIH developments have been counted in 28 neighborhoods across the city and 21 MIH projects had been built (Stein 2021: 19). What is interesting here is that most of these MIH sites are in areas of Manhattan, the Bronx, and Brooklyn that are either in the process of gentrification or among the most severely rent-burdened neighborhoods with one of the city's highest poverty rates. Furthermore, the affordability levels do not generally correspond to the income levels of the residing low-income community (Kober 2020: 10; Stein 2021).

According to Kober, there were only two MIH sites in 2020 that included market-rate units – both still under construction at the time. One is the Bedford-Union Armory redevelopment in Crown Heights, Brooklyn, a 15-story residential tower with 250^2 of the 400 units listed as "affordable housing" (ibid.: 11). The second site is 601 West 29th Street in West Chelsea, Manhattan, adjacent to the High Line and the $25 billion Hudson Yard development.[3] The proposal for 601 West 29th Street involved a 58-story building with 990 residential units, with 234–247 units listed to be "affordable housing." So far, these two developments seem to be the only ones that meet the condition of MIH, though the Bedford-Union Armory is a redevelopment heavily subsidized by city funding and tax credits. In addition, the Armory redevelopment is located on city-owned land, meaning it could have easily required more "affordable housing" from the developer as a condition for the 99-year lease on the Armory property than it was able to reclaim through MIH and other public subsidies (ibid.: 11). Kober highlighted in his report that the development at 601 West 29th Street in West Chelsea has so far been "the only site that meets the conditions required for the success of an unsubsidized MIH development" (ibid.: 11).

To understand and evaluate why there are so few units produced through the MIH program, I will examine the public review process of the two aforementioned redevelopment projects as well as two further redevelopment proposals in Manhattan whose application for MIH was rejected. One redevelopment is the so-called Adorama development proposal located in Chelsea, Manhattan. The other is the Sherman Plaza development proposal in Inwood, Manhattan. I chose these two examples because both were considered "test cases" for the city's new MIH program. The four cases make a good comparison because of their geographical location: while the Adorama and 601 West 29th Street redevelopments are located in one of the wealthiest areas of New York City, the Bedford-Union Armory and Sherman Plaza redevelopments are located in predominantly low-income communities of color experiencing gentrification (Table 3.1).

As mentioned above, planning obligations for inclusionary housing in London – in contrast to New York City – can be applied to every new development proposal

Table 3.1 Housing Demographics for the Studied Neighborhoods Compared to New York City Level

	New York City	Inwood	Crown Heights/ Lefferts Garden	Chelsea/Clinton	
		Sherman Plaza site	Bedford-Union Armory site	Adorama site	601 West 29th Street
Median household income	$60,010	$53,050	$51,790	$103,540	
Poverty rate	18.9%	22.2%	18.3%	12.7%	
Heritage and ethnicity	—	70.1% Hispanic/ 17.8% white	66.3% Black/ 19.8 white	60.9% White	
Homeownership rate	32.0%	9.6%	16.7%	21.9%	
Median sales price per unit, condominium ($2017)	$900,000	$295,080	$450,000	$1,465,230	
Rental vacancy rate	3.6%	1.7	3.6%	6.6%	
Median rent, all ($2017)	$1,380	$1,330	$1,320	$2,280	
Median rent, asking	$2,800	$2,050	$2,020	$3,750	
Severely rent-burdened households	29.3%	32.3%	33.1%	20.9%	
Severely rent-burdened households, low-income households	45.6%	45.5%	46.5%	44.5%	

Source: Compiled by the author from NYU Furman Center (2017).

that involves the creation of more than ten residential units. That might explain why, in purely statistical terms, the delivery of "affordable housing" through inclusionary housing agreements in London has been used more effectively than in New York City. Between 2015–16 and 2018–19, roughly 12,000 "affordable housing" units have been delivered through Section 106 agreements.[4] This accounts for about 40 percent of all the "affordable homes" delivered in the same period. During that time, about 22,000 "affordable homes" funded through S106 agreements have been given planning permission (Ministry of Housing, Communities and Local Government (MHCLG) 2019).[5] This, however, does not mean that the creation of "affordable housing" through Section 106 agreements adequately addresses the housing shortage in London. As already mentioned above, there is no guarantee that developers will fulfill their planning obligations. Many go back and re-negotiate the percentage of "affordable housing" to be provided and usually end up having to provide less than was previously agreed upon. Another concern is the small number of social housing that has been provided. Of the 12,000 "affordable units" delivered, only 6 percent have been social rent, compared to 38 percent affordable rent and 56 percent shared ownership (ibid.).

The first two cases I selected are both located in affluent neighborhoods of London. Each case represents a typical way of how developers are able to lower the amount of "affordable housing" to be provided or get out of providing any "affordable housing" at all. For example, in the luxury residential redevelopment at 56 Curzon Street in the Inner London borough City of Westminster (Osborne 2014), the developer accepted to make a £5 million cash-in-lieu payment to the Council, instead of having to provide "affordable housing" on-site. The second is the Battersea Power Station redevelopment site – one of London's biggest redevelopment projects –, located on the South Bank of the Thames, in the South West London Borough of Wandsworth. The luxury project plans were primarily criticized in the press when the developer renegotiated the Section 106 agreements, nearly halving the number of "affordable housing" in the negotiation process on the basis of the financial viability assessment of the project (i.a. Cuffe 2017; Kollewe 2017).

The other two cases I selected are neighborhoods with primarily low-income residents. Tower Hamlets, Hackney, and Newham are among the boroughs with the highest portion of people living in poverty in London (Trust for London 2014). Both development proposals – Bishopsgate Goodsyard development spanning the border between Hackney and Tower Hamlets, and the so-called Boleyn Ground development in the London Borough of Newham (Table 3.2) – have been heavily criticized by the local community for not including enough "affordable housing" and that which agreed upon being far from affordable for most low-income households.

One main difference between the cases studied is that in New York City all planning applications were negotiated under the de Blasio administration, while in London all of them were negotiated or began to be negotiated under the Johnson government. In other words, they are still part of what I call in Chapter 2 the second phase of inclusionary housing, whereas in New York City, they are part of what I call the third phase. This has to do with the fact that my main research phase in London took place in the spring of 2016 when Boris Johnson was still mayor.

Table 3.2 Housing Demographics for the Studied Boroughs Compared to Inner London Level

	Inner London	Newham	Tower Hamlets/ Hackney	Westminster	Wandsworth
		Boleyn Ground site	Bishopsgate Goodsyard site	56 Curzon Street	Battersea Power Station site
Modeled Household median income estimate 2012/2013	£40,290	£28,780	£34,930/£35,140	£47,510	£47,480
Median house price	£495,000	£485,000	£415,000/£485,000	£920,000	£557,000
Homes owned outright, (2014) %	14.6	9.4	7.0/11.1	17.1	17.7
Rented from Local Authority or Housing Association (2014) %	32.1	31.4	41.6/45.4	27.8	19.3
Housing Waiting list	227,549	17,453	19,124/11,238	4,453	3,846

Source: Compiled by the author from Greater London Authority (GLA 2016a).

Whether the decision-making of planning applications in London changed under the Khan government is, therefore, subject for further research. The argument I make in this chapter, however, presupposes little change between governments, as most decisions are made at the local level by Borough Councils.

In terms of data, I evaluate different kinds of empirical material and sources, mainly planning documents, reports, and newspaper articles. While in New York City, I am further able to draw on official video footage of the public review process, I have to rely primarily on written documents for those concerning London. In New York City, I have further been able to closely examine the so-called Adorama development proposal as well as the Sherman Plaza development proposal through participant observation in the public review process, as well as attending activist meetings and interviewing people involved. Likewise, I attended meetings in London with key activists involved in the protest against the Bishopsgate Goodsyard development plans.

Even though I do not see these case studies as representative of all cases – each case is negotiated on an individual case-by-case-basis – I have, nevertheless, observed certain recurring patterns and features during my analysis of the eight cases studied. As such, I will mostly discuss the cases in terms of their recurring characteristics rather than their particular context.

Negotiating Inclusionary Housing in Affluent Neighborhoods

In the four cases studied in London and New York City that are located in affluent neighborhoods, there was clear evidence of local governmental austerity-driven urban entrepreneurship during the planning process. In following a pro-growth agenda, local governments adhered to the priorities of higher levels of government and developers' interests rather than their own "affordable housing" targets. The four cases, thus, illustrate two distinct forms of the negotiation process: first, allowing payments in lieu and, second, being reluctant in adopting measures to place "affordable housing" requirements on developers.

The "Free Ride" – Exempting Developers from Inclusionary Housing Requirements by Allowing Payments in Lieu

The first form of the negotiation process I examine relates to how developers were able to negotiate themselves out of providing any "affordable housing" on-site and to pay instead into an "affordable housing" fund, and I show how developers have twisted arguments that have generally been used in favor of "affordable housing" provision. By comparing the 56 Curzon Street development in the City of Westminster London (Box 3.1), to the so-called Adorama redevelopment project in Chelsea, Manhattan (Box 3.2), recurrent features in the local governments' role in inclusionary housing in low-poverty neighborhoods become evident. Both neighborhoods are among the most lucrative real estate areas in their respective city, where land is expensive and scarce.

In the case of the 56 Curzon Street development in Mayfair in the City of Westminster, London, the real estate and private equity investment company Brockton Capital applied for planning permission in January 2013 to demolish and redevelop the existing eight-story building at 56 Curzon Street. The existing building contained 31 self-contained physically separate residential units

---

Box 3.1   London: 56 Curzon Street redevelopment

- Location: Mayfair
- Borough: City of Westminster
- Housing target: 30%
- Developer: Brockton Capital
- Original offer by the   25 units (no affordable
  developer: housing)
- Overall units: 31
- Affordable housing: 0
- Payment in lieu: £5m
- Planning approval: 2013

---

subdivided into 81 smaller studios and apartments. The developer wanted to convert it into an eight-story building comprising 25 luxury residential units (GLA 2013: 2). Although the floor space in the proposed building would nearly double, the total number of residential units and density would have been reduced compared to original specifications. In other words, the 25 proposed units would be very large. In addition, no "affordable housing" would be provided on-site.

Since the loss of residential housing and density would not increase the number of housing units on-site, the scheme did not comply with London Plan policy (ibid.: 5). Unwilling to decide on the application alone, and because the application was considered of potential strategic importance, the Westminster City Council notified the Mayor of London Boris Johnson about the application.

According to a GLA report, Johnson advised the developer to revise the development plans in compliance with London Plan policy as it "results in a loss of housing due to the applicant choosing to include several exceptionally large units within the development" (ibid.: 5). This is what Bob Colenutt describes as the typical "dilemma" (Colenutt 2020: 109) in the negotiation process: while city and local authorities want more density so that they can extract more planning gain via "affordable housing," developers want less density in order to build more or bigger private housing units and have less obligations to build "affordable housing" (ibid.).

The aforesaid report by the GLA further states that "affordable housing" is usually required on-site, and only in exceptional circumstances can it be provided off-site or through payment in lieu (GLA 2013: 5). Often times developers argue that they need to provide the "affordable homes" in a separate block or with a separate entrance – a "poor-door" – so future "affordable housing" residents would not have to pay the higher service charges. In this case, the developer, however, used the "poor door argument" to avoid the obligation to provide any "affordable housing" on-site (Osborne 2014). In the planning report, the developer's argumentation is stated as follows:

> The applicant has stated that onsite provision of 'affordable housing' would result in significant design inefficiencies due to the need for separate entrances and building cores and there would be deficiencies in the quality of affordable accommodation. Furthermore, it states that the provision would impact on the viability of the scheme and that the high level of service charge is unlikely to be attractive to a registered provider. The applicant states it has also explored opportunities for offsite provision but has not found a donor site.
>
> (GLA 2013: 5)

After Westminster City Council had rejected a revised proposal of 27 residential units in May 2013, it approved the revised offer of 31 residential apartments in July 2013 (Bourke 2013). According to the developer as stated in the subcommittee of Westminster City Council, "the increase to 31 units is the maximum feasible 'having regard to commercial viability'" (Westminster City Council Planning Application Subcommittee 2013: 169). It was, further, accepted by the City Council that it would not be viable for the development scheme to provide "affordable housing" on-site, instead the requirement would be an "affordable housing" payment in lieu of £6,83 million. The developer offered instead to pay an "affordable housing" contribution of about £5 million in addition to about half a million pounds for local improvements of public spaces (Westminster City Council Planning Application Subcommittee 2013: 170). This offer by the developer was ultimately accepted by the Westminster City Council. Though the Council has set an overall "affordable housing" target of 30% in the borough as part of its core strategy, it accepted the scheme without any "affordable housing" on-site. This, however, is not a unique decision, as "Westminster City Council has approved similar plans in the past" (Gower 2013).

In New York City, a developer tried to get out of MIH requirements along similar lines by arguing that the special planning approval it was seeking was not a rezoning and, thus, would not trigger MIH. In 2016, the developer Acuity Capital Partners was seeking a special permit from the City Planning Department (CPC) to build a 17-story condominium

Box 3.2 New York City: Adorama redevelopment	
• Location:	Ladies' Mile District
• Neighborhood:	Chelsea, Manhattan
• Developer:	Acuity Capital Partners
• Original offer by the developer:	66 units (no affordable housing)
• Overall units:	66 units
• Affordable housing:	0
• Payment in lieu:	Yes
• Planning approval:	2016

with 66 residential units on a parking lot between 17th and 18th Streets in the Ladies' Miles Historic District in Chelsea. The proposal incorporated the renovation and maintenance of the two adjunct smaller buildings, one of them home to the historic Adorama camera shop. Due to its proximity to the shop, the application has become known as the Adorama special permit. Since current zoning on-site only allowed up to six-story buildings, the developer wanted to transfer air rights[6] from the historic buildings to the new development in order to build the 66 residential units instead of the 40 units allowed. This would be an increase of 26 residential units. For the transfer of air rights, the developer, however, needed a special permit from the City Planning Commission. Since a significant increase in density would make the project subject to the new MIH program, this triggered an intensive debate between the developer and local governmental actors on whether this proposal would be a rezoning that involves a "significant increase in residential floor area"[7] over what would otherwise be allowed to be developed on that site. The question was, therefore, not how much value recapture could be claimed but whether it would be legal to reclaim anything at all.

In the public hearing of the CPC, which I attended, a representative of the developer insisted that it was not a rezoning and, thus, the application was not subject to MIH. The representative went on to argue the following: "We are not increasing the residential floor area, we are only increasing what we are entitled to."[8] In contrast, members of the respective Community Board 5 (CB5) and the Manhattan Borough President Gale Brewer, who have advisory powers, together with housing advocates and community groups argued that 26 units would be a significant increase in residential floor area and urged the Commission to reject the proposal unless MIH would be applied. The CPC, however, approved the special permit with seven votes and three absentees – the minimum that was required. In an interview with the New York Times, the chairman of the CPC, Carl Weisbrod, defended the commission's position by stating that:

[w]e were 100 percent clear when we did M.I.H.[9] that it applied when you created new residential capacity, and not simply when you applied to move

your existing capacity around. [.] We have, as I think is universally recognized, the most far-reaching mandates around, and to do that, we pushed the program to the limits of what is legally defensible. We do not want to push it to the point where it could be easily legally challenged.

(Chaban 2016)

By the time the project had passed the CPC and was to be reviewed by the City Council, the press had already criticized the developer for not being willing to create the much-needed "affordable housing" in New York City (Kaufmann 2016) and the City Council for potentially "opposing 'affordable housing'" (Chaban 2016). In the public hearing of the Subcommittee on Zoning and Franchise of the City Council, a representative of Acuity Capital Partners announced that the developer had offered to make a payment in lieu into a separate fund where it would dedicate a portion of its profits to "affordable housing" elsewhere in the neighborhood. I include here an extract from the subcommittee hearing about a discussion between the developer's special counsel Valerie Campbell and Council Member Corey Johnson who represents Council District 3, which includes the neighborhood of Chelsea where the Adorama project is located:

COUNCIL MEMBER JOHNSON:	So, if MIH does not apply here but if the borough president and the community board and state senator Krueger and others believe that even though we are not setting precedent because city planning has already deemed that it does not apply, so it's out of scope for me to try to apply MIH? […]
VALERIE CAMPBELL:	That is basically, you know, what we have proposed.
COUNCIL MEMBER JOHNSON:	And that ends up being four and a half thousand… 5,000?
VALERIE CAMPBELL:	5,000 square feet.
COUNCIL MEMBER JOHNSON:	5,000, five and half thousand square feet. So, five and a half thousand square feet end up being how many units are you approximating?
VALERIE CAMPBELL:	Five or 6,000, I… yeah 5.5.
COUNCIL MEMBER JOHNSON:	Five and a half units. And so, if we were looking again at MIH even though it didn't apply here by city planning's definition, we would then say that for buildings that were under a certain number you don't have to build on-site. HPD and city planning are in the process of promulgating rules related to an 'affordable housing' fund for the community board where the money would stay in that particular community district. And so, in that instance

we would come up with a calculation on what five and half units, or five units, or six units, whatever we rounded up or rounded down to, whatever that number ends up being and that potentially would be a reasonable way to still have the applicant in the spirit of trying to help towards 'affordable housing' in a local neighborhood and not build on-site because they would have been exempt under MIH anyway. That would be a potential way to participate and to give. Is that all accurate?

VALERIE CAMPBELL: Yes, that is accurate.

COUNCIL MEMBER JOHNSON: And is that what the applicant is stating they're willing to do today?

VALERIE CAMPBELL: I think Elliot, you know, set forth what his proposal is right now. Obviously, we do not have the HPD regulations. We don't know what their calculus would be. We proposed a calculus which is based on 25 percent of the profits attributable to that…

COUNCIL MEMBER JOHNSON: And you're willing to do that because the council has some power here in deciding this special permit?

VALERIE CAMPBELL: We are willing to do that because we understand that this is an important issue for the council, the community board and this is something that the developer is willing to do.

(New York City Council Subcommittee on Zoning and Franchises 2016a: 60ff[10])

As I sat through the public hearing at the CPC that day, and as I listened to the number of residential units to be built, the residential floor area to be increased, and the proposed limits on the building size not once did I hear the issue of the value to be reclaimed for social benefit come up. As the hearing extract shows, the discussion about 5,500 square feet translated into about 5.5 "affordable housing" units to be created – a very small number of units that – as Council Member Johnson pointed out – would not have to be built on-site anyway.

Similar to the redevelopment of 56 Curzon Street in London, the developer offered to make a voluntary payment in lieu. In this way, the developer would not have to build these few "affordable units" elsewhere. In contrast to the development project at 56 Curzon Street in London, the amount of payment in lieu was, however, never mentioned in the public hearings. As an "affordable housing" fund had not yet been established by the city, the City Council could only base its planning decision on the assumption that the developer would stand by its word. As far as I have been able to determine, no commitment was put in writing between the developer and the City Council. Ultimately, despite concerns expressed by civil society and local governmental actors, the City Council ended up approving the condominium project in Chelsea in September of 2016 without any MIH requirements in place.

What has become evident in both cases is that developers used the payment in lieu as a way to get out of inclusionary housing requirements. While in the case of 56 Curzon Street, the developer was in a position to drop the amount required for an "affordable housing" payment triggered by this scheme by almost two million pounds, it was enough for the developer in the Adorama case to just express the willingness of commitment rather than having to guarantee the payment of a certain amount in order to get planning permission. This can also be attributed to the vague formulation of the MIH regulation, which offers developers loopholes to get out of "affordable housing" obligations or, as in the Adorama case, to offer a vague commitment to a payment in lieu. It further shows how local authorities in both cases were trying to be flexible in the negotiation process to enable the development to go ahead in favor of the developer. Thereby, they were willing to reduce the planning contributions to a minimal contribution in the form of a payment in lieu rather than obliging the developer to contribute to the much-needed "affordable housing" on-site.

Local Authorities' Reluctance in Adopting Measures to Increase "Affordable Housing" Provisions On-Site

By again relating two development projects from each city, I show how developers negotiated the inclusionary housing requirements down, while local authorities showed little interest in adopting appropriate measures to increase "affordable housing" provisions from development schemes. This reluctance of local governments to hold developers accountable for providing "affordable housing" is what I call the second way local governments negotiate in favor of urban growth and developer interests.

One of the prime MIH examples is the development project of 601 West 29th Street in West Chelsea. It was mentioned in the Manhattan Institute's report as the only MIH development that had actually met the conditions of MIH at the time (Kober 2020: 11). The major rezoning of 2005 in both West Chelsea and the Hudson Yards during the Bloomberg administration was also one of the first that included the so-called *"Designated Areas" Inclusionary Housing*

Box 3.3   New York City: 601 West 29th Street and 606 West 30th Street redevelopments

- Location: 601 West 29th Street/606 West 30th Street
- Neighborhood: West Chelsea, Manhattan
- Developer: Douglaston Development/ Lalezarian
- Original offer by the developer: 1200 units (25% affordable housing)
- Overall units: 1200 units
- Affordable housing: 25% MIH (option 1)
- Planning approval: 2018

Program (IHP).[11] According to a report by the Office of Council Member Brad Lander that reviewed the effectiveness of NYC's inclusionary zoning program from its inception in 2005–13, the developers' participation in the program proved to be "extremely strong" (Ullman, Freedman-Schnapp, and Lander 2013: 4) in producing "affordable housing" units on Manhattan's West side. In the Hudson Yards and West Chelsea rezoning areas, 1,441 IHP units have been generated out of 7,752 total units, which make up 18.6% of the total developments (ibid.: 12). The rezoning has not only spurred an unprecedented real estate boom in the area but also sparked a process of hypergentrification (Navarro 2015). Since then, the continuously rising rents rank among the highest in the city (NYU Furman Center 2016: 117).[12] The median sales price per unit in a condominium, for example, was about one and a half million dollars. The median household income of the population was about $104,000 in 2016. At the same time, the neighborhood ranks among those in the city with the greatest income inequality. About 20 percent of the people living in the district at the time were severely rent-burden. Among low-income households that percentage increased to 44 percent (NYC Furman Center 2017: 75).

In 2018, the two developers[13] jointly requested from the Department of City Planning the approval of a rezoning of the development sites from light industrial to commercial and residential use as well as the transfer of air rights from the Chelsea Piers along the Hudson River Park to construct two mixed-use skyscrapers comprising roughly 1,200 residential units, of which about 300 would be "affordable housing." As in the Adorama case, the debate here circled around fulfilling the minimum MIH requirements. In the West Chelsea development projects, both developers chose from the beginning option one of the MIH program, setting aside 25 percent of housing for households with incomes averaging 60% AMI. The willingness of the developers in the West Chelsea cases to provide "affordable housing" on-site was from the beginning very much connected to their request of a special permit from the CPC to shift the very lucrative but unused air rights from the Chelsea piers at Hudson River Park to their development sites. In doing so, the developers would be allowed to increase the maximum floor area of the building to the maximum of 12 Floor Area Ratio (FAR), which would not have been possible without the special permit. Thus, the change of the zoning map from light industrial to commercial and residential use and the transfer of air rights to permit high-density residential development created such substantial economic value that the MIH requirements did not seem to be much of an issue to the developer. Instead, a rather critical issue for planning permission was the amount of money the community would receive for the transfer of the development rights. A member of the respective Community Board 4 (CB4) – which voted to deny the project unless certain conditions such as a maximum height of the building were met – pointed out the importance of reclaiming value from the project for community benefit:

> [T]he price of the transfer rights is critically important for those of us in West Chelsea because it offsets the rapid and tremendous growth with the protection of our community, our neighborhood and our special resources.
>
> (New York City Council Subcommittee
> on Zoning and Franchises 2018: 116)

In accordance with the CB4 and the Hudson River Park Trust, a public corporation owned in partnership by New York State and the City, it was determined that the money from the transfer of air rights would be used for renovation and maintenance of the Hudson River Park as well as other future park improvements within the area. Prior to the Uniform Land Use Review Procedure (ULURP) process, the Hudson River Park Trust commissioned an independent appraiser who determined that the value of development rights for transfer to the two sites would be in total 48 million dollars. But while the Hudson River Park Trust accepted this amount as compensation for the air rights, CB4 and other community members questioned whether this amount was adequate compensation for the Trust. A critical point during the ULURP process was, thus, the question of how the value of the air rights was assessed. The said member of the community board doubted the determined value of the air rights and urged the City Council to review the assessment:

The transfer of development rights from Hudson River Park Trust to Douglaston and Lalezarian is a very large number that will do a lot of great things along the river but please don't be misled by the total number in and of itself but instead look at how it was calculated, I think we're getting shortchanged, and we should be receiving more for these rights based on looking at square foot costs in our neighborhood.

There are a number of examples you can use where development rights have been transferred. In private transactions between landlords and developers we're seeing prices in the ranges of 800 to 1,000 dollars per square foot. Recently the City Planning Commission recommended setting the price for the transfer rights of West Chelsea at 635 dollars to provide resources for the housing fund. The trust itself sold development rights to St. John's Terminal in West Village for 500 dollars yet in this case Hudson River Park Trust and the two development teams arrived at a price that is surprisingly below what would be expected at only 300 dollars per square foot.

(New York City Council Subcommittee
on Zoning and Franchises 2018: 117)

The CPC and City Council, however, ended up approving the development proposal, justifying its decision on the grounds that "the receiving site […] would appropriately assume transferred floor area in a quantity and a set of uses to significantly support the much-needed improvements and capital maintenance in the Park" (CPC 2018: 32). It further noted that "[t]he project would also bring a substantial amount of 'affordable housing' to the area, which will contribute to the diversity of the residential stock in Manhattan Community District 4" (ibid.: 37) and "will support the objectives of the Inclusionary Housing Program" (ibid.: 40). The approved zoning change, however, was a huge gift to the developers. They were now allowed to create a 58-story and a 37-story building in one of the most lucrative real estate locations in New York City that would have not been possible without the changing of the zoning map. While the rezoning and the acquisition of the development rights of the Hudson River Park created substantial value, the provision of the minimal amount of 300 "affordable housing" units and the donation of 48 million dollars to the Park Trust seem in this context like a great deal in favor of the developers.[14]

Even though it seemed obvious that the development projects stood to gain enormous economic value from the rezoning allowing a high-density residential development, the City Council was reluctant to ask the developer to provide more "affordable housing" than was officially required or for deeper affordability options. According to an NYU Furman Center report, "in neighborhoods with high rents, mandatory inclusionary zoning with an increase in density can encourage the development of more 'affordable housing'" (NYU Furman Center 2015: 4) It is assumed that the density added through the rezoning creates enough value to cross-subsidize "affordable housing" units without additional public subsidies. Thus, given the high market rents and turnover expected in this West Chelsea location, it is reasonable to assume that "the projects would allow them to do better economically" (New York City Council Subcommittee on Zoning and Franchises 2018: 120), as argued by a representative of the respective Community Board on the City Council's Subcommittee on Zoning and Franchises in reference to the agreed-upon minimum amount of affordable housing.

In short, the development projects could be seen as a success for the new MIH program and as an anti-displacement measure by placing about 300 "affordable housing" units in a neighborhood that has extremely low opportunities for low-income households to move to. At the same time, these developments are placed within an area that already experienced an unprecedented real estate boom and will, thus, contribute to fueling the upward spiral of real estate capital, and the few "affordable housing" units are only a drop in the ocean otherwise known as the housing affordability crisis.

Located near the Thames in the South West borough of Wandsworth, the Battersea Power Station redevelopment is one of London's biggest redevelopment projects to date (Kollewe 2015). It is the centerpiece of the vast Nine Elms "Opportunity Area" created in 2012 to redevelop the last remaining industrial stretch of river in central London into a new

---

Box 3.4   London: Battersea Power Station redevelopment

- Location: Nine Elms
- Borough: Wandsworth
- Housing target: Wandsworth: 33%, Nine Elms: 15%
- Developer: Battersea Project Land Company Ltd
- Original offer by the developer: 3,444 units (15% affordable housing)
- Overall units: 3,444
- Affordable housing: 9%
- Planning approval: 2015 (renegotiation 2017)

---

mix-use neighborhood. According to the journalist Steavenson (2017), the redevelopment involves "£15bn of investment, 25 different sites to be built over 25 years, 16 developers, 16,000 new homes, 25,000 new jobs and over half a million square meters of mixed use development" (Steavenson 2017). Due to the overall missing infrastructure in the area, the "affordable housing" requirements in Nine Elms are only a minimum of 15 percent, compared to the at least 33 percent "affordable housing" target in the rest of the borough (Wandsworth Council 2018: 16).

The original planning permission granted in 2011 entailed 3,444 residential units of which 517 were "affordable housing," equating to 15 percent "affordable housing." A new planning permission granted in 2015 increased the overall number of housing to 4,239 and accordingly also increased the "affordable housing" number to 636 units, equaling still no more than 15 percent. In 2017, however, citing technical and financial problems, the developer was able to renegotiate the terms of "affordable housing," dropping the number of "affordable housing" from 636 to 386 units. This was a 40 percent reduction from the prior plans. In return, the developer promised to deliver the proportion of the now 9 percent affordable homes three years earlier than anticipated. The developer further stated that the other 250 affordable units, which would equate to the 636 affordable units, will "be subject to an end of scheme review to determine whether they would be financially viable" (Wandsworth Council 2017).[15]

European commercial property consultancy company BNP Paribas (BNPP) was commissioned by Wandsworth Council to review the applicant's viability assessment and later confirmed the development proposal by stating that a "provision of 'affordable housing' at a reduced level of 9% would still represent the maximum reasonable level" (ibid.). With respect to the later construction of the remaining 250 units, BNPP, however, acknowledged that "it is very unlikely that these units will be delivered" (ibid.). In other words, there was no guarantee that the remaining 250 units proposed would be delivered after an end of scheme review. BNPP further advised the Council that "in return for putting these units at risk, the Council could potentially benefit from additional affordable housing […] (in the form of on-site units […] and a payment in lieu)" (ibid.). In case of delivery, the "affordable housing" provision would then equate to the overall housing target set at a minimum of 33 percent by Wandsworth Council. BNPP stated that the decrease in "affordable housing" was nevertheless consistent with the Council's other priorities, such as ensuring the extension of the Northern Line, the job creation through the development as well as securing the maximum number possible of "affordable housing" (ibid.). BNPP is only one of several property consultancy companies advising local councils in London as well as developers on the negotiation of S106 agreements. In the literature, it has been argued that viability assessments through private consultancy companies usually lead to a drop in "affordable housing" requirements (Layard 2019; Minton 2017: 35).

As a result of BNPP's viability assessment of the reduced "affordable housing" proposal, Wandsworth Council approved the variations to the S106 agreement without any conditions. The Council was able to make this decision without public consultation since the developer only asked for a variation of the S106 agreement and not for new planning permission. However, the drop in "affordable housing" was widely criticized in the press (i.a. Cuffe 2017; Kollewe 2017) as it clearly illustrates how the local authority was compelled to relax the minimal "affordable housing" in exchange for more housing completion.

The cases studied in this subsection clearly illustrate some of the difficulties local authorities face when dealing with powerful developers and consultants. In all cases except West Chelsea, the local authorities ended up relaxing their "affordable housing" requirements in exchange for the development to be able to proceed and, thus, privileging of economic growth over their commitment in tackling the affordable housing shortage.

Negotiating Inclusionary Housing in Low-Income Neighborhoods

In contrast to the cases studied in affluent neighborhoods in both cities, local authorities have generally been able to increase the "affordable housing" provision during the planning process in low-income neighborhoods. In all four cases that follow, I identified three interrelated and mutually dependent aspects that have been crucial in the planning process and implementation of inclusionary housing in low-income neighborhoods. The first aspect relates to the level of government. In all cases studied, planning applications and activities have been differently supported as well as contested at various scales of government. While developers have in all cases tried to keep "affordable housing" obligations to a minimum, local governments have generally been more engaged in increasing the number of "affordable housing" in low-income neighborhoods than in affluent ones due to greater pressure from the local communities in low-income areas affected by redevelopment. While city governments or agencies have generally been more accommodating to developers to ensure that the development schemes were able to go ahead, local authorities have generally been less pliant and have shown greater support for "affordable housing."

The second aspect relates to the concept of affordability. In all four cases, the proposed developments would bring an influx of affluent people to neighborhoods where gentrification was already unfolding, thereby exacerbating the process of gentrification rather than counteracting it.

The third and very crucial aspect in the planning processes in low-income neighborhoods is community organization and pressure. In all four cases studied so far, community groups in low-income neighborhoods pushed for higher proportions of "affordable housing" units as well as for deeper affordability levels, whereas in affluent neighborhoods, community pressure played little or no role – this should come as no surprise since the interests of market-rate residents tend to align with those of developers when it comes to "affordable housing."

Local Authorities' Engagement in Developers' Planning Applications

There is clear evidence in the cases studied so far that the decisions taken by local authorities during the planning process were aimed at putting pressure on the developer to increase the provision of "affordable housing."

In the two cases in New York City, two council members of districts at the center of controversial developments were under enormous pressure from local community residents and groups to either push for more units and deeper affordability or reject the project altogether. Although, the developers of the Sherman Plaza redevelopment project in Inwood, Manhattan and the Bedford-Union Armory redevelopment in Crown Heights, Brooklyn chose from the beginning to comply with the MIH requirements – choosing option two of the MIH rules – the local community vehemently opposed the development plans.

The plans for the redevelopment of the vacant Bedford-Union Armory – operated and maintained by the New York National Guard from early 1900 until 2011 – into a recreation center, nonprofit offices, and housing had initially called for 330 rentals. About half of them were initially planned to be "affordable housing" and a total of 60 units were intended to be condominiums, of which 20 percent would be "af-

---

Box 3.5   New York City: Bedford Union Armory redevelopment

- Location: 1555 Bedford Avenue
- Neighborhood: Crown Heights, Brooklyn
- Developer: BFC Partners
- Original offer by the 330 rentals (50% affordable
  developer: housing), 60 condos
                                       (20% affordable housing)
- Overall units: 414 rental units
- Affordable housing: 60% (250 units, 109 units
                                       MIH (permanently
                                       affordable), 141units
                                       (only affordable for a
                                       certain period of time,
                                       and 10% for homeless
                                       people))
- Planning approval: 2017

---

fordable" (Warerkar 2017a). The redevelopment, however, faced fierce criticism from both local residents and local governmental actors, who argued that since the development is on land owned by the city it should be 100 percent "affordable housing." As the development made its way through the ULURP, the CPC voted in favor of the development plans, in spite of the Community Board (CB) and the then Borough President Eric Adams recommending disapproving the application. Further into the process, the local Council Member Laurie Cumbo also came out against the development plans. In approving applications, the City Council usually defers to the vote of the local council member.

However, a last-minute deal was worked out between the developer and the city: the city promised to put in $50 million to subsidize the additional "affordable housing" (Holliday Smith 2017) to enable the development proposal to go ahead, while the developer dismissed the initially proposed luxury condos altogether and instead offered 414 rental units, of which 250 units would be "affordable housing" below or at 60 percent of the AMI. Despite major protests and criticism from local community groups and residents, Council Member Cumbo ended up supporting the development. In the City Council's subcommittee public hearing in November 2017, Laurie Cumbo announced her decision and expressed her pride about the achieved "affordable housing" numbers:

> Today, I am proud that we have revised the Bedford Union Armory project that now lives up to the values of the community, and what I have fought so hard to achieve. [...] I'm proud to say that the original project included 67 units at or below 60% AMI. Only 67 units. Today, as a result of my negotiations with the Administration, pressure from the community, and local elected officials, the luxury condominiums not only have been eliminated, but we now have

60% of the units that represents 250 units will be affordable at the 60% AMI level or below. […] We stood up for real affordability and we won.

(Cumbo cited in New York City Council
Committee on Land Use 2017: 9)

Most local community groups and residents, however, strongly opposed plans to build market-rate housing on land owned by the city. From the balcony of the City Council Chamber reserved for the public, many voiced their anger and disapproval by shouting, "The city is not for sale! Kill the deal!" (Holliday Smith 2017).

The Sherman Plaza redevelopment is located at 4560 Broadway on the border between Washington Heights and Inwood. In March 2016, the developers sought planning permission for a rezoning that would turn the existing parking garage into a 23-story residential building in which 30 percent of the residential floor area would be set aside for "affordable housing" (option two of the MIH

Box 3.6   New York City: Sherman Plaza redevelopment

- Location: 4560 Broadway
- Neighborhood: Inwood, Manhattan
- Developer: Acadia Reality Trust
- Original offer by the   356 units (30% affordable
  developer: housing)
- Overall units: 356
- Affordable housing: 50 % (177 units), of which
                             30% MIH (with Deep
                             Affordability Option),
                             and 20% additional
                             affordable housing
- Planning approval: rejected

---

program). Facing criticism from the local community, the developer proposed a revised scheme that included the commitment to the Deep Affordability Option of the MIH requirements (see Table 1.3 in Chapter 1). The local Community Board as well as the Manhattan Borough President recommended approval of the proposed development scheme. In June 2016, the CPC followed suit and passed the developer's proposal. As the scheme continued its way through the ULURP, opposition against the proposed development did not abate. In addition to voicing their disapproval at the various public hearings, local groups held several rallies, petitions, and meetings with local Council Member Ydanis Rodriguez. Under this constant pressure, the developer ultimately committed to an additional 20 percent affordable housing, which represented 50 percent of the 356 total housing units – the goal Council Member Rodriguez hoped to achieve.

However, in the public hearing of the Subcommittee on Zoning and Franchise that I attended, it became public that the developer's commitment of the additional 20 percent "affordable housing" depended on additional subsidies. The following extract from the public hearing presents the developer's vague commitment to the additional "affordable housing" units that was subsequently criticized by the local community:

COUNCIL MEMBER GENTILE: Thank you. Thank you, Mr. Chairman. I'm just
                             curious about the extra 'affordable housing'.
PAUL TRAVIS: Right.

COUNCIL MEMBER GENTILE:	What guarantees are there that you will actually produce the extra 'affordable housing'?
PAUL TRAVIS:	That's an excellent question. We can and will commit to it. There will be a regulatory agreement with either HPD or the housing development corporation, which will lay out all the income levels and the number of units. So that will ultimately provide the guarantee of affordability.
COUNCIL MEMBER GENTILE:	So, there will be some kind of an agreement you're saying with HPD?
PAUL TRAVIS:	Correct, either HPD or the housing development corporation, depending on the program.
COUNCIL MEMBER GENTILE:	So, is the additional 'affordable housing' dependent on a subsidy that you receive from HPD or some other city agency?
PAUL TRAVIS:	Correct.

[…]

COUNCIL MEMBER GENTILE:	Right, so, you're proposing on the condition that there's a subsidy for…
PAUL TRAVIS:	Correct. […] Until a year ago, I guess you would have looked at a project like this and you would have said well obviously you're going to apply for a 421A. 421A currently does not exist. We hope it will again at some point. So, there's just always things that we don't control that have impact on us. But we are committed to finding a mechanism to providing 50 percent affordability.

(New York City Council Subcommittee on Zoning and Franchises 2016b: 42ff[16])

After this question round between the developer and one of the committee members, there was a murmur in the public audience. It became obvious during the review process that the developer did not have a concrete plan of how to provide the additional 20 percent of affordable units. And since the Deep Affordability Option of MIH only allows the additional use of subsidies if more than the required "affordable housing" percentage would be provided, it became clear to everybody in the room that day that there was no guarantee that the developer would later add other options like the Deep Affordability Option of MIH or provide the 20 percent "affordable housing" – as they promised to do (Fieldnote 2016/06/12). Since the developer chose option two of the MIH program, the only "affordable housing" required would be 30 percent for residents with incomes averaging 80 percent AMI ($62,150 per year for a family of three). Elisabeth Lorris Ritter who testified on behalf of the local Community Board and originally registered to testify in favor of the project was outraged about this new information:

> [O]n the basis of the developer's testimony this morning my reservations may actually rise to the point of opposition. [...] I am shocked to hear that the blend of 'affordable housing' that I understood to be 20 percent at 40 percent AMI and 30 percent at a blended average of 80 percent AMI, which is what you presented at the city planning commission, is going to be 30 percent at a blended rate of about 103 percent AMI. You also said that the project wasn't dependent on any public subsidies but on further questioning from Council Member Gentile, thank you very much for bringing that to light, you allowed that the 20 percent additional 'affordable housing' is contingent on subsidies.
>
> (Ritter cited in New York City Council Subcommittee on Zoning and Franchises 2016b: 85)

The approval of the development plans would, thus, allow the developer to build 70 percent of the units as market-rate apartments, which would be unaffordable for most of Inwood's low-income residents. The affected local community continued to protest against the development plans, putting enormous pressure on local Council Member Rodriguez who ended up withdrawing his support for the proposal – the very next day, the City Council rejected the development project. In the final City Council meeting on August 16, 2016, Ydanis Rodriguez justified his rejection to the other Council members as follows:

> I listen to my community's loud and clear voices for and against it. We had many meetings with developers and administration, and at the end of this process we decided that we didn't have everything in place to support the Broadway and Sherman rezoning.
>
> (Rodriguez cited in New York City Council 2016: 48)

What becomes evident here is that as long as development projects reflected the mayor's housing plan, city government officials and agencies have generally defended them. For example, the CPC approved all of the developed projects studied in New York City, despite major criticism from local governmental bodies. The Mayor of New York City may have the power to veto the City Council's decision, but ultimately the council can override the mayoral vote by a two-thirds majority. And as local council members usually get the last word over what happens in their district, the council as well as the mayor are rather reluctant to override their decisions. The rejection of the Sherman Plaza development plans by the City Council was, however, publicly criticized by the Mayor, framing it as a lost opportunity to build much-needed affordable housing. In the famous weekly #AskTheMayor series of the Brian Lehrer Show on New York Public Radio, de Blasio commented on the City Council's rejection of the development plans as follows:

> This is a very local situation, but I have to say I'm disappointed. I have great respect for Council Member Rodriguez, we work very closely together. But

here's the bottom line: Now this community has lost the chance to have a building that would have been 50 percent 'affordable housing', which is an extraordinary win for the community.

(de Blasio cited in Lehrer 2016)

What is obvious here is that de Blasio favored the plan primarily "because it reflects the mayor's housing policy in general: to foster mixed-income projects in which developers include affordable units and other community benefits in exchange for being allowed to build more apartments than they could without the government's say so" (de Blasio cited in Lehrer 2016). As such, de Blasio considered "affordable housing" of any kind as a "win for the community" (ibid.).

The same is true for the Bedford-Union Armory development in Crown Heights, New York City. The mayor endorsed the project, hoping that the residents and local governmental representatives would "get behind the project" (Warerkar 2017b). But in the case of the Bedford-Union Armory development, the de Blasio administration was actually misapplying the MIH strategy to city-owned land as the city would have been able to dictate the terms for "affordable housing" development beyond MIH requirements. In a rapidly gentrifying low-income neighborhood, where speculators drive up land prices and public land is scarce, the city could have taken the opportunity to transform an underused parcel of land into much-needed affordable housing. Building on city-owned land saves, after all, the considerable costs involved in buying overpriced land (Shaw 2018: 214).

As with the Sherman Plaza redevelopment in New York City, local communities' opposition to two proposed developments with very few "affordable housing" units prompted local authorities in London to take various measures to increase the "affordable housing" provision.

The first case is the redevelopment of the former football stadium Boleyn Ground in the London borough of Newham. The developer Galliard Homes had originally stated in 2015 that it was not really viable to deliver "affordable housing" on-site. However, under pressure from the local council, the

---

Box 3.7 London: Boleyn Ground redevelopment

- Location: Upton Park
- Borough: Newham
- Housing target: 35–50% (with 60% social rent)

- Developer: Galliard Homes
- Original offer by   838 units (6%
  the developer: "affordable housing")
- Overall units: 838
- Affordable housing: 25% social rent/ affordable rent: 25% intermediate housing: 25%
- Planning approval: 2016

---

developer was willing to commit to 6 percent (51 units) "affordable housing" on-site of the overall 838 residential units in planning. The 6 percent offered were planned as shared ownership units (GLA 2016b: 2). To verify the developer's financial viability assessment, the Council then appointed a private consultant company. Among other things, the consultant concluded that the "sales values had been

underestimated by a considerable degree" and that the "build costs were overesti-
mated (by some 35%)" (ibid.: 3). The consultant further advised the Council that 20
percent profit "was unreasonable considering that that level of profit was set at the
height of the credit crunch, and a more appropriate profit level would be 10-15%"
(ibid.: 3). In effect, this practice by Galliard Homes to overestimate the construction costs and to include a profit as high as 20 percent into their viability calcula-
tions can be seen as another tactic of how developers across the country have tried
to keep their "affordable housing" obligations to a minimum (Colenut 2020: 107).

In response, Galliard Homes submitted a revised scheme, offering 22 percent
"affordable housing." This was then further revised, and in March 2016 Newham
Council approved the scheme with 25 percent "affordable housing" of which 60 percent was intermediate housing and 40 percent "affordable housing." Though the
borough was in high need of "affordable housing," the revised scheme included no
social rent. As such, Newham Council reneged on its own Newham Core Planning
Strategy, which states that large developments should have 35–50 percent "affordable
housing" of which at least 60 percent should have social rent (Newham Council
2017: 4). Newham Council justified its planning decision by arguing that it would
invest £18 million to provide the public subsidy necessary to deliver the additional
10 percent "affordable housing" to reach the borough's minimal target (GLA
2016b: 4). But as Paul Watt accurately states, "pouring public money into the scheme
to boost the 'affordable housing' numbers goes against the spirit of planning obligations, which are obligations *on the part of the developer to the local authority"* (Watt
2018: 127). Perhaps most striking of all is that in spite of governing one of the most
economically deprived boroughs in London, Newham Council chose to invest large
amounts of taxpayer money to increase its "affordable housing" numbers just so that
the development could
proceed.

Similarly, the de-
velopers of the Bish-
opsgate   Goodsyard
development   initially
offered in 2014 to pro-
vide 10 percent "afford-
able housing" of the
approximately   1,350
homes to be created on
the approximately 4.2
hectares of former rail-
way land in the heart
of Shoreditch, which
spans the two boroughs
of Hackney and Tower
Hamlets. This small
amount   of   "afford-
able housing" had been

**Box 3.8   London: Bishopsgate
Goodsyard redevelopment**

- Location: Shoreditch
- Boroughs: Tower Hamlets/Hackney
- Housing target: Tower Hamlets: 35–50%
                              (with 70% social rent)
                              Hackney: 50% (with
                              60% social rent)
- Developer: Joint Venture between
                              Hammerson and
                              Ballymore
- Original offer: 1,356 units (10%
                              "affordable housing")
- Overall units: 500
- Affordable housing: 50% social rent/affordable
                              rent: 25% intermediate
                              housing: 25%
- Planning approval: 2020

justified with the developer's viability assessment, which remained confidential to even the councilors of Tower Hamlets and Hackney deciding on the matter.

The scheme faced immense criticism and numerous protests from local groups appalled by the size of the project as well as its lack of "affordable housing." In 2015, Hackney's Mayor Jules Pipe, who had no decision-making power over the proposed development scheme, weighed in on the controversy by resorting to unusual means: he launched his own petition on change.org against the scheme, calling on his own council to reject the planning application as well as on the mayor of London to withdraw his support for the scheme. He argued that the development plans are "based primarily on cashing in on luxury flats way beyond the means of most Hackney or Tower Hamlets residents" and that they "are wholly inappropriate for this part of Shoreditch and do nothing to address London's housing crisis" (Pipe 2015). The petition attracted more than 11,000 signatures. Tower Hamlets and Hackney Councils' planning committees then rejected the development plans in December of 2015 on the grounds of the severe impact on the area's character, the loss of light to the surroundings as well as the lack of "affordable housing" and business space, among other issues.

After the councils' planning committees had voted for the refusal of the development scheme, the Mayor of London Boris Johnson removed the right of the councils to decide on the £800 million scheme, as requested by the developers. In contrast to New York City, the mayor in London has the right to overrule local planning committees if they regard a rejected development as of potential strategic importance to London. In such cases, the mayor then becomes the local planning authority for the application. During his time in office from 2008 to 2016, Boris Johnson has taken over 19 planning applications, of which 17 were granted planning permission.[17] In the case of the Bishopsgate Goodsyard redevelopment, the public hearing was scheduled on April 18 in 2016, about two weeks before the mayoral election. In the end, the hearing was postponed after Johnson's own planning officers advised him to reject the application, leaving the decision to his successor Sadiq Khan.

In 2020, a revised scheme in which the total number of new homes was reduced from 1,356 to 500 units but with 50 percent "affordable housing" units on-site was passed by the GLA. However, the overall reduction in homes meant that the approved 50 percent affordable homes, which equate to 250 units, are less than the initial 10 percent "affordable housing," which would have been about 350 "affordable housing" units. This does not mean that the revised scheme is worse than the initially proposed plans, as the developers also reduced the height in the scheme, offered more "affordable" workspace for local businesses, and included new community and cultural spaces as well as a new public park. While Hackney Council's planning committee supported the revised development scheme, Tower Hamlet's councilors continued to oppose the application, calling for more affordable and family sized homes (Wright 2020). Furthermore, of the 50 percent approved "affordable housing" units only 18 percent were to be social rent, which the campaign Reclaim the Goodsyard organized by Weavers Community Action Group called "woefully inadequate" (GLA 2020: 52) in the public consultation process. Even though the approved scheme now represented the councils' overall "affordable housing" targets of 50 percent, it failed to reach the social rent target of 70 percent in Tower Hamlets and 60 percent in Hackney.

What has become evident in all four cases in London and New York City is that local authorities have taken measures to increase the "affordable housing" provisions on-site. These measures have included using the power to reject or to advise to reject, questioning viability assessments, and reminding developers of higher policy requirements as well as, more unusually, petitioning as was seen in one case in London.

What has further become evident in all four cases is that although city and local governments have generally increased the overall affordable housing targets within the respected development proposals, they could have done a lot more to achieve a greater number of affordable housing units. In other words, apart from the development scheme in Inwood, primarily city but also local governments have taken decisions to ensure that the development schemes were able to proceed. The prime example for this has been the Bishopsgate Goodsyard development scheme in London where Boris Johnson "called in" the application after the two boroughs in question signaled their objection to the schemes. But also, in the case of Newham, the Borough Council was even willing to invest £18 million to boost the "affordable housing" provision. In the case of the Bedford Union Armory redevelopment, the local council member ended up supporting the application, despite the local community board and the Brooklyn Borough President voting against it.

That both city and local governments are willing to prioritize the number of affordable homes provided over whether they are actually affordable to the local community is evidence of the market-oriented nature of their housing policies.

The Unaffordability of "Affordable Housing"

As described in the Introduction, "affordable housing" in both cities has commonly been regarded as a benefit to the community and it is a planning ideal for inclusionary housing. The question of how much value can be recaptured from market-rate development, however, is very much connected to the question of how much impact the development will have on the residing community. It is, thus, not only a question of how much "affordable housing" can be recaptured but also a question of whether residents can afford the newly created "affordable housing" and how the development might trigger a wave of new-build gentrification and displacement.

While authorities in all four cases pushed for a higher proportion of "affordable housing," they were less interested in the affordability of these units for the residing community. The question of how much value can be recaptured is, thus, inevitably connected to the type of "affordable housing" provided on-site.

In London, both applications proved to be controversial, primarily because they were both below the local councils' core targets of between 35 and 50 percent "affordable housing" of which at least 60 percent should have been social rent.[18] While in the Boleyn Ground case in Newham no social rent was provided, the developer of the Bishopsgate Goodsyard development scheme only offered 18 percent of the 50 percent "affordable housing" proposed. In the two cases studied, the larger portion of "affordable housing" accounted for shared ownership homes, which is determined by the London Plan for households with an annual median income of up to £80,000. However, this is way above the estimated median household income set by the GLA, which is between £29,000 in Newham and £35,000 in Tower Hamlets and Hackney (GLA 2016a). Social rent by contrast is usually determined through the national guideline board, while what is deemed "affordable rent" is set at the local level and requires a rent of no more than 80 percent of the local market rent. In areas that are already experiencing gentrification pressures such as Uptown Park in Newham and Shoreditch in Tower Hamlets/Hackney, 80 percent of the local market is still beyond what most low-income households would be able to afford. Moreover, the London Plan also specifies that the proportion of shared ownership homes should not exceed 40 percent of the total supply of "affordable housing." In Chapter 2, I have already argued that there has been a trend toward intermediate housing and more moderate to middle-class incomes in the evolution of inclusionary housing in London. In both cases presented, the higher proportion of intermediate homes further reinforces this trend toward the middle class.

Similarly, in New York City, both applications have been criticized for not providing enough "affordable housing" for the lowest-income households. Even though the Bedford Union Armory redevelopment committed to no more than 60 AMI for all "affordable housing," which in 2016 equated to about $50,000 annual income for a family of three, this only mirrors the median household income of the area.[19] The Sherman Plaza development included "affordable housing" levels up to 135 percent of the AMI, which equates to an annual household income of about $130,000 as of 2016. Since "affordable housing" in New York City is determined at the city level,[20] the determined affordability levels often fail to be "affordable" for households at the lower income levels in Inwood or Crown Heights. In 2016, the AMI for the New York City region was $81,600 for a family of three (100% AMI). In other words, 80% of the AMI was $65,250, which would correspond to option two of the MIH program and was well above what has been determined as the median household income in Inwood (Table 3.1).

As we can see in Tables 3.1 and 3.2, the London Boroughs of Newham and Tower Hamlets/Hackney as well as the Inwood and Crown Heights neighborhoods in New York City are all relatively "poor" compared to the rest of the city. In both cities, the areas where the development schemes were located are significantly below the city-level median household income. That means that a majority of very low-income households will not be able to access the greater portion of the "affordable housing" provided in each scheme. In particular with New York City, this city-wide institutionalized form of AMI, thus, prioritizes higher geographic scales, which in the cases studied in this subsection, functions at the expense of local low-income neighborhoods and residents.

Apart from the rejected Sherman Plaza development, the development schemes discussed here will inevitably bring major changes to the area. At least 50 percent of the housing created in these developments will be market-rate, which in practice means luxury housing in areas that are primarily low-income. As Tom Angotti and Sylvia Morse have already emphasized, this in turn will "lead to rising land values and rents and has a ripple effect on the surrounding area" (Angotti and Sylvia 2016: 70).

According to them, this will further "result in substantial displacement" (ibid.) of the local low-income population through what Marcuse called "displacement pressure" (Marcuse 1985). In this sense, by giving planning permission to large development schemes that will primarily attract people with higher incomes relative to the median income of the local community, city and local governments have engaged in what I call a form of *gentrification through the back door*.

It is this *gentrification through the back door* that local residents and community groups affected by development fear and what has led them to engage in "planning-related activism" (Watt 2018: 125) to push for a higher amount of actual "affordable housing" in private development applications.

Community Efforts to Challenge Inclusionary Housing-Related Planning Practices

As seen in this subchapter, a very high degree of community organization[21] and activism was involved in all four cases of which the main aim was to pressure local authorities to either increase the "affordable housing" provisions and make them affordable for low-income residents or to cancel the development scheme altogether.

In each case, local community members and groups often backed or organized by city-wide community organizations formed powerful campaigns to fight against specific planning applications, which they saw as an opening of their community to more luxury development and, hence, gentrification. Public participation in the review process usually comprises only a few minutes of testimonies at local hearings. Moreover, many citizens who have testified have often felt their concerns and objections were ignored or outright rejected. For those reasons, citizens, activists, and community organizations have generally had to engage in various tactics to get themselves heard, including lobbying the council, writing objection letters to the city government or local council members, as well as in community activism involving demonstrations and marches, petitions and informational workshops, and even the production of alternative development proposals.

With respect to the Boleyn Ground development plan in London, Paul Watt outlined two local campaigns that were directed against the small amount of "affordable housing" as well as the absence of social rent within the development scheme. One of them was organized by Newham Citizens, who form part of the wider alliance The East London Citizens Organization (TELCO)[22] that aimed at pressuring the council to lift the "affordable housing" provision to 35 percent, which would equate to the minimum of Newham Council's housing target. The second campaign was called BOLEYNDEV100 organized by local community residents that fought for 100 percent social housing on-site (Watt 2018: 126). They submitted 700 objection letters to the council and sent eleven speakers to testify at the Strategic Planning Committee on their behalf (BOLEYNDEV100 2016). The two above-mentioned campaigns agitated for a higher provision of "affordable housing."

Organized by several neighborhood groups, the More Light More Power (MLMP) campaign rallied against the potential impact of the Bishopsgate Goodsyard development on the local community, calling on the local council and the GLA to reject the scheme. One of their main concerns that gave the campaign its name was the forecasted reduction of 43 percent of sunlight for the surrounding area due to the development's proposed height. In addition, they criticized the associated demolition of historic 19th-century factory buildings and the development's small amount of affordable working and living space.[23] In 2020, the MLMP campaign supported the revised schemes, arguing that "there is currently more to gain by influencing key aspects of the proposals, than campaigning for outright refusal" (MLMP 2020). In the meantime, a separate campaign emerged called the Reclaim the Goodsyard[24] organized by Weavers Community Action Group that remained opposed to the development scheme, arguing that it "remains an over-development of the area, with an excessive provision of commercial and retail space and an under-provision of 'affordable housing' for local people" (Wright 2020).

With regards to the Inwood and Crown Heights cases, the council members of the district came under immense pressure from the local community. Since the local community in Inwood was very well organized and came together in the neighborhood coalition Northern Manhattan Not for Sale (NMN4S), they were able to place immense pressure on Council Member Ydanis Rodriguez to stop the Sherman Plaza development. The coalition was initially formed to fight against the proposed Inwood rezoning – as described in Chapter 2 – but stands more broadly for real affordable housing and against the gentrification of their neighborhood.[25]

In the case of the Bedford Union Armory in Crown Heights, local residents and community groups and other citywide community organizations, such as New York Communities for Change (NYCC),[26] assembled under the slogan #killthedealforreal. They pressured the local Council Member Laurie Combo, who was in the middle of a reelection campaign, to reject the development project unless 100 percent affordable housing was provided. Further, they argued for the site to be converted into a community land trust (del Valle 2017) – a non-profit corporation that acquires land and empowers tenants to jointly use and manage the land.

All these community campaigns against the development projects studied in this chapter were to a certain degree successful in organizing increases in the amount of "affordable housing" provided. The most successful of all was probably the NMN4S campaign organized by the eponymous coalition. The fight against the Sherman Plaza redevelopment was the only planning-related community struggle that was able to stop the development scheme entirely. It also happened to be the one that I was able to intensively follow during my fieldwork. As the development application made its way through the ULURP, I attended several public hearing meetings where several members of the NMN4S campaign testified vehemently against the plans, criticizing primarily the height, mass, and scale of the building that was seen to be out of context, its negative impact on the surrounding designated landmarks[27] as well as the lack of housing that would be affordable for the local community. Outside the ULURP, I attended several rallies, a community forum organized by NMN4S as well as various organizing meetings at which it was continually pointed out by participants that for them MIH signaled nothing but gentrification and displacement (see Figure 3.1).

Figure 3.1 (a) and (b) Inwood's residents and local community groups protesting against the
        Sherman Plaza redevelopment, August 2016. (c) Local residents from Inwood and
        Washington Heights at the New York City Council Subcommittee on Zoning and
        Franchises, July 12, 2016. (d) Council Member Ydanis Rodriguez announcing his
        rejection of the Sherman Plaza redevelopment, August 15, 2016. (*Continued*)

Source: © Yuca Meubrink

Figure 3.1 (Continued)

As New York City experienced an affordable housing crisis, the local community feared that the development project could open Inwood up to developers. Many were worried that the influx of wealthy new residents would drive up housing, retail and food prices in the neighborhood. For example, David Friend, a resident who testified during the ULURP, argued:

> While the developers and elected officials have been negotiating, they are trying to distract residents via promises of a handful of 'affordable housing' in the proposed building, this will in no way counterbalance the thousands of local families who are likely to be displaced as a result of opening the floodgates to luxury market-rate housing in our neighborhood. Gentrification is already underway and landlords are already doing everything they can to get long-term tenants out to flip their units out of the stabilized system.
>
> (David Friend 2016)

Many residents and local community groups warned public officials that the upzoning would cause direct and indirect displacement. Ava Farkas from Metropolitan Council stated:

> We have a huge and valuable housing stock of rent stabilized buildings in Washington Heights and Inwood. And a building that is going to create a majority of the units for [middle-income households] is really going to raise the income level for people in Inwood and incentivize other landlords to try to push out and harass tenants in the surrounding rent-stabilized buildings.
>
> (Farkas cited in New York City Council Subcommittee on Zoning and Franchises 2016b: 67)

In the end, protests organized by the local community paid off: at a spontaneous press conference in front of Sherman Plaza at 4650 Broadway on the evening before the final vote in the City Council, Ydanis Rodriguez announced that he was going to vote against the proposal. When Ydanis Rodriguez came to the point of announcing his final decision tensions were running high. He ended up saying that he would not be moving forward with the development and that he would vote against it. The following quote is taken from my fieldnotes of the reactions of the local community as well as of Ydanis Rodriguez's after he announced his decision:

> The crowd of local residents surrounding him cheered and shouted. They could not believe it. Ydanis himself was finally smiling. I guess a lot of pressure had just fallen from him. He tried to calm the crowd to announce his decision in Spanish but the people were already cheering, and hugging each other. Many had tears in their eyes. It felt like a real victory for the community.
>
> (Fieldnote 2016/08/15)

However, in the aftermath of the Council's rejection of the proposal, the developer Acadia Reality Trust, who had bought the land of 4560 Broadway for $18.25 million in 2005, sold the property to the investment company FBE Limited for $26 million in April 2018. Shortly after, FBE Limited sold the site to the joint venture of the two developers, The Arden Group and Hello Living for $55 million (Mazzocchi 2018), more than double the amount that FBE Limited paid and more than triple the amount Acadia Reality Trust had paid in 2005. After the joint venture broke down, The Arden Group planned a 19-story mixed-use development with 222 residential units of which 30 percent would be "affordable housing" (Hallum 2023). As the developer plans to comply the development project with all the applicable zoning regulations, they can, however, develop the building as-of-right, meaning it does not require any approval from the city (Londono 2018).

Neighborhood Inequalities Reinforced

The different approaches taken by each city when engaging with developers illustrate how city and local governments produce different outcomes across various neighborhood contexts, depending on the wealth of the neighborhood.

In the four case studies of developments in affluent neighborhoods, I identified two ways in which developers were able to keep the "affordable housing" provision to a minimum. It was evident that local authorities were compelled to relax the "affordable housing" in exchange for more completions.

In the four case studies of developments in low-income communities, local authorities were able to increase the "affordable housing" provisions. I identified how the local authority's engagement, along with community pressure and the question of the affordability of "affordable housing" were crucial aspects in the planning process. Together they illustrate that community pressure on local authorities results in higher numbers of "affordable housing" and deeper affordability levels than originally proposed by the developer. By contrast, these three aspects played no, or at most a minor, role in the planning process in affluent neighborhoods. Despite the efforts of local authorities, it became also clear that in low-income communities inclusionary housing is likely to accelerate gentrification and displacement processes.

These differences in implementation of inclusionary housing could further stem from different party alliances of the local authority in question – an aspect that I have not touched upon in my analysis. In the two cases studied in London, the three local councils of Newham, Tower Hamlets, and Hackney were at the time all Labour-led, while the affluent boroughs of City of Westminster and Wandsworth were both led by Conservative City Councils. These findings match also those of the scholars Li and Guo (2020) who conclude that "developments in Labour jurisdictions tend to include more affordable housing" (Li and Guo 2020: 987). However, complicating matters, in New York City, the local council members of the three neighborhoods of Inwood, Crown Heights, and Chelsea were all Democrats. Considering that estate demolitions in London have been pursued by Conservative as well as Labour councils, including Lambeth Council as discussed in Chapter 2, it is questionable whether party alliance is a decisive aspect in this regard. Given the US two-party system does not directly compare to the English multi-party system, it would be important to study more specific examples of how inclusionary housing policies play out differently across neighborhoods to substantiate my findings.

All in all, my findings suggest how inclusionary housing practices reinforce the market-driven approaches adopted by city and local governments no matter what neighborhood the development is located in. Except for one, all development proposals studied were eventually approved by the authority in question. Of the eight development plans studied, in only three cases – one in London and two in New York City – were local authorities able to reach their own "affordable housing" targets or inclusionary housing requirements. But in these three cases, most of the housing created – affordable or not – is far from being affordable to the residing low-income community. This illustrates the city and local governments' pro-growth interests at the expense of much-needed affordable housing. The stipulation of "affordable housing" obligation through inclusionary housing practices, thus, "offers merely a chimera that allows developers to buy off planners [and city and local governments] and construct evermore elite housing towers" (Graham 2015: 641) – an aspect that I will touch upon in Chapter 4. This may not be surprising given the budgetary deficits city and local governments are facing due to years of austerity measures and the pressure they are under from higher levels of government to meet housing targets. For the most vulnerable parts of local communities, this however means that they will experience even more displacement pressures as more and more luxury housing units are developed in their community. Given the hope that has been associated with inclusionary housing policies – in particular in New York since the implementation of MIH – this paints a rather disenchanting picture of inclusionary housing practices in both cities.

Fieldnotes

Meubrink, Yuca. Participant observation of the New York City Council Subcommittee on Zoning and Franchises, July 12, 2016.

Meubrink, Yuca. Participant observation of the press conference of Ydanis Rodriguez, Sherman Plaza at 4650 Broadway, Manhattan, New York City, August 15, 2016.

Notes

1 For a continuous update on MIH sites, see NYC's Department of Housing and Preservation's Inclusionary Housing Sites Map: https://hpd.maps.arcgis.com/apps/webappviewer/index.html?id=6d3f09240876403097c6d37a3c467917.

2 The 250 "affordable housing" units account for about 60 percent of the overall units provided. Thirty percent of these are MIH units, while the additional units are subsidized through various public programs.

3 The Hudson Yard development is not only the most expensive development project in US history but comprises 11 hectares also one of the largest (Tyler and Bendix 2019). Nevertheless, only 107 "affordable housing" units have been set aside as part of the planning deal under the Bloomberg administration's voluntary inclusionary housing program. Since the pandemic, the Hudson Yards is now on the edge of bankruptcy (Kuttner 2021).

4 I do not differentiate between the number of homes that are S106 nil grant or S106 partial grant-funded units.

5 Statistics were compiled by the author from the specified source.

6 Air rights are the right to build or develop the space above a property. Unused air rights can be transferred in limited circumstances to another surrounding zoning lot.

7 New York City's Zoning Resolution, Article VII, Chapter 4, Section 74–32: https://zr.planning.nyc.gov/article-vii/chapter-4/74-32 (last accessed: January 21, 2021).

8 Employed by law firm Kramer Levin – who counts Acuity Capital Partners as one of its clients – Valerie Campbell expressed these statements during the public review process before the public City Council Committee meeting on June 22nd, 2016. https://www.youtube.com/watch?v=01OioWQJLtM (last accessed March 27, 2020).

9 The more common abbreviation of Mandatory Inclusionary Housing is MIH.

10 This extract has been edited by the author for better readability.

11 The other major area in 2005 was Greenpoint/Williamsburg.

12 Only the Financial District and Midtown in Manhattan had higher median asking rents.

13 The developer Douglaston Development coordinated their development plans at 601 West 29th Street with the developer Lalezarian, who proposed to develop a neighboring building at 606 West 30th Street. Both development proposals adjoin the Hudson Yard and West Chelsea rezoning area that had created an enormous real-estate value increase on the surrounding blocks (Kober 2020: 11). Even though the City Council passed both development plans in the same meeting, the report by the Manhattan Institute (Kober 2020) does not list 606 West 29th Street as an MIH site. In the subsequent analysis, the development at 606 West 30th Street will frequently be mentioned in connection with the development at 601 West 29th Street since both are often mentioned jointly in planning documents.

14 By 2023, the construction of both developments have been completed with 1212 rental units in total, of which 305 are designated for affordable housing, ranging from 40 to 100 AMI for households with annual incomes between $26,000 and $144,000 (Londono 2023; Young and Pruznick 2023).

15 As of 2023, the developer has delivered a block of 386 affordable homes in some distance from the power station. None of the affordable housing units are inside the power station (Kollewe 2022). As far as I can tell, there is no news on the remaining 250 affordable homes.

16 This extract has been edited by the author for better readability.
17 For more information, see https://www.london.gov.uk/what-we-do/planning/planning-applications-and-decisions/public-hearings/past-public-hearings (last accessed: January 23, 2021).
18 In Newham and Tower Hamlets, the overall affordable housing target is 35–50 percent affordable housing of which 60% in Newham (Newham Council 2017: 4) and 70% in Tower Hamlets (Tower Hamlets Council 2013: 11) should have social rent. In Hackney, the overall affordable housing target is 50 percent of which 60 percent should have social rent (Hackney Council 2015: 62).
19 In 2021, the housing lottery for the first 55 affordable housing units of the redeveloped Bedford-Union Armory opened, with an Area Median Income ranging of 30 percent for four of the units, 40 percent for six units, 50 percent for another six units and 60 percent for the remaining 39 units. Of the affordable apartments, about 76 percent are studios and one-bedroom units and another 22 percent are two-bedroom units. There is only one single three-bedroom, which is set at 60 percent AMI with an eligible incomes range between $54,412 and $88,800 for households of three to seven people (Hubert 2021).
20 The Area Median Income of New York City is determined on the Median Family Income of the five boroughs plus Putnam County.
21 By community organizations, I am encompassing a large number of different actors and organizations such as grassroots (housing) movements and coalitions, tenant rights membership organizations, neighborhood advocacy groups, labor unions, faith-based community groups, and charities.
22 TELCO is the founding Chapter of Citizens UK, an alliance of over 80 civil society institutions comprised of trade unions, faith groups, charities, schools and universities.
23 For more information on the campaign, see http://www.morelightmorepower.co.uk/ (last accessed: January 23, 2021).
24 For more information, see http://www.goodsyard.org/ (last accessed: January 21, 2021).
25 For more information, see https://www.metcouncilonhousing.org/campaign/northern-manhattan-is-not-for-sale/ (last accessed: January 21, 2021).
26 New York Communities for Change is a community-based non-profit organization based in New York City. Founded in 2010, it is one of several successors of the left-wing housing advocacy organization *Association of Community Organizations for Reform Now* (ACORN) that had suffered a funding scandal in 2009 that turned out to be baseless but nevertheless has damaged the image of ACORN. NYCC is a leading voice in neighborhood and national issues and fights against social and economic injustice. For more information, see https://www.nycommunities.org/ (last accessed: January 23, 2021).
27 There are two designated landmarks in the immediate vicinity of the Sherman Plaza: the Cloisters, a branch of the Museum of Metropolitan Art located in a recreated medieval monastery, is situated on the top of a hill in the northern end of the Fort Tyron Park. Both the monastery and the park are listed on the National Register of Historic Places and are two out of only ten city-designated Landmarks of New York City.

References

Angotti, Tom. 2016. "Land Use Zoning Matters." In *Zoned Out! Race, Displacement, and City Planning in New York City*, edited by Tom Angotti and Sylvia Morse, 18–45. New York: UR.
Angotti, Tom, and Morse Sylvia. 2016. "Racialized Land Use and Housing Policies." In *Zoned Out! Race, Displacement, and City Planning in New York City*, edited by Tom Angotti and Sylvia Morse, 46–71. New York: UR.
BOLEYNDEV100. 2016. "Newham Council Sides with the Rich. Again." BOLEYNDEV100. March 11. https://boleyndev100.wordpress.com/.

Bourke, Joanna. 2013. "Brockton Wins Mayfair Consent" *Estates Gazette*, July 17. https://www.egi.co.uk/news/brockton-wins-mayfair-consent/.

Chaban, Matt A. V. 2016. "Why, in One Case, the de Blasio Administration Opposes Affordable Housing." *The New York Times*, August 9. https://www.nytimes.com/2016/08/09/nyregion/a-manhattan-condominium-project-tests-de-blasios-fledgling-housing-program.html.

City Planning Commission (CPC). 2018. "City Planning Commission Report in the Matter C 180129A ZSM." New York City: City Planning Commission. https://www1.nyc.gov/assets/planning/download/pdf/about/cpc/180127.pdf.

Colenutt, Bob. 2020. *The Property Lobby: The Hidden Reality Behind the Housing Crisis.* Policy Press.

Cuffe, Grainne. 2017. "Battersea Power Station Developer Nearly Halves Number of Affordable Homes." *Wandsworth Guardian*, June 22, 2017. https://www.wandsworthguardian.co.uk/news/15364937.battersea-power-station-developer-nearly-halves-number-of-affordable-homes/.

Friend, David. 2016. "Testimony to Be Submitted to the New York City Planning Commission Meeting." *New York City Planning Commission*, May 25. Retrieved via FIOA request.

Fuller, Crispian. 2018. "Entrepreneurial Urbanism, Austerity and Economic Governance." *Cambridge Journal of Regions, Economy and Society* 11 (3): 565–85. https://doi.org/10.1093/cjres/rsy023.

Fuller, Crispian, and Karen West. 2017. "The Possibilities and Limits of Political Contestation in Times of 'Urban Austerity.'" *Urban Studies* 54 (9): 2087–2106.

Gower, Patrick. 2013. "London Mayor Blocks Mayfair Apartment Plan Citing Size." *Bloomberg*, May 15. https://www.bloomberg.com/news/articles/2013-05-14/london-mayor-blocks-exceptionally-large-mayfair-apartment-plan.

Graham, Stephen. 2015. "Luxified Skies." *City* 19 (5): 618–45.

Greater London Authority (GLA). 2013. "Planning Report D&P/3005/0356: Curzon Street, Mayfair in the City of Westminster." Greater London Authority. https://www.london.gov.uk/sites/default/files/public%3A//public%3A//PAWS/media_id_217425///56_curzon_street_report.pdf.

———. 2016a. "London Borough Profiles and Atlas." London Datastore. https://data.london.gov.uk/dataset/london-borough-profiles.

———. 2016b. "Planning Report: West Ham Stadium, Boleyn Ground, Green Street, Upton Park, London." Greater London Authority. https://www.london.gov.uk/sites/default/files/public%3A//public%3A//PAWS/media_id_286111///west_ham_stadium_report.pdf.

———. 2020. "London's Population." London Datastore. https://data.london.gov.uk/dataset/londons-population.

Hackney Council. 2015. "Development Management Local Plan." Hackney Council. https://hackney.gov.uk/development-management-dpd.

Hallum, Mark. 2023. "Arden Group Lands $150M Loan to Build Inwood Residential Building." *Commercial Observer*, April 19. https://commercialobserver.com/2023/04/arden-group-lands-150m-loan-to-build-inwood-residential-building/.

Holliday Smith, Rachel. 2017. "Brooklyn Armory Deal, and Larger De Blasio Development Debate, Move Toward Term Two." *Gotham Gazette*, December 11. https://www.gothamgazette.com/city/7360-brooklyn-armory-deal-and-larger-de-blasio-development-debate-move-toward-term-two.

Hubert, Craig. 2021. "Affordable Housing Lottery Opens for 55 Units at Bedford Union Armory, Starting at $367 a Month | Brownstoner." *Brownstoner*, 30. Juni. https://www.brownstoner.com/real-estate-market/affordable-housing-brooklyn-bedford-union-armory-1089-president-street-crown-heights-lottery-opens/.

Kaufmann, Sarah. 2016. "NYC Developer Really, Really Doesn't Want Affordable Housing in Its New Chelsea Building." *Patch*, September 8. https://patch.com/new-york/chelsea-ny/developer-really-really-doesnt-want-affordable-housing-its-new-chelsea-building.

Kober, Eric. 2020. "How Has de Blasio's Inclusionary Zoning Program (MIH) Fared?" New York City: Manhattan Institute. https://www.manhattan-institute.org/deblasios-mandatory-inclusionary-housing-program.

Kollewe, Julia. 2015. "Battersea Is Part of a Huge Building Project – But Not for Londoners." *The Guardian*, February 14. https://www.theguardian.com/business/2015/feb/14/battersea-nine-elms-property-development-housing.

———. 2017. "Battersea Power Station Developer Slashes Number of Affordable Homes." *The Guardian*, October 5. http://www.theguardian.com/uk-news/2017/jun/21/battersea-power-station-affordable-homes-almost-halved-by-developer.

———. 2022. "Battersea Power Station Set For Public Opening After 10-year Development." *The Guardian*, June 21. https://www.theguardian.com/business/2022/oct/05/battersea-power-station-set-for-public-opening-after-10-year-development.

Kuttner, Robert. 2021. "A Tale of Two Developments: Affordable Housing or Subsidized Ultra-Luxury?" *The American Prospect*, February 9. https://prospect.org/api/content/2d556eba-6a5c-11eb-a355-1244d5f7c7c6/.

Layard, Antonia. 2019. "Planning by Numbers: Affordable Housing and Viability in England." In *Planning and Knowledge: How New Forms of Technocracy Are Shaping Contemporary Cities*, Mike Raco and Federico Savini. Bristol: Policy Press, 213–24. https://policy.bristoluniversitypress.co.uk/planning-and-knowledge.

Lehrer, Brian. 2016. "#AskTheMayor About Your Free NYC ID." *The Brian Lehrer Show*. WNYC. https://www.wnyc.org/story/askthemayor-about-your-free-nyc-id/.

Li, Fei, and Zhan Guo. 2020. "Will Mandatory Inclusionary Housing Create Mixed-Income Communities? Evidence From London, UK." *Housing Policy Debate* 30 (6): 972–93. https://doi.org/10.1080/10511482.2020.1787482.

Londono, Vanessa. 2018. "Hello Living Acquires 4650 Broadway for $55 Million, Releases New Renderings." *New York YIMBY* (blog). November 15. https://newyorkyimby.com/2018/11/hello-living-acquires-4650-broadway-for-55-million-releases-new-renderings.html.

———. 2023. "Housing Lottery Launches for 70 Units at 606 West 30th Street in West Chelsea, Manhattan." *New York YIMBY* (blog). April 28. https://newyorkyimby.com/2023/04/housing-lottery-launches-for-70-units-at-606-west-30th-street-in-west-chelsea-manhattan.html.

Lowndes, Vivien, and Alison Gardner. 2016. "Local Governance Under the Conservatives: Super-Austerity, Devolution and the 'Smarter State.'" *Local Government Studies* 42 (3): 357–375. https://doi.org/10.1080/03003930.2016.1150837.

Marcuse, Peter. 1985. "Gentrification, Abandonment, and Displacement: Connections, Causes, and Policy Responses in New York City." *Urban Law Annual; Journal of Urban and Contemporary Law* 28 (1): 195–240.

Mazzocchi, Sherry. 2018. "Does Hello Broadway Mean 'Bye, Neighborhood'?¿Hello Broadway Significa 'Adiós Barrio'?" *Manhattan Times News*, November 28. https://www.manhattantimesnews.com/does-hello-broadway-mean-bye-neighborhoodhello-broadway-significa-adios-barrio/.

Ministry of Housing, Communities and Local Government (MHCLG). 2019. "Affordable Housing Supply Statistics (AHS) 2019–20. Live Tables – 1011S, 1011C." Government UK. https://www.gov.uk/government/statistical-data-sets/live-tables-on-affordable-housing-supply#live-tables.

Minton, Anna. 2017. *Big Capital: Who Is London For?* UK: Penguin.

More Light More Power (MLMP). 2020. "More Light More Power Statement" More Light More Power (Blog). http://www.morelightmorepower.co.uk.

Navarro, Mireya. 2015. "In Chelsea, a Great Wealth Divide." *The New York Times*, October 23. https://www.nytimes.com/2015/10/25/nyregion/in-chelsea-a-great-wealth-divide.html.

New York City Council. 2016. "Transcript of the Minutes of the City Council Stated Meeting." New York City Council. https://legistar.council.nyc.gov/View.ashx?M=F&ID=464 1693&GUID=073273DC-8DC7-418D-9876-8B622AC97070.

New York City Council Committee on Land Use. 2017. "Transcript of the Minutes of the Committee on Land Use." New York City Council. https://legistar.council.nyc.gov/View.ashx?M=F&ID=5677314&GUID=9025B3CC-B154-4950-9877-585AEAFFC3A8.

New York City Council Subcommittee on Zoning and Franchises. 2016a. "Transcript of the Minutes of the Committee on Zoning and Franchises." New York City Council, September 7. https://legistar.council.nyc.gov/View.ashx?M=F&ID=4677971&GUID=68ED 2D6B-A4E7-4CEC-B050-0CE03C9A8AD9.

———. 2016b. "Transcript of the Minutes of the Committee on Zoning and Franchises." New York City Council, July 12. https://legistar.council.nyc.gov/View.ashx?M=F&ID= 4565731&GUID=0E600C87-4325-4C38-B406-314F49CF4FFB.

———. 2018. "Transcript of the Minutes of the Committee on Zoning and Franchises." New York City Council. https://legistar.council.nyc.gov/View.ashx?M=F&ID=6280638&GUID= 37513BB6-7198-41E7-ADD6-722DD072B7A5.

Newham Council. 2017. "London Borough of Newham: Local Plan and Community Infrastructure Levy Viability Assessment." Newham Council. https://www.newham.gov.uk/ downloads/file/904/newhamlocalplanviabilitystudy.

New York City Office of the Mayor. 2021. "Mayor de Blasio Announces 200,000 Affordable Homes Built or Preserved during this Administration." The Official Website of the City of New York. December 22. http://www1.nyc.gov/office-of-the-mayor/news/853-21/ mayor-de-blasio-200-000-affordable-homes-built-preserved-during-this-administration.

NYU Furman Center. 2015. "Creating Affordable Housing Out of Thin Air: The Economics of Mandatory Inclusionary Zoning in New York City." New York City: NYU Furman Center. http://furmancenter.org/files/NYUFurmanCenter_CreatingAffHousing_ March2015.pdf.

———. 2016. "State of New York City's Housing & Neighborhoods – 2016 Report." NYU Furman Center. https://furmancenter.org/research/sonychan/2016-report.

———. 2017. "State of New York City's Housing & Neighborhoods." New York City: NYU Furman Center. https://furmancenter.org/research/sonychan/2017-report.

Osborne, Hilary. 2014. "Poor Doors: The Segregation of London's Inner-City Flat Dwellers." *The Guardian*, July 25. http://www.theguardian.com/society/2014/jul/25/poor-doors-segregation-london-flats.

Panton, Mark, and Geoff Walters. 2018. "'It's Just a Trojan Horse for Gentrification': Austerity and Stadium-Led Regeneration." *International Journal of Sport Policy and Politics* 10 (1): 163–83. https://doi.org/10.1080/19406940.2017.1398768.

Pipe, Jules. 2015. "Reject the Bishopsgate Goods Yard Planning Application." Change.org. 2015. https://www.change.org/p/boris-johnson-withdraw-your-support-for-two-luxury-skyscrapers-in-hackney-e14fa61f-1f0b-459b-a533-714209514f9b.

Shaw, Randy. 2018. *Generation Priced Out: Who Gets to Live in the New Urban America.* Oakland, California: University of California Press.

Steavenson, Wendell. 2017. "London's Nowhere Neighbourhood." *Prospect Magazine*, April 7. https://www.prospectmagazine.co.uk/magazine/londons-nowhere-neighbourhood.

Stein, Samuel. 2018. "Progress for Whom, Toward What? Progressive Politics and New York City's Mandatory Inclusionary Housing." *Journal of Urban Affairs* 40 (6): 770–81. https://doi.org/10.1080/07352166.2017.1403854.

Stein, Samuel. 2021. "Assessing de Blasio's Housing Legacy: Why Hasn't the "Most Ambitious Affordable Housing Program" Produced a More Affordable City?" Community Service Society (Jan.). https://www.cssny.org/publications/entry/assessing-de-blasios-housing-legacy.

Tower Hamlets Council. 2013. "Affordable Housing Supplementary Planning Document." Tower Hamlets Council. https://democracy.towerhamlets.gov.uk/mgIssueHistoryHome. aspx?IId=35278&PlanId=99&RPID=0.

Trust for London. 2014. "Poverty Rates by London Borough." Trust for London. 2014. https://www.trustforlondon.org.uk/data/poverty-borough/.

Tyler, Jessica, and Aria Bendix. 2019. "Hudson Yards Is the Most Expensive Real-Estate Development in US History. Here's What It's like inside the $25 Billion Neighborhood." *Business Insider*, May 15. https://www.businessinsider.com/hudson-yards-tour-of-most-expensive-development-in-us-history-2018-9.

Ullman, Seth, Michael Freedman-Schnapp, and Brad Lander. 2013. "Inclusionary Zoning in New York City: The Performance of New York City's Designated Areas Inclusionary Housing Program since its Launch in 2005." *Office of Council Member Brad Lander.* https://www.scribd.com/doc/160544058/Inclusionary-Zoning-in-New-York-City-The-performance-of-New-York-City-s-Designated-Areas-Inclusionary-Housing-Program-since-its-launch-in-2005.

Valle, Gaby del. 2017. "Crown Heights Residents Protest Development at Bedford-Union Armory." *Gothamist,* March 8. https://gothamist.com/news/crown-heights-residents-protest-development-at-bedford-union-armory.

Wandsworth Council. 2017. "Wandsworth Council Meeting: Battersea Power Station Site. Deed of Variation to the Section 106 Agreement." Wandsworth Council.

———. 2018. "Wandsworth Local Plan. Site Specific Allocations Document" Wandsworth Council. https://www.wandsworth.gov.uk/media/3755/local_plan_site_specific_allocations.pdf.

Warerkar, Tanay. 2017a. "Embattled Bedford-Union Armory Project Is Endorsed by Mayor de Blasio." *Curbed NY,* July 13. https://ny.curbed.com/2017/7/13/15966632/crown-heights-armory-de-blasio-support.

———. 2017b. "Bedford-Union Armory Redevelopment Loses Condos, Gains More Affordable Housing." *Curbed NY,* November 21. https://ny.curbed.com/2017/11/21/16686288/bedford-union-armory-redevelopment-affordable.

Watt, Paul. 2018. "'Social Housing Not Social Cleansing': Contemporary Housing Struggles in London." In *Rent and Its Discontents. A Century of Housing Struggle,* edited by Neil Grey, 117–135. London: Rowman & Littlefield.

Westminster City Council Planning Application Subcommittee. 2013. "56 Curzon Street, WJ8PB". City of Westminster, item no. 4. https://committees.westminster.gov.uk/Data/Planning%20Applications%20Committee/20130716/Agenda/item%2004%20-%2056%20curzon%20street,%20w1.pdf#search=%22Curzon%20Street%22.

Wright, Charles. 2020. "Bishopsgate Goodsyard Plans Recommended for Approval by City Hall Planners." *On London* (Blog). November 27, 2020. https://www.onlondon.co.uk/bishopsgate-goodsyard-plans-recommended-for-approval-by-city-hall-planners/.

Young, Michael, and Matt Pruznick. 2023. "3ELEVEN Completes Construction at 601 West 29th Street in West Chelsea, Manhattan." *New York Yimby* (Blog), September 15. https://newyorkyimby.com/2023/09/3eleven-completes-construction-at-601-west-29th-street-in-west-chelsea-manhattan.html.

4 Vertical Segregation by Design

How Inclusionary Housing Developments Contribute to a Vertical Gentrification Movement

So far this study of inclusionary housing policies and practices has illustrated how and why city and local governments in both London and New York City have used the provision of "affordable housing" to place new-build mixed-income developments into primarily lower-income neighborhoods, thereby laying down the path to new-build gentrification and displacement years ahead of the new homes and residents. In Chapters 2 and 3, I concentrated on the horizontal dimension of the socio-economic and spatial practices as well as the consequences of inclusionary housing. In this chapter, I explore the vertical aspects of inclusionary housing distribution and its relation to gentrification processes.

In the literature, it has been well documented that once built, these large, high-density, self-contained mixed-income developments add new buildings and social character to existing neighborhoods (i.a. Davidson and Lees 2010; Lauermann 2022) and, in turn, promote gentrification rather than socially mixed communities. Mark Davidson, for example, analyzed social mixing within the context of new-build gentrification by focusing on the relationship between the gentrifying residents and the incumbent communities in three neighborhoods undergoing new-build gentrification in London. He pointed out that the particular nature of new-build gentrification has played an important role in generating what Butler and Robson (2003) have called "social tectonics" (Butler and Robinson 2003). These "social tectonics" are characterized above all by the fact that spatial proximity does not necessarily lead to social proximity. The question of scale and proximity of different social and ethnic groups has become a key issue in discussions about the connection between social mix policies and gentrification. Most studies discuss the social impact and "neighborhood effects" of these new-build developments (i.a. Bridge, Butler, and Lees 2012; Davidson and Lees 2010; Lees 2008). In other words, they have primarily focused on the horizontal aspect of gentrification.

Less attention has been given to the lived experiences of social mixing within mixed-income developments and even less to how it relates to the actual physical arrangement of "affordable housing" units within otherwise market-rate developments. While some scholars have concentrated on the physical aspects and design solutions for integrating different tenure types within mixed-income developments, they have neglected its concomitant vertical dimension of segregation and gentrification (Lawton 2013; Levin, Arthurson, and Ziersch 2014; Roberts 2007;

DOI: 10.4324/9781003468479-5

Tiesdell 2004). Other scholars engaged with urbanism's vertical dimension, meanwhile, have neglected aspects of design and the nature of individual buildings (i.a. Graham 2015; Lauermann 2022; Maloutas and Spyrellis 2016; Marcińczak and Hess 2020).

In this chapter, I examine the physical arrangement and design outcomes of inclusionary housing programs in London and New York City in the context of new-build gentrification. Thereby, I connect these two seemingly separate debates on vertical segregation and design practices in order to demonstrate how inclusionary housing practices exhibit various forms of vertical social differentiation and distancing – a practice I call vertical segregation by design. I further draw on Bourdieu's thesis on social and appropriated physical space to provide an explanatory framework.

I deliberately do not address the issue of whether one design outcome provides more or less social interaction between residents with different socioeconomic statuses than another. The reason for this is partly because it does not fit within the scope of this study, but also partly because I am examining the socioeconomic effects and socio-spatial practices of inclusionary housing rather than how residents mix in and through such forms of housing. The focus of this chapter is, thus, to show which design concepts of social mixing are envisioned, and whether once such a development is built, its design would, in principle, create the opportunity for different tenures to mix. The question of whether they create socially meaningful mixed communities is debatable and, thus, a subject for further research.

Regarding the selection of my case studies, I have chosen mixed-income housing developments that exhibit three different forms of vertical segregation by design: two cases previously discussed in the Introduction, namely, those displaying the practice of "poor doors," and the remaining chosen after reviewing the press and the literature. In all cases, I draw my findings primarily from my own observations of the respective developments. In addition, I base my findings on participant observations while attending a barbecue in New York City and a protest action in London, as well as on several short conversations with residents, doormen, and activists. Furthermore, I analyzed planning documents and press articles of the cases under consideration.

In the following, I begin with introducing my analytical framework before I discuss the three different forms of vertical segregation by design.

Theoretical Considerations of Vertical Segregation by Design

The Relation Between Social, Physical, and Appropriated Physical Space

While some scholars explain classical gentrification processes through Bourdieu's concept of habitus by focusing on the consumption practices, education, or the aesthetic of the built environment (i.a. Bridge 2001; Butler 2003; Watt 2008), Davidson argues that new-build gentrification generates a distinct interaction between the gentrifiers and the incumbent residents that cannot solely be explained through the concept of habitus. According to Davidson, the relation between those two groups is primarily "presented, shaped, and mediated by the architecture, marketing, and built form of gentrifying developments created by real estate developers" (Davidson and Lees 2010: 537). As such, he calls for more focus on the influence of the built environment and real estate capital on the creation of differences between the gentrifiers and the generally lower-income incumbent residents (Davidson 2008).

While Davidson focuses on how the "social class continues to operate and be structured in the neighbourhood context," drawing on Bourdieu's thesis on the relative structuring of class identity, I focus rather on the built form of mixed-income housing developments themselves, as well as the perceptions of planning authorities and developers regarding the social mix behind them. In doing so, I pick up on Davidson's call to concentrate on how the built environment and real estate capital increasingly shape the creation of socio-economic differences.

Although it has been used more commonly to understand how people and social groups with high capital accumulation shape urban spaces more than social groups with less capital at their disposal, Bourdieu's concept of the interaction of physical, social and appropriated physical space (Bourdieu 1991) appears helpful toward explaining gentrification processes. According to Bourdieu, space is "socially constructed and marked" (Bourdieu [1991] 2018: 108) and the construction of space – the physical environment – is determined by people with high capital accumulation and shaped according to their needs (ibid.: 109). This means that people with less capital have fewer opportunities to shape spaces and their perceptual and interpretive schemes are less likely to be found in space. Hence, it is the people with high capital accumulation that appropriate spaces, which are "the sites where power is asserted, and no doubt under the most invisible form, that of symbolic violence as unperceived violence" (ibid.: 108). Bourdieu further points out that "[a]rchitectural spaces[…]are no doubt the most important components of the symbolism of power because of their very invisibility" (ibid.: 108). Hence, architectural spaces are designed according to the needs of groups with high capital accumulation such as local planning authorities and developers. As developers design the apartments according to the needs and desires of future market-rate residents, those groups indirectly also shape the design of mixed-income developments. In other words, the design and accessibility of buildings depend largely on the form of capital available to individuals.

Lower-income people are, thus, situated almost always in space regulated and ruled by those who own capital. The social space that people of lower income inhabit is reflected more often than not in their location in the physical space appropriated by those of higher income. According to Bourdieu, the ability to appropriate space "allows one to keep at a distance undesirable persons and things as well as to bring in closer desirable ones" (ibid.: 110). That means that people with capital often make accessibility to the spaces they have constructed as difficult as possible for others, such as exclusion through codes of dress or interaction, or, in a more extreme form, by sealing themselves off in gated communities. In turn, the physical space is not only shaped by people but people are also shaped by the way the physical space is constructed (ibid.: 112). In other words, the way physical space is shaped has an effect also on the way people behave, interact, or socially mix.

It is this theoretical issue of (in)accessibility to the appropriated physical space of mixed-income developments that "affordable housing" tenants and market-rate residents face and how that relates to new-build gentrification processes that I will explore in this chapter.

Linking the Debates on Vertical Urbanism with Discussions About Urban Design and Social Mixing

"Affordable housing" provision has many different facets, and the physical arrangement and urban design outcomes of social mix policies are highly variegated and differ in context and form. In the literature on urban design in socially mixed communities some general aspects can, however, be distinguished that are of direct importance for the analysis of the built form of inclusionary housing policies and practices. These aspects include the degree of mixing of different tenure types, the architectural appearance of tenure types, as well as other design elements such as communal spaces, carports, and garages. A common feature of almost all studies that look at the spatial arrangement of different tenure types is that they primarily ask whether there are urban design strategies that facilitate successful implementation of the tenure mix.

First, with respect to the degree of mixing of different tenure types, Groves et al. (2003) and Tiesdell (2004) offer each a typology of different urban design models that describe the degree of integration or separation of different tenure types. Groves et al. (2003: 36), who studied the neighborhood Bourneville in Birmingham, England, found four models of tenure mix: the integrated model, the segmented model, the segregated model, and the monolithic. According to Groves et al., the integrated approach is defined in terms of the "affordable" units being side by side with and indistinguishable from market-rate units. The segmented approach describes "affordable housing" as that divided from the market-rate units through small blocks (ibid.: 36f). The segregated model applies where the "affordable housing" is geographically separated from the market-rate housing or homeownership, and the monolithic model can also be described as the single tenure model. In terms of the degree of integration and segregation, Tiesdell (2004), who concentrates on the inclusion of "affordable housing" within market-rate developments, is more specific than Groves et al. He considers six urban design strategies in relation to the layout and the appearance of the market-rate and "affordable housing" units within a development project. These urban design strategies range from the "affordable housing" being segregated from, clustered, or pepper-potted within market-rate housing with either different or similar appearance (Tiesdell 2004: 204).

The second aspect relates to the visual appearance of mixed-income developments that have primarily been discussed in terms of their degree of difference. Roberts (2007), who examines three mixed-income communities in the UK, assesses whether what she calls a "tenure blind" approach should be adopted as a "universal approach" in all new mixed-income developments. She defines a "tenure blind" approach as "affordable housing" being "pepper-potted" within and indistinguishable from market-rate housing (Roberts 2007: 187). She concludes:

> Even if the design and layout do not conform to an ideal notion of tenure blind development provided that the layout draws on established principles of urban design and no stigma can be attached to the social housing through its visual appearance, then a degree of social interaction between different income groups is facilitated and resident satisfaction levels are high.
>
> (Roberts 2007: 201)

In one of her case studies, however, the social housing units were more attractive than the private ownership homes, and she acknowledges that the outcome might have been different if it would have been reversed (ibid.: 199).

The third aspect refers to differences in tenure that are not only architectural. Roberts refers in this context primarily to cars, carports, garages, and "personalization" of dwellings that show "an immediate indicator of [ones] absence [or] lack of it" (ibid.: 199). Lawton (2013) has further reflected on communal spaces. He examined the urban design perspective of urban practitioners such as urban planners, architects, and management personnel in Amsterdam, looking at the micro-politics of such communal spaces as courtyards, stairwells, and lifts. His findings suggest that there is a "desire for separation of communal social space within socially-mixed apartment blocks" (Lawton 2013: 113), based on the expectations of the future purchasers or renters of the market-rate housing. His research, therefore, suggests that social mix should take place "at a scale above that of the internal spaces of the staircases or corridors" (ibid.: 114). Levin et al. (2014: 30) concur with Lawton's findings that social mix on the block level is disliked by private residents. As a consequence, Levin et al. show that the design of the buildings studied – also in Amsterdam – that contained the "pepper-potted" model "has resulted in the lack of shared spaces for public and private residents and, therefore, a lack of opportunities for social mixing" (ibid.: 31).

However, since 2014, there seems to be a gap in the literature on urban design strategies in mixed-income developments – interestingly right at the time when the "poor door" debate surfaced in the press. The gap has partly been filled by a more recent debate on vertical segregation and the more overarching debate of vertical urbanism, which has for the most part evolved in the last decade (i.a. Graham and Hewitt 2013; Graham 2015; Harris 2015, Maloutas and Spyrellis 2016; Marcińczak and Hess 2020; Nethercote and Horne 2016). The concept of vertical urbanism seeks to highlight the vertical expressions of urban power, sovereignty, and space. Some of the studies have primarily focused on vertical urban housing and have occasionally picked up on the "poor door" phenomenon (i.a. Graham 2015). In the context of housing, scholars have focused primarily on vertical segregation (i.a. Maloutas and Spyrellis 2016; Marcińczak and Hess 2020) or gentrification (Graham 2015; Lauermann 2022) caused by luxury high-rise housing development.

Stephen Graham, who refers primarily to the global cities London, New York City, and Tokyo, demonstrates how "current elites are taking over the urban skies through housing towers built for the super-rich in various cities" (Graham 2015: 621). However, in other big cities such as Hong Kong, this can also be the case in reverse, with informal communities settling on rooftops (Wu and Canham 2010). With respect to mixed-income developments, Graham points out that [c]ontroversially, many such towers are designed with separate, utilitarian "poor doors" which shift lower-income tenants far away from the luxurious foyers for affluent residents (Graham 2015: 634). Lauermann argues – similar to Mark Davidson – that these new vertical developments reshape the built environment of a neighborhood, which "leads to a new kinds of social displacement patterns, as older and more 'affordable housing' is replaced, and new architecture encloses vertical space in new ways" (Lauermann 2022: 773). These new ways have, however, rarely been analyzed in detail, other than some studies of social and ethnic stratification of residents in mixed-income developments in Athens, Greece (Maloutas and Spyrellis 2016) and Bucharest, Romania (Marcińczak and Hess 2020). Using large-scale data sets, Thomas Maloutas and Stavros N. Spyrellis (2016), for example, found that the "quality and price differences between the upper floors [which are occupied by wealthier households] and the lower floors were – and continue to be – very significant" (Maloutas and Spyrellis 2016: 34).

However, the debate on vertical segregation and gentrification has generally neglected the urban design elements and physical arrangement of the "affordable housing" units in favor of a focus on the vertical dimension. I, therefore, apply the concept of vertical segregation of residents within new-build developments more broadly, focusing on the physical arrangement and the urban design of mixed-income developments as a product of inclusionary housing policies. The social and ethnic stratification by floor of residence is just one example of what I call vertical segregation by design.

By engaging in the debate on vertical segregation and discussions on the integration of "affordable housing" from the perspective of urban design, I argue that the three aspects mentioned earlier – the degree of mixing of different tenure types, the architectural appearance of tenure types, as well as non-architectural elements – can also be considered in terms of their vertical arrangement. By adding the vertical dimension to the analysis of urban design outcomes of inclusionary housing developments, I illustrate how even the most "integrated" approaches to inclusionary housing continue to show elements of exclusion and segregation.

Vertical Segregation by Design in London and New York City

Inclusionary housing developments in London and New York City produce different degrees of social mixing or ways of how "affordable housing" is included in market-rate housing – from separate blocks or doors to pepper-potting within one building. Local planning authorities in both cities have policies that specify urban design criteria and housing layouts, by which they can direct developers in issues related to the amount of "affordable housing" provided as well as to its affordability, location, and design. Hence, the urban design outcome, as Tiesdell (2004) points out, is often a consequence of the negotiation process between the local planning authorities and the developer. Issues like "affordable housing" distribution, access to amenities for all residents, and equal facilities in both affordable and market-rate apartments can all be issues for negotiation. The urban design strategy may, however, also depend on several other factors that Tiesdell calls "micro design factors" (Tiesdell 2004: 205) such as the size of the development, its proportion as well as the type of "affordable housing" to be provided, or other factors that affect marketability such as riverfront views, nearby parks, or noise pollution caused by traffic. All these issues have often represented possibilities for compromises with the developer in the negotiation process, where local authorities have, for example, lowered their preferences on design issues in exchange for more "affordable housing."

Due to the scope, complexity, and opacity of negotiations in relation to urban design practices, it is difficult to generalize urban design practices of inclusionary housing developments in any specific location, much less predict the actual outcome in advance. As such, I primarily focused my research on studying the built outcomes of negotiations rather than the negotiation process itself and the extent to which certain urban design outcomes of the developments in this chapter encourage or "inhibit the very possibility of mixing" (Davidson 2012: 238).

In the following, I discuss three different expressions of vertical segregation by design in mixed-income developments that I identified from my case studies in New York City and London.

Segregation through Separate Entrances and Tenure Type

The so-called "poor doors" practice is probably the most palpable and shocking form of vertical segregation by design within mixed-income developments. As already touched upon in the Introduction, the "poor doors" have similar expressions in New York City and London, despite different planning systems and inclusionary housing policies.

In both the Extell development on Riverside Boulevard and the Relay development in London, for example, market-rate residents enter through a glassy revolving door that leads to a spacious lobby boasting a chandelier, armchairs, and concierge, while "affordable housing" tenants are forced to go down a narrow alley to enter the building through an unassuming door (Figure 4.1). In compliance with planning legislation, "affordable housing" is "included" in the developments. But through their location, blandness, and simplicity in style, they are marked as distinct and do not fit into the rest of the building that is marked as a luxury high rise. The distancing or spatial distribution of power with unequal symbolic appropriation (Bourdieu [1991] 2018: 110) is further accentuated in the marketing and naming of the separate units of the developments. In London, the name Relay Building refers only to the market-rate units. The "affordable housing" element, in contrast, has its own name: Houblon Apartments. It even has its own separate address: Tyne Street. Similarly, the Extell development in New York City has two

Figure 4.1 (a) Relay Building with separate entrances for the private market residents and (b) the "affordable housing" tenants in Tower Hamlets, London. (c) Riverside Boulevard Development with a main entrance for private market residents and (d) a side alley to the "affordable housing" entrance on the right behind the garbage in Manhattan, New York City. (*Continued*)

Source: © Yuca Meubrink

Figure 4.1 (Continued)

different addresses, a prestige address for the market-rate residents, called One Riverside Park, and another address for the "affordable housing" element, called 40 Riverside Boulevard.

In London, separate entrances, however, are not the only urban design elements that lead to the separation between different income groups. At the Relay Building, the elevator of the "affordable housing" element only goes to the five lowest floors of the 22-story building. The bottom two floors are designated for social rent, and the other three floors are for those households with affordable rent or intermediate housing. Tenants have access only to their own floor. The "affordable housing" element, thus, is not only isolated from the wealthier residents but is also vertically separated by the different types of "affordable housing." In this way, the mingling of affordable residents between floors is discouraged by the design of the building.

Moreover, even though both entrances are protected from uninvited visitors – either through a code as in case of the "poor door" or through a concierge as in the case of the entrance for the higher income residents, I was able to access the "affordable housing" segment more easily – either through asking for access or just walking in with somebody else. In contrast, it is no coincidence that apart from the lobby, the staircases, elevators, or common spaces of the luxury area were not accessible to me as a field researcher. This accentuates the different thresholds inscribed in the urban design and is fortified by security personnel at the entrance.

To summarize, the two examples show how lower-income tenants "included" in the market-rate developments are shifted away from the luxurious street-facing entrance to a side entrance around the corner. There are no common paths or meeting places for the "affordable housing" and market-rate residents until they reach the busy main street. Once on the street, the residents of both entrances disappear into the anonymity of the big city. This architectural separation of tenure types represents an expression of segregation by design. While previously, social segregation took place primarily on a horizontal level through different boroughs, streets, or houses, now additional vertical segregation of social classes is created on different floors within a residential building with different entrances.

Figure 4.2 Baltimore Wharf development on the Isle of Dogs, Tower Hamlets, London.
Source: © Yuca Meubrink

Segregated Beneath and Behind Waterfront Condominiums

There seems to be a tendency in London to visually differentiate not only between market-rate and affordable units by using different entrances but also by type of "affordable housing." The £330 million, 45-story high Baltimore Wharf tower (Figure 4.2) is just one of many luxury residential towers that have been built or will be built on the Isle of Dogs (Bloomfield 2014). According to Tower Hamlets Council, at least 25 percent of the almost 3,000 apartments will be "affordable" housing (Tower Hamlets Council 2012). In the case of the Baltimore Tower, which was developed by Galliard Homes and was completed in 2017, the 366 market-rate apartments were fully sold long before completion, with apartment prices starting at around £480,000 (Spittless 2014). This is significantly more than most London-ers can afford on an average annual income of around £25,000 (see HM Treasury 2014). According to the Guardian, 87 percent of the market-rate apartments were sold to foreign investors (Booth 2017) – a fact that is often criticized in the litera-ture (i.a. Atkinson 2020; Glucksberg 2016) because much of the market-rate hous-ing is simply Pieds-à-terre.

At the foot of the Baltimore Tower, there are seven residential blocks with dif-ferent entrances depending on the socio-economic status of the residents. Most of the blocks are hidden from the waterfront (Figure 4.2). Of the total 1,110 apart-ments, about 35% are "affordable housing" (Tower Hamlets Council 2012). The facades of the apartment blocks show a clear division between the private and rental units as much as between the different types of "affordable housing." The apartments of the private residents have dark brown bricks on the facades, large windows with dark glass panes, and metal balconies.

In contrast, the facades of the apartments of the lower-income residents are beige, the windows smaller and equipped with light panes (Figure 4.3). Of the

Figure 4.3 (a) Private market blocks and (b) the "affordable housing" blocks at the Baltimore Wharf development on the Isle of Dogs, Tower Hamlets, London.

Source: © Yuca Meubrink

roughly 400 "affordable" apartments, only a few come with balconies. These balconies face inward and are mostly located on the long side of the beige part of the building. The different forms of "affordable" housing are spatially separated from each other by different entrances. While the apartments accessible via the courtyard are for social or affordable rent, the apartments accessed on the outer side are for intermediate housing (Meubrink 2016: 159).

Although it appears that the division of the blocks is mainly on the horizontal dimension, the vertical dimension is underscored by the fact that the aesthetic of the market-rate apartments, such as the color of the bricks and large windows, is more consistent with the aesthetic of the Baltimore Tower than the lighter colored "affordable housing" blocks.

But it is not only the design of the facades that shows the division of social classes. The market-rate and "affordable housing" units are linked via two interconnected courtyards that show clear differences in design: The courtyard for the private owners has exits to the driverless Dockland Light Railway station Cross-harbour on one side and Oakland Quay overlooking Canary Wharf on the other. In the center of the courtyard for private residents, there are two rows of concrete flowerbeds and a row of black concrete benches flooded with water. The courtyard appears unused, and there is no seating that would invite people to linger, meet and chat (ibid.). This is also an indication that many of the market-rate residents use their apartments on a temporary basis, if at all, and the developer seems to have known this in advance.

Furthermore, since the private residents have other communal areas available to them within their apartment building, as described in the next subsection of this chapter in more detail, there appears to be no reason for them to meet in the open courtyard, which is technically accessible to all. Thus, the courtyard for the private tenants serves more of a symbolic than practical function.

In the courtyard for "affordable housing" residents, there are some raised flower beds and a playground for children of the families living in the "affordable housing" units (Figure 4.3). In the courtyard of the market-rate units, the children from the playground are, however, not welcomed and will be admonished by the facility manager if they try to cross over from the courtyard of the "affordable housing" units (Fieldnote 2015/08/15).

In New York City, the Williamsburg Community Apartments at The Edge development in Brooklyn show a similar expression of vertical segregation by design. The Edge is one of the few developments that participated in the voluntary inclusionary housing program under the Bloomberg Administration and included 20 percent "affordable housing" in its otherwise market-rate condominium development. Sale prices for the condos range from approximately $400,000 to almost $3 million (Barbanel 2008). Even though the luxury towers and the "affordable housing" components share the same developer, there are clear differences in their architectural design (Figure 4.4).

After systematically observing "poor doors" in London, I developed a clear sensitivity for the architectural differences in the design of "affordable housing" units included in market-rate developments. Similar to the Baltimore Wharf

Figure 4.4 The Edge condominium towers at Williamsburg, Brooklyn standing out from the
        surrounding community.

Source: © Yuca Meubrink

development, the "affordable housing" blocks are adjacent to The Edge luxury
high-rises. While the two blue glassy condominium towers face the new pier as
well as a new park and the Manhattan skyline, the four-story "affordable housing" blocks face onto Kent Avenue that runs through Williamsburg and Greenpoint.
They are lined with brown and beige tiles, have smaller windows, and as far as I
could tell they have no balconies or courtyards (Figure 4.5).

Just as in the case of the Baltimore Wharf development, the "affordable housing"
is denied a waterfront view. The "affordable housing" renters were not allowed to
"pass through the spacious lobbies guarded by doormen, and they had no access to
the Olympic-size glass-covered pool or other amenities" (Susser 2012: 50) included
in the high-rises – a fact that the scholar Ida Susser (2012), who wrote a comprehensive ethnographic study about Greenpoint-Williamsburg in the 1970s and restudied
the area after the 2005 rezoning, had already pointed out two years before the "poor
door" phenomenon was coined and branded a scandal by the press in 2014.

In both cases mentioned above, the "affordable housing" is located beneath and
behind the waterfront condominiums. The social distance despite spatial proximity, thus, is primarily created through the vertical structure of the developments in
which luxury towers and their amenities are inaccessible to the "affordable housing" residents.

Separation through Amenities

In contrast to London, the separation of mandated "affordable housing" elements
on-site through separate entrances or blocks is less commonly found in New York

Figure 4.5 (a) The Edge condominium towers and (b) the adjacent "affordable housing" elements beneath and behind the condominium towers in Williamsburg, Brooklyn.

Source: © Yuca Meubrink

City. The enclosure of amenities and facilities like parking spaces, courtyards,
gyms, pools, or any other common areas are perhaps the most readily apparent form
of "affordable housing" segregation within mixed-income developments in the city.

In response to the "poor door" debate, the New York State Legislature as well
as the de Blasio administration and City Council tried to design their housing programs in such a way as to not stigmatize "affordable housing" residents. Clos-
ing the 421-a program's loophole in 2015, the New York Legislature stated that
"all dwelling units in an eligible multiple dwelling must share the same common

entrances" (New York City Department of Housing, Preservation and Development 2019). It further stated that all units must also share the "common areas" and "shall not be isolated to a specific floor or area of an eligible multiple dwelling" (ibid.). MIH, which was crafted in the midst of the "poor door" uproar, requires that all units must not only share the same entrance but must also have access to the same amenities if the "affordable housing" units and the market-rate buildings are within one building. Nevertheless, developers were still allowed to build a separate low-income building next to the market-rate building as long as its design didn't disadvantage the "affordable housing" tenants.

This legislation in New York's inclusionary housing approach can be characterized by what Groves and Tiesdell both call the most "integrated approach," where the "affordable housing" and the market-rate units are indistinguishable in terms of their appearance and are pepper-potted within the development (Groves 2003: 36; Tiesdell 2004: 204). MIH, however, left private developers the scope to indirectly separate market-rate from "affordable housing" tenants by investing in amenities and facilities that are inaccessible for "affordable housing" tenants. In a mixed-income development in Queens, for example, part of a large balcony was fenced off to "affordable housing" tenants (Briquelet 2014).

From what I've gathered through my research, it would appear that "affordable housing" tenants in New York City have the right to access amenities only when they pay the corresponding fees. Put simply, "affordable housing" tenants' access to shared amenities is curtailed by the presence of fees.

Living in a building in which the "affordable housing" units have been pepper-potted throughout it and are indistinguishable from the market-rate units, one of my interviewees told me that he paid a fee to gain access to shared amenities: "It is about 60 bucks per month, and I thought it does not make a big difference to the already high rent. But not being able to use the various terraces would definitely be a loss" (Interview with Harrison 2017).

I knew Harrison through a circle of friends, who invited me to a potluck on the 13-floor terrace of his 52-story mixed-income tower building in Brooklyn. The terrace was like an open courtyard with a barbecue space and various areas to hang out for those who have paid the monthly fee. Harrison told me that he had to put down an additional deposit of $500 to use the barbecue area.

At one point during the barbecue, Harrison invited everybody to the rooftop terrace to see the sunset. When we got there, there were already other people sitting there, chatting and enjoying the view over the city. It felt like the place to be in the building. On the rooftop, there were also other luxury facilities like a huge TV room, a reading room, and other salon-like areas for just hanging out (Fieldnote 2017/08/19). This is in line with what Graham noted by quoting a study of Michael Panacci:

> In a study of condo developments in Toronto, architecture researcher Michael Panacci found that the top of the building podiums, complete with lighted lagoons and luxury bars, often tend to be more active than the real street below which lies outside the highly securitized building entrance.
>
> (Panacci quoted in Graham 2015: 630)

The surrounding neighborhood in which Harrison lives also felt less active in comparison to the life of the rooftop terrace, which despite not having a bar was a popular place for people to bring their own drinks to spend the evening. Below, the streets were almost empty, full of construction sites, with few shops and no bars. Graham calls the more active life in a condo "a simulated urbanity but one that is elitist, controlled, sterile and removed from the wider public city" (Graham 2015: 630). Since Harrison pays the fee, he has access to this "simulated urbanity" and the gated community created through its restricted access. This resonates with what Davidson points out with respect to the interaction of new residents with their local community. According to him, the on-site facilities accentuate the lack of concern with the local neighborhood (Davidson and Lees 2010: 535). According to Bourdieu, "[o]ne can physically occupy a locale without inhabiting it properly" (Bourdieu [1991] 2018: 111). In this case, Bourdieu was referring primarily to habitual aspects such as wearing the "right" clothes or behaving in the "right" way. But he would probably agree that financial capital, which allows you to pay a fee for amenities, is also a decisive factor in how one inhabits a space. For tenants of "affordable housing," this means that even if their apartments are "pepper-potted" throughout the building, they are still largely excluded from the amenities and the "simulated" community these create. Therefore, many are reduced to mingling with those from other floors in such spaces as the lobby, condo corridors, elevators, and exit-only staircases.

Although facilities and amenities are considered "micro factors" (Tiesdell 2004: 205) in the design of a building, these factors can just as profoundly modify or subvert the possibility of social mixing. The same applies to the distribution of "affordable housing" within a development. The MIH program requires that "affordable housing" should be distributed throughout 65 percent of any given development. However, except for the West Chelsea development on 601 West 29th Street, in none of the developments outlined in Chapter 3 was the issue of amenities discussed during the negotiation process. Regarding the West Chelsea development, the Community Board 4 (CB4) to the City Planning Commission had urged the developer to construct and distribute "affordable housing" units in such a way that its occupants had equal access to the building's amenities, such as courtyards. It further recommended to distribute "affordable housing" throughout at least 80 percent of the proposed building. While the developer ended up committing to providing all apartments with the same finishes and to reducing the amenity fees for lower-income residents during the planning process, the issue of the equal distribution of "affordable housing" units remained a concern. In the public hearing of the Subcommittee of Zoning and Franchise, this concern was raised by several members of the community board:

LEE COMPTON: Good morning Mr. Chairman, my name is Lee Compton, I am the Co-chair of the community board 4's Chelsea Land Use Committee [...]. We are disappointed that the affordable units to be generated by the projects will be segregated in the lower floors, we believe that economic integration can be a vehicle to achieve social and racial integration. We ask that you mandate a broader distribution of affordable units than the applicants have proposed.

(NYC City Council Subcommittee Zoning and Franchise 2018: 112)

JOE RESTUCCIA: My name is Joe Restuccia, I am the Co-chair of the Housing, Health and Human Services Committee of Community Board 4. I want to piggyback again on the issue of this integration. The developers have committed to about 65 or 67 percent integration, the truth is they can do better, their projects economically allow them to do better, they have a philosophical difference with us. We need to push them to get to a higher number because the truth is in these buildings people don't care where you live, it's all about people mixing together and that to us is a big issue, its economic, racial and ethnic integration.

(NYC City Council Subcommittee Zoning and Franchise 2018: 120[1])

With extremely low opportunities for low-income households to move to areas like Chelsea, the Community Board 4 generally puts a lot of emphasis on socio-economic diversity and integration in mixed-income buildings (Manhattan Community Board Four (MCB4) 2018). Since the developer had already agreed to set aside 25 percent of the residential floor area for families making an average of 60 percent AMI, there was little leverage for the city government to increase the amount of "affordable housing." The members of the community board, however, tried to push the distribution percentage to the maximum. As a response, the developer committed about 68 percent, which is slightly more than required, and, thus, this was presented as a success:

JUSTIN SHERMAN: […] In terms of distribution on floors, as I mentioned MIH regulations require distribution of the affordable units on 65 percent, we expect to be able to exceed that currently estimated at 67, 68 percent.

(NYC City Council Subcommittee Zoning and Franchise 2018: 107)

Nevertheless, the distribution of the 25 percent "affordable housing" share across 65 percent of the building does not require an even distribution. It is very likely a vertical hierarchy exists in the building, where the lower-income units are relegated to their lower floors.

Vertical Gentrification of Mixed-Income Housing

The focus of this chapter was to show which ideas of mixing are reflected in the built form and the physical arrangement of mixed-income developments and whether once a development is built, its design would, in principle, create the opportunity for different tenures to meet. I have illustrated how mixed-income developments that include "affordable housing" on-site still show characteristics of segregation by design. I have also shown the major role that the notion of verticality plays in keeping "affordable housing" distinct from market-rate housing within mixed-income developments.

The examples mentioned above show how the urban design of these different forms of "inclusionary" housing discourages the very possibility of mingling of different income groups. The design of the buildings and courtyards or the inclusion of restricted amenities represent barriers for the different classes to socially mix. Some of these design elements have also a historical dimension: views or addresses, for example, have always been an element of social distinction. What is new, however, is the use of such elements of social distinction within a building complex. These design elements predetermine the tectonic relations described by the social scientists Tim Butler and Garry Robson (2003).

Although both cities have persevered in removing barriers to social mixing through certain urban design requirements, inclusionary housing developments continue to limit the opportunities for different tenures to meet and mingle. In London, the exclusion is more direct and visible than in New York City as different tenures are more often visibly separated through the architecture of the entrances, facades, or buildings themselves. In New York City, the exclusion is in most cases less direct and, therefore, less visible than in London. The "affordable housing" units are largely more interspersed with market-rate units than in London. Nevertheless, accessibility is still limited through separate common areas and through the investment in amenities that are restricted to those who can afford the monthly fee.

In both cities, the exclusive physical arrangement of "affordable housing" elements confirms Tiesdell's observation that the decisions concerning the layout and urban design outcome have been oriented toward "protecting the value of the market-rate housing from the perceived negative externality of the affordable units" (Tiesdell 2004: 210). In all cases discussed above, lower-income tenants are given the possibility to enter a space from which they would typically be excluded: luxury housing development. But they have been either hidden from view – by a physical "poor door" or an entirely separate block – or excluded by restricted access to common areas. As Bourdieu noted, these "locus[es] and place[s] occupied by [the lower-income tenants] in appropriated physical space are indicators of [their] position in social space" (Bourdieu [1991] 2018: 107).

This vertical segregation by design, thus, opens – in some cases literally – a back door to vertical gentrification. The image of the vertical city, with its luxury apartments, spacious common areas, and stunning views over the city, remains an elite image. Many affordable housing tenants are denied entry to this gentrified luxury city erected literally above them. In other words, "affordable housing" "integration" tends to lead to vertical segregation by design, and thereby contributes to a vertical enclosure of space.

Interview

Interview Harrison. 2017. Interview with Harrison, affordable housing tenant, conducted on 09/22/2017 by Yuca Meubrink in New York City, USA.

Fieldnotes

Meubrink, Yuca. Observation of the Baltimore Wharf development, Isle of Dogs, Tower Hamlets, London August, 15, 2015.
Meubrink, Yuca. Participant Observation of a barbecue organized by an "affordable housing" tenant, 250 Ashland Place, Fort Green, Brooklyn, New York City, August, 19, 2017.

Note

1 I edited this excerpt slightly for better readability.

References

Atkinson, Rowland. 2020. *Alpha City: How London Was Captured by the Super-Rich*. London: Verso.
Barbanel, Josh. 2008. "A Barometer in Williamsburg." *The New York Times*, March 16. https://www.nytimes.com/2008/03/16/realestate/16deal2.html.
Bloomfield, Ruth. 2014. "London's Tall Building Boom." *The Wall Street Journal*, März. http://www.wsj.com/articles/SB10001424052702304256404579449440635372128.
Booth, Robert. 2017. "Foreign Investors Snapping up London Homes Suitable for First-Time Buyers." *The Guardian*, June 13. https://www.theguardian.com/society/2017/jun/13/foreign-investors-snapping-up-london-homes-suitable-for-first-time-buyers.
Bourdieu, Pierre. [1991] 2018. "Social Space and the Genesis of Appropriated Physical Space." *International Journal of Urban and Regional Research* 42 (1): 106–14. https://doi.org/10.1111/1468-2427.12534.
Bridge, Gary. 2001. "Bourdieu, Rational Action and the Time-Space Strategy of Gentrification." *Transactions of the Institute of British Geographers* 26 (2): 205–16. https://doi.org/10.1111/1475-5661.00015.
Bridge, Gary, Tim Butler, and Loretta Lees. 2012. *Mixed Communities: Gentrification by Stealth?* Bristol: POLICY PR.
Briquelet, Kate. 2014. "Luxury Building Fences off Low-Rent Tenants' Terraces." *New York Post*. December 7. https://nypost.com/2014/12/07/luxury-bulding-fences-off-rent-stabilized-tenants-terraces/.
Butler, Tim. 2003. "Living in the Bubble: Gentrification and Its 'Others' in North London." *Urban Studies* 40 (12): 2469–86. https://doi.org/10.1080/0042098032000136165.
Butler, Tim, and Garry Robson. 2003. *London Calling: The Middle Classes and the Remaking of Inner London*. Berg 3PL.
Davidson, Mark. 2008. "Spoiled Mixture: Where Does State-Led 'Positive' Gentrification End?" *Urban Studies* 45 (12): 2385–405.

————. 2012. "The Impossibility of Gentrification and Social Mixing." In *Mixed Communities: Gentrification by Stealth?*, edited by Gary Bridge, Tim Butler, and Loretta Lees. 233–50. Bristol: Policy Press.

Davidson, Mark, and Loretta Lees. 2010. "New-Build Gentrification: Its Histories, Trajectories, and Critical Geographies." *Population, Space and Place* 16 (5): 395–411.

Glucksberg, Luna. 2016. "A View from the Top: Unpacking Capital Flows and Foreign Investment in Prime London." *City* 20 (April): 238–55. https://doi.org/10.1080/13604813.2016.1143686.

Graham, Stephen. 2015. "Luxified Skies." *City* 19 (5): 618–45.

Graham, Stephen, and Lucy Hewitt. 2013. "Getting off the Ground: On the Politics of Urban Verticality." *Progress in Human Geography* 37 (1): 72–92. https://doi.org/10.1177/0309132512443147.

Groves, Rick, Alan Middleton, Alan Murie, and Kevin Broughton. 2003. *Neighbourhoods That Work: A Study of the Bournville Estate, Birmingham.* Bristol: Policy Press.

Harris, Andrew. 2015. "Vertical Urbanisms: Opening up Geographies of the Three-Dimensional City." *Progress in Human Geography* 39 (5): 601–20. https://doi.org/10.1177/0309132514554323.

HM Treasury. 2014. "Impact on households: distributional analysis to accompany Budget 2014." HM Treasury. https://www.gov.uk/government/uploads/system/uploads/attachment_data/file/293738/budget_2014_distributional_analysis.pdf.

Lauermann, John. 2022. "Vertical Gentrification: A 3D Analysis of Luxury Housing Development in New York City." *Annals of the American Association of Geographers* 112(3): 772–80. https://doi.org/10.1080/02723638.2021.1956112.

Lawton, Philip. 2013. "Understanding Urban Practitioners' Perspectives on Social-Mix Policies in Amsterdam: The Importance of Design and Social Space." *Journal of Urban Design* 18 (1): 98–118. https://doi.org/10.1080/13574809.2012.739546.

Lees, Loretta. 2008. "Gentrification and Social Mixing: Towards an Inclusive Urban Renaissance?" *Urban Studies* 45 (12): 2449–70.

Levin, Iris, Kathy Arthurson, and Anna Ziersch. 2014. "Social Mix and the Role of Design: Competing Interests in the Carlton Public Housing Estate Redevelopment, Melbourne." *Cities* 40 (October): 23–31. https://doi.org/10.1016/j.cities.2014.04.002.

Maloutas, Thomas, and Stavros N. Spyrellis. 2016. "Vertical Segregation: Mapping the Vertical Social Stratification of Residents in Athenian Apartment Buildings." *Journal of Mediterranean Geography* 127 (November): 27–36. https://doi.org/10.4000/mediterranee.8378.

Manhattan Community Board Four (MCB4). 2018. "Letter about 601 West 29th Street, Inclusionary Housing Plan to Maria Torres-Springer, Commissioner of the Department of Housing, Preservation and Development," December 12. https://www1.nyc.gov/html/mancb4/downloads/pdf/december-2018/20-letter-to-hpd-re-601w29th-st-inclusionary-housing-application.pdf.

Marcińczak, Szymon, and Daniel Baldwin Hess. 2020. "Vertical Segregation of Apartment Building Dwellers During Late State Socialism in Bucharest, Romania." *Urban Geography* 41 (6): 823–48.

Meubrink, Yuca. 2016. "Segregation Durch Architektur Als Produkt Londoner Wohnungspolitik." In *Jahrbuch StadtRegion: Schwerpunkt: Planbarkeiten. Herausforderungen Und Dynamiken Räumlicher Planung*, edited by Frank Othengrafen, Brigitta Schmidt-Lauber, Christine Hannemann, Jörg Pohlan and Frank Roost, 152–66. Opladen Berlin Toronto: Budrich, Barbara.

Nethercote, Megan, and Ralph Horne. 2016. "Ordinary Vertical Urbanisms: City Apartments and the Everyday Geographies of High-Rise Families." *Environment and Planning A: Economy and Space* 48 (8): 1581–98. https://doi.org/10.1177/0308518X16645104.

New York City Department of Housing, Preservation and Development. 2019. "Tax Incentives: 421a." NYC Department of Housing Preservation and Development. https://

web.archive.org/web/20190808115734/https://www1.nyc.gov/site/hpd/developers/tax-incentives-421a-main.page (last accessed: January 3, 2022).

Roberts, Marion. 2007. "Sharing Space: Urban Design and Social Mixing in Mixed Income New Communities." *Planning Theory & Practice* 8 (2): 183–204. https://doi.org/10.1080/14649350701324417.

Spittless, David. 2014. "The Docklands, Diamond': First Family Homes in Canary Wharf Are Unveiled." *Evening Standard*, July 23.

Susser, Ida. 2012. *Norman Street: Poverty and Politics in an Urban Neighborhood*, Oxford University Press. http://www.oxfordscholarship.com/view/10.1093/acprof:oso/9780195367317.001.0001/acprof-9780195367317.

Tiesdell, Steven. 2004. "Integrating Affordable Housing Within Market-Rate Developments: The Design Dimension." *Environment and Planning B: Planning and Design* 31 (2): 195–212. https://doi.org/10.1068/b2998.

Tower Hamlets Council. 2012. "Delegated Officer Report for Former London Docklands Sport Area, 36 Limeharbour, London." Tower Hamlets Council. https://development.towerhamlets.gov.uk/online-applications/files/5DCF3541DCC4599D993288EF9367A3D7/pdf/PA_12_01923-724292.pdf.

———. 2014. "Tower Hamlets Approves Canary Wharf Group's Wood Wharf Development." 2014. http://www.towerhamlets.gov.uk/news__events/news/december_2014/wood_wharf_approved.aspx.

Watt, Paul. 2008. "The Only Class in Town? Gentrification and the Middle-Class Colonization of the City and the Urban Imagination." *International Journal of Urban and Regional Research* 32 (1): 206–211. https://doi.org/10.1111/j.1468-2427.2008.00769.x.

Wu, Rufina, and Stefan Canham. 2010. *Portraits from Above: Hong Kong's Informal Rooftop Communities*. Hong Kong: Peperoni Books.

5 Limited Accessibility to and Affordability of "Affordable Housing" as a Form of Gentrification

Throughout this book, I have demonstrated the tensions between "affordable housing" as defined from a policy perspective and housing affordability as experienced by the individual. What is considered "affordable housing" in policy terms may not be affordable to those who are eligible for it. As outlined in the Introduction, housing affordability in housing policy and planning is often expressed in terms of standardized norms of what constitutes 'affordable housing' in New York City and London. Similarly, housing affordability is often defined in terms of the ratio of housing costs to income, which is about one-third of the renter's income. These institutionalized notions of "affordable housing" and affordability often neglect what individuals would consider affordable (Stone 2006).

In this chapter, I explore the tension between the "affordable housing" offered in mixed-income developments and the individual experiences of tenants living in "affordable housing" as well as people looking for "affordable housing." In Chapter 4, I examined how the urban design and the physical structure of inclusionary housing developments can exclude "affordable housing" tenants from accessing certain amenities and in turn impede the possibility of mixing "affordable housing" tenants with market-rate residents. Complementing this, I demonstrate in this chapter how alongside certain income percentages and numerical targets, there are other factors that play a role in excluding lower-income households from gaining access to "affordable housing."

I argue that there are several structurally embedded factors that make it harder for people of lower incomes to gain access to "affordable housing" than for moderate- and middle-class income people. Similarly, I argue that there are several factors that make it harder for people on lower incomes to afford an affordable housing despite being eligible. In both cases, this results in an influx of wealthier people into "affordable housing." This limited accessibility to and affordability of the "affordable housing" apartments, thus, reproduces rather than counteracts class patterns of privilege and inequality.

In the first section, I focus on the accessibility of "affordable housing" units available. I discuss the evident gap between who is eligible for "affordable housing" and who ends up getting an "affordable housing" apartment. By using the NYC housing lottery as an example, I examine individual experiences and struggles to get an "affordable housing" apartment. The chapter then moves forward to the individual

DOI: 10.4324/9781003468479-6

experiences of "affordable housing" residents both in New York City and London by examining whether affordability continued to be a problem for those able to get hold of an "affordable housing" apartment. Each section illustrates how access to as well as affordability of "affordable housing" for those on the lower end of the income band is more limited than for those on the higher ends of the income band.

In terms of my sources, I primarily used ethnographic methods such as interviews and participant observation in this chapter. I interviewed several residents in "affordable housing" as well as a housing association director in charge of the "affordable housing" lottery process at 461 Dean Street, Brooklyn, New York City. I chose this housing lottery in particular because I was able to observe this process by attending informational sessions and also interviewing a "winner" in that specific housing lottery. In addition, I support my empirical findings with data obtained from press articles as well as secondary reports and literature.

Accessible for Whom?

Who gets "affordable housing" is a very complex question, and, therefore, is difficult to answer. What types of households end up living in "affordable housing"? Besides the fact that the profile of new tenants depends obviously on who applies, it largely depends on the allocation system. The allocation systems in both cities work very differently. However, in both, developers have no ability to select who will live in the "affordable housing" units. The selection process is usually administratively based and conducted by the local authority or housing associations.

In New York City and many other cities in the US, such as in Boston, Chicago, or San Francisco, it is common to allocate "affordable housing" through a lottery process. The "affordable housing" lottery in New York City is organized by housing associations that are usually government-sponsored or non-profit across all five boroughs. All interested households must apply through a housing lottery website, which is officially known as NYC Housing Connect[1]. For each development, housing associations have to hold a separate housing lottery, and to qualify, one needs to fall within a specific income range based on the AMI. The range varies from lottery to lottery.

In the following, I critically examine the NYC housing lottery system, which claims that each applicant has an equal chance of selection. In particular, I illustrate how the system's allocation procedure is structured, and how its structure fails to provide for those with the greatest housing needs. In doing so, I will show to what extent the American Dream as an ideal of equality of opportunity is associated with this allocation procedure. In doing so, I identify six factors that show the limited access that low-income households have to "affordable housing." These factors include (1) the sheer number of applications and the associated low odds of obtaining "affordable housing," (2) the lack of "affordable housing" for families with four or more members; (3) the income gaps between the income bands; (4) the bureaucratic hurdles related to required documentation; (5) threshold issues related to automatic exclusion if income is too low or if the 30 percent rule is applied; and (6) the uneven distribution of "affordable housing" within the different income bands.

This unequal management of the NYC housing lottery shows how an allocation system shapes the local politics of housing by applying unfair constraints on certain applicants. The outcome of this allocation system is, thus, an emergent politics of housing in which "affordable housing" is used as a gentrification and displacement mechanism.

This analysis of the NYC allocation system is, however, not intended as a statement about the London allocation system. The allocation system in London – in contrast to the NYC housing lottery system – is more segmented, works differently from borough to borough, and operates on priority listings or first-come-first-serve bases. In addition, the allocation process in London differs depending on the type of "affordable housing." If one wants to rent an apartment with social rent, one must apply through its local authority, which places one on a waiting list called Housing Register. Using a range of criteria that may vary from borough to borough, the local authority then determines the priority of the applicants. The allocation system of affordable rent functions similarly, only that in this case it is housing associations that determine the priority list. Likewise, to get a shared ownership apartment, one has to register with the Help to Buy agent, who then sees whether one is eligible for properties that one wants to apply for. Although my research suggests that it is likely that the London allocation system also includes unfair constraints on applicants in most need of housing, further research would be needed to get a precise assessment of the London allocation system.

The Inequality of the NYC Housing Lottery System[2]

"It is kind of like a ball that rolls around," says the executive director of a prominent housing association[3] in response to my question about how the "affordable housing" lottery process works. The non-profit housing association has a long tradition in community-based organizing and today develops and manages housing for low- and moderate-income residents throughout New York. It is further one of several other "affordable housing" providers that manage the application processes of NYC "affordable housing" lotteries.

The interview took place in the director's small office on the 11th floor of a 23-story office building in Downtown Brooklyn. While waiting in a small anteroom for her to receive me, I imagined what it would be like to sit here while waiting to be interviewed after being selected in the housing lottery: What must it be like to sit here full of hope for a better and possibly affordable apartment, and at the same time full of fear that you might somehow mess up the interview? A few minutes later, a friendly young assistant led me into the director's office, who was sitting at her desk and barely visible behind stacks of papers. As I learned in the course of the interview, these were the applications from people whose numbers had been drawn in the housing lottery for 461 Dean Street in Prospect Heights, Brooklyn. About 83,000 households applied for the 181 affordable units available (Fieldnote 2016/08/24).

This sheer number of applications presents the first barrier to people applying for the housing lottery as it minimizes the chance of receiving an "affordable housing" apartment. The director explained to me that applications have significantly increased since 2012, when applications for the housing lottery could be filled out and submitted online. One of the main reasons she cited for this is the fact that once an account is created and a single online application is completed, it is fairly easy to reapply for other housing lotteries. It literally only requires one click. Nevertheless, the director believes that marketing the apartments is still very important. While the city sets some basic mandatory criteria for circulating information about the appropriate housing lottery citywide, the director is committed to doing more. She attends community meetings, schools and churches to make sure the neighborhood knows about the preference they receive in the "affordable housing" lottery. But it's a "double-edged sword," she acknowledged, because "on the one hand, the more you inform, the more people apply, but on the other hand, we're trying to focus on the local neighborhood to maintain or increase socioeconomic and ethnic diversity" (Interview with the Executive Director 2016).

I first met the director at an informational meeting for the "affordable housing" lottery for 461 Dean Street in Fort Greene, Brooklyn, which she moderated. 461 Dean Street was the first building of the $4,9 billion Pacific Park development to be completed. The developer, Forest City Ratner, rebranded the site – formerly known as Atlantic Yards – as Pacific Park and planned to build 16 high-rise buildings and the Barclays Center arena. The housing association signed the original housing pledge with Forest City Ratner (Oder 2016).

At the informational meeting, the auditorium was packed. The almost exclusively Black American audience reflected a large part of the population from the nearby of Bedford Stuyvesant. Historically, the Bedford-Stuyvesant neighborhood, which remains marked by poverty to this day, has been a cultural center for African Americans in Brooklyn. Similar to Bushwick to the east, Fort Greene to the west, and Crown Heights and Prospect Heights to the south, this neighborhood is increasingly subject to gentrification processes, which is particularly evident in the displacement of African Americans from the area. Nevertheless, Bedford Stuyvesant remains a predominantly Black African community, according to a 2015 study by the New York City Department of Health. About 33 percent of people live below the poverty line, which is about one-third more than New York as a whole. Meanwhile, the unemployment rate is at 17 percent, the incarceration rate is more than double that of the New York area as a whole, and the rent burden is about 55 percent of monthly income (NYC Health 2015).

Newly constructed, mixed-income buildings, such as the 32-story high-rise on Dean Street, largely attract higher-income families to the area, contributing to the gentrification of the neighborhood and the displacement of the surrounding population. The housing lottery info session in the nearby neighborhoods is intended to encourage the resident population to apply for the new 'affordable' housing. The director, therefore, touted the apartments to the audience in a PowerPoint presentation as "beautiful apartments with fantastic views, parquet floors, and gorgeous courtyards" (Fieldnote 2016/05/16).

The rent for the apartments is based on income and is divided into income levels, ranging from $20,675 (for a studio i.e. living and kitchen area in one room) to $144,960 (for a two-bedroom apartment) in the case of 461 Dean Street. As the director explained the different income brackets, the attendees of the info session began asking questions. The questions addressed the hurdles for those on low income to access "affordable housing" that I identified during my research, such as the number of rooms, affordability, and income gaps as well as the difficulty in obtaining the necessary documents.

One of the first questions was related to what I identified as the second barrier: the number of bedrooms. With regards to the availability of "affordable housing" at 461 Dean Street, there were no three-bedroom apartments on offer: "Does this mean that a family with more than four members cannot apply?" asked a woman from the audience. "Yes, that's true," the director admitted, while at the same time advising those families to wait for the next housing lottery, which would soon open at 535 Carlton Avenue, around the corner from 461 Dean Street, where three-room apartments would be available (Fieldnote 2016/05/16). The new building on Carlton Avenue had three-bedroom apartments – 15 out of 297 apartments, to be exact, which is about five percent. But only one of those 15 three-bedroom apartments was in the lowest income bracket, meaning for households of up to six people with annual incomes between $29,863 and $42,040. Meanwhile, there were seven three-bedroom apartments in the highest income bracket for households between $129,258 and $173,415 annually.

Since there are generally only specifications regarding the percentage of the floor space of "affordable" housing to be included and average affordability levels, but not the size or concrete affordability levels, it is more profitable for developers to build primarily studios and one-bedroom apartments in the higher income brackets than two- or three-bedroom units. In the case of 461 Dean Street, for example, about eighty percent of the apartments are studios and one-bedroom apartments, and only six percent of the apartments are in the lowest income bracket. Statistics in this regard also show that "housing lotteries favor young single people"(Weaver 2016). According to an article in the online newspaper DNAinfo, about 40 percent of those who obtained an "affordable" apartment through the housing lottery between 2013 and 2015 were between 25 and 34 years of age, of whom half were single, and only four percent over 62 (Weaver 2016).

Other questions from the audience touched upon the issue of income gaps, which I identified as the third barrier. Applicants are placed into certain income tiers when they apply. But there are gaps between the income bands. This caused a stir among the participants at the information session, as it is a factor that excludes certain people from the lottery. Income bands vary from building to building, which is why it is a stated goal of the director to minimize the gaps between these income bands set by developers in agreement with the city. In the case of Dean Street, there were nonetheless gaps of up to $19,000 between two rather lower-income levels, while the income bands tended to overlap in the higher-income ranges. The result is that the lottery is skewed towards households on higher incomes than those on lower ones. When participants realized that if they fell into these gaps, they would not be eligible at all, some people got up and left the room, obviously angry or disappointed.

The topic that really riled those attending the most was what I considered the fourth barrier: the obtaining of documents upon selection in the housing lottery. While the director was still reading the list of documents to have at hand for the interview, the participants were already raising their arms for questions. Applicants have to submit several documents from their employer, their bank, and their landlord to disclose their monthly salaries, their tenant files, and their creditworthiness. In particular, questions are asked about their financial situation or criminal record, as applicants can be rejected if they have debt obligations (including rent or credit card payments) or a criminal record. It is also possible for housing associations to reject applicants based on low creditworthiness alone, as this can be seen as an indicator of financial instability. The director of the housing association pointed out that some of the documents – such as a birth certificate – may be difficult to gather for those born outside the US and/or who do not have one and recommended that those affected deal with such formalities as soon as possible (Fieldnotes 2016/05/16).

Renting the American Dream

When New York City Councilmember Robert E. Cornegy, who represents parts of Brooklyn's Bedford Stuyvesant and Crown Heights districts, entered the info session room to address his constituency, he echoed the director's rhetoric. In an almost preachy tone, he told the audience, "you have to stay engaged, it is a long process, you have to focus and commit to it. This is the American Dream" (Fieldnotes 2016/05/16).

By referring to "winning" the housing lottery as the fulfillment of the American Dream, he invoked an American ideal that is considered a key aspect of American culture. The American Dream is a national ethos that has its origins in the founding of the nation and the mystification of life on the frontier, where an opportunity for prosperity and individual success should be available to all, regardless of social and economic differences. Much like the Declaration of Independence (1776), which states that "all men are created equal" and have the "inalienable right to life, liberty, and the pursuit of happiness," the American Dream also makes this optimistic promise of equal opportunity, meaning that anyone and everyone can succeed with hard work and determination. The goals of the dream, or the notion of success, changed throughout American history. While self-realization and the pursuit of economic and social prosperity were the central goals of the American dream before World War II, from the 1950s onward, success was defined primarily by the attainment of certain status symbols, such as a car or homeownership. Owning a house on one's own lot and being able to move about freely by car became an integral part of the American dream, reflected primarily in suburban life (Jobs 2014: 20).

According to social scientist Richard Florida, in large, expensive cities like New York, where housing is increasingly unaffordable, the notion of "renting" an apartment in the city has recently become for many a "viable path to their achieving of the American Dream" (Florida 2013). Like hardly any other city, New York stands for the idea of the American Dream – be it the Statue of Liberty as a symbol of freedom and justice, the Empire State Building as once the tallest building in the world, or the Rockefeller Center as a sign of self-realization and the inconceivable wealth of an ambitious businessman. Thus, for most New Yorkers, "winning" the housing lottery seems to literally be a fulfillment of the American dream of owning a home – to use the rhetoric of politician Cornegy.

At first glance, a lottery and the American Dream seem far apart, if not the opposite. While a lottery is based on luck and chance, the American dream is imagined to be achieved only through self-discipline and hard work. On second glance, however, both are based on the liberal ideal of the right to equal opportunity. This means, in theory, that everyone has the opportunity to 'win' the lottery regardless of one's socioeconomic background. By invoking the ideal of the American Dream in the context of the housing lottery, Council Member Cornegy sought to inspire those present at the meeting to believe that through self-discipline and hard work, by continuously applying and submitting all required documentation on time, each and every one of them had an equal chance to "win" an "affordable housing" apartment.

The Unaffordable American Dream

The reality of people in need of "affordable housing" in New York is, however, different from what the political rhetoric of the American Dream implies. Even though the director is aware of this fact, she did not tell the attendees during the information session that everybody with an income below 30 percent of the AMI – defined as extremely low-income – is not eligible for "affordable housing":

> Basically, you are lying to them, right? You are like: 'Sure apply here but in fact, you can't get in. [...] So the first thing that happens when you print out the lottery log is you reject everyone for being too poor.'
> (Interview with the Executive Director 2016)

That means that everybody who is below the threshold of the lowest income band gets immediately rejected. In the case of 461 Dean Street, the threshold was about $22,000 (annual income) for a one-bedroom apartment. This is what I identified as the fifth barrier to accessibility. "You can't imagine," she goes on, "we send out like a thousand rejection letters" (Interview with the Executive Director 2016). Yet, as the director explained to me, there is another hidden factor behind why people get rejected. As described earlier, the household income must fall between certain income bands. But additionally, another rule is applied: the rule that rent should not be over 30 percent of your income. By looking at an example from the "affordable housing" units available at 461 Dean Street, a one-bedroom apartment for two persons costs roughly between $28.000 and $36.000 (income band 2). Thus, when underwriting the loan, the 30 percent rule is set right in the middle at about $32.000. That is how the rent is calculated, and, in this case, the rent is set at $770. As the director later admitted, "So, the problem is that automatically when you do that, the people at the bottom of the band, won't get an apartment because you are applying the 30% rule" (ibid.). In other words, if the household income is about $28,000 and the person applies for a one-bedroom apartment, that person is likely to be rejected as 'too poor' because of the 30 percent rule, even though he or she is officially eligible for "affordable housing."

Besides these inherently structural reasons, there are several other reasons for why people aren't eligible. Harrison, a man in his mid-30s whom I interviewed and who had invited me to the barbecue I described in Chapter 4, told me what he thought might be the main reason for rejection:

> I think the most common reason though, is that between the time of applying and getting an interview your life changes. Like one guy had applied legitimately alone and then lived with his girlfriend a year later when he got pulled. I mean it was just him on the application, so they weren't eligible anymore. But he wasn't trying to trick anybody, and he was willing to pay the higher rent with the higher income, but he wasn't eligible. Another woman applied when she was living in this community board district for this building actually, because she was living in the area but again nine or ten months later when she was finally pulled, she'd moved down the street and just literally over the border of the community board district, and then she wasn't eligible. She got pushed to the bottom of the list.
>
> (Interview with Harrison 2017)

Harrison has been selected in the lottery at 461 Dean Street. After constantly being held off for a year, he summarized this time period as follows:

> It is an exhausting and really difficult process, and every time I went it was always very intense in the space, piles of papers everywhere, people losing things, applicants were crying and so unhappy, other applicants angry, many applicants like myself just afraid and quiet and trying to be respectful. It was a frustrating situation. […] It is an enormous bureaucracy and you are treated as… Yeah, I mean everything you say is very suspect. I feel, like, the people who interview you, the way the process is set up, they are assuming that you are lying to them and you have to prove that you are innocent. Kind of guilty until proven otherwise. And that adds to the stress, the anxiety. And you think about it every single day like a co-worker in my office was also going through the exact same process just a few months behind me, and she is reliving everything I went through, which is every time your phone buzzes in your pocket, you think it's them calling, every few minutes checking your e-mail, there are message boards online where people share information about specific buildings or about the whole lottery process, and it is addictive looking at them. You are on the hook for this thing, and you are doing everything you can, and it's kind of a competition and there is so much uncertainty and for months and months you are literally thinking about it first thing when you wake up and the last thing when you go to sleep. And I thought it's just me, but the more I talk to people, I realize it's many people going through that process.
>
> (Interview with Harrison 2017)

Another woman that I interviewed – who was self-employed – told me that she got rejected for not being able to show on her paychecks the estimated income for the entire year since the year was not over yet. Moreover, on account of her last three years of tax returns, she was about $300 short for the income band she applied for, and, thus, was immediately told in the interview that she was not eligible:

> He did the math and he was like: "Sorry, you didn't make up enough money." [...] I don't think he asked me anything else. He just sat there, did the math and then he just collected all my paperwork and was like: "Well, we need to keep this because sometimes they audit us." So, he took all my paperwork. But I was really bummed. It was studios and one-bedrooms on 43rd and 11th [in Midtown, Manhattan] for like $800 with a washer and dryer.
>
> (Interview with Jenna 2017)

The fact that many people, even after being notified that they have been selected in the housing lottery, are rejected further along in the process – whether because they cannot get the documents together in time, have moved to a different part of town, their income has changed over time or somehow do not pass the interview – illustrates how the lottery's notion of equal opportunity for all is pure illusion. As argued earlier, it is the structurally embedded barriers mentioned above that make it harder for people in lower-income brackets to gain housing through the lottery. Added to this is the fact that no "affordable housing" is being built through the inclusionary housing program for people with annual incomes below $20,000. For them, the promise of all New Yorkers having the equal opportunity to get their hands on "affordable" housing and fulfill the American Dream degenerates into an empty one. The fact that many low-income people are now aware of this is clearly illustrated by what the director said later in the interview:

> Like, when I go out and do this training or outreach in low-income neighborhoods, not the 461 Dean St. neighborhood, but like out in Bushwick, not the gentrified Bushwick, you know, the real Bushwick, and I used to go out and would say like: "So how many have applied for the lottery?" Then everyone would raise their hand. But then, how many have heard back? Nobody heard back. Nobody... you know, maybe one person got an apartment – ridiculous. Now, when I go and ask how many people have applied, nobody raises his or her hand. And I was so confused, and I said: "You guys aren't applying for these lotteries?" And they were like, well we are too poor, we stopped applying. And like, I make $20.000 and [...] I looked on the website at how many apartments for [...] families making $20.000 or $24.000 there were, and there were none.
>
> (Interview with the Executive Director 2016)

At the same time, the chances of "winning" the housing lottery are much higher for households with incomes of up to about $150,000 per year than in the low- or middle-income range (Oder 2017). This is the sixth barrier to accessibility that I identified during my research. For these higher-income households, the American Dream is a real possibility. As the Dean Street housing lottery shows, for the two highest income levels, the application numbers were sometimes far below 5,000, while in the lower-income bands they ranged between 15,000 and 25,000. In other words, applicants in the highest income levels are up to five times more likely to have their number come up in the housing lottery than applicants in the lowest income level.

The lottery held at 461 Dean Street, with about 83,000 households applying, was the largest lottery held in New York City at that time. However, this high number of applications has become standard for newly built, mixed-income development projects in Brooklyn or Manhattan today. The housing lottery conducted a little later by the same housing association at 535 Charlton Street drew more than 93,000 applications (Bellafante 2017). The 53-story apartment building at 250 Ashland Place, a new development near Downtown Brooklyn and a stone's throw from 461 Dean Street received more than 82,000 applications for its 282 "affordable housing" units (Laterman 2016). In Manhattan, more than 104,000 households applied for 160 Madison Avenue in Midtown, just a block from the Empire State Building (Zimmer and Chiwaya 2015), and some 88,000 households applied for 55 "affordable" apartments located on 40 Riverside Boulevard on the Upper West Side (Navarro 2015). "You might as well play the lottery, you probably have a better chance of winning," the director joked in the interview, before adding, more seriously: "But that's the reality of people in need in New York" (Interview with the Executive Director 2016).

The fact that people stopped applying altogether, or are rejected because they are "too poor" or because they cannot provide the documentation required for 'affordable housing' points to a tenant selection strategy by housing associations that are based on control and stigmatization. Still, many low-income tenants will feel that it is their fault when their applications are rejected. In this way, the lottery system, which not only favors higher-income tenants, but, more perversely, proclaims itself to be a system open to all, is able to pass a structural problem as an individual one.

In the next section, I will show that even if people are eligible and lucky enough to get an "affordable housing" apartment, it does not necessarily mean that they *feel* that they can actually afford it.

Affordable for Whom?

A first glance, the answer to the question above seems quite simple – institutionalized income norms and standards define who is eligible for "affordable housing." Measured against these standards and norms, one would assume that households that have managed to successfully go through an intensive application process, should not experience housing affordability problems,[4] yet – as I demonstrate in this section – they often do. Examining whether people living in "affordable housing" apartments in New York City and London face affordability problems, I focus primarily on moderate to median-income households as those are the ones that inclusionary housing is increasingly designed for. In doing so, I identify four structurally embedded factors that cause tenants of "affordable housing" in the lower-income range to experience greater affordability issues than residents of "affordable housing" in the upper-income range. These include (1) the social norms that create exclusivity; (2) the market dynamics that drastically reduce affordability over time as prices rise; (3) the lack of long-term preservation of the 'affordable housing' units; and (4) specific contract-related disadvantages.

"Money Is Tight in My Affordable Apartment": Residents' Experiences of
Affordability of Their "Affordable Housing" in New York City

"Money is tight in my affordable apartment" (E-mail Harrison 2018). This was how Harrison described his housing situation about a year after he had moved into one of these newly built, mixed-income developments in Brooklyn. It was not at 461 Dean Street but one around the corner at 250 Ashland Place. As he is in the rather higher income bands, he was lucky enough to get be drawn not only once but twice in the housing lottery, which gave him the privilege to choose the apartment he preferred. This shows again how people with relatively higher incomes have a higher chance of "winning" the "affordable housing" lottery than people with lower household incomes.

His sentence above intrigued me though, as it sums up the problem in a simple, clear, and straightforward statement: "Affordable housing" does not mean that it is actually affordable to the people eligible for it. And while this is nothing new, and unaffordability has been a constant concern in the gentrification literature, in particular for low-income tenants (i.a. Minton 2017, Stein 2018; Watt 2018), I was still surprised to hear this statement from Harrison who is considered to have a moderate- to middle-income. In New York City, moderate- to middle-income translates into an annual income of between $80,000 and $130,000 for a single household. Harrison pays about $2,150 a month for his one-bedroom, "affordable housing" flat, excluding the fees for amenities such as access to the rooftop terrace or the fitness studio. He is a senior policy advisor for the office of the Mayor of New York City and annually earns about $78,000.

With his annual income, Harrison qualified for income band two, which has set the annual income earnings of a single household for a one-bedroom apartment at between $74,983 and $99,825. But if you apply the "30 percent rule," a different picture emerges: described earlier as the fifth barrier to accessibility, the 30 percent rule is set right in the middle of the respective income band. In the case of income band two, for which Harrison is eligible, the annual income is set at about $87,404. That means that if your income is on the higher end of the band, you pay even less than 30 percent, but if your income is at the lower end of the income band, such as in the case of Harrison, you spend more than 30 percent of your income on rent. That leads to a situation in which even people like Harrison – not to mention people with much lower incomes – feel that they cannot financially afford their "affordable" flat despite having a moderate income.

Still, what all my interview partners in New York City had in common is that they were delighted about their luck to "win" the housing lottery and to get a new and clean flat in one of Manhattan's or Brooklyn's most trendy neighborhoods, while paying only a fraction of the general market-rates. One of my interviewees, for example, said: "I tell people that I won the lottery. Yeah, I am a little braggy (laughing)" (Interview with James 2017).

The question of affordability, however, was rarely expressed explicitly. It was more often mentioned as a side note when talking about the extra monthly fees for the amenities or other additional fees that my interviewees did not anticipate. This issue is related to the first factor that I summarized as social norms. One of my interviewees who has an "affordable housing" flat in Hell's Kitchen, Manhattan, remarked that before moving in, he had not considered that it is customary to tip each concierge about $50 to $100 at Christmas, and that he actually cannot afford it (Interview with Max 2016). When asked about how he feels about living in a building with a concierge, another interviewee living in an "affordable housing" flat in Fort Green, Brooklyn, had this to say:

> At Christmas time, I think, it is expected to tip everyone. I am not sure about the amount. So, I need to research on that. I have a friend whose parents have, like, a fancy building in Midtown. I mean this is a condo, so they own it, but I think everyone is expected to kind of have money. He said they give everyone on average like $100 and there are like 25 people. And so, I was like, oh gosh, I can't afford that. [...] I would have to move out on January First if I do that (laughing).
>
> (Interview with James 2017)

For James, it was his first time living in a building with a doorman. Although at the beginning he was a little bit unsure how to act around the doorman, overall he was happy to live in a building with a doorman: "It took me a while to adapt. I mean, do I say hello every time? If they are busy, do I just walk by or is that rude or whatever? But it is nice, and they are very friendly guys" (Interview with James 2017).

In terms of interacting with other tenants in the building, James told me that he knew two people before moving in:

> Yeah, I knew two people. I think you've met them at the party, Kathe and Mike. They are paying market rate. They have a one-bedroom on the 17th floor. I haven't actually visited them on their floor since I moved in.
>
> (Interview with James 2017)

As mentioned in Chapter 4, I was invited to a barbecue on a terrace in a building where I also met James. It was not so surprising then that James knew people who could afford to pay market-rate in a newly-built development given his income and his job as a contractor for the federal government. It also confirmed what I have noticed about the accessibility of 'affordable housing' units: The lottery's 'winners' are mainly moderate to middle-income earners, as more affordable apartments are reserved for them. And based on my interviews, it was mainly young aspiring professionals living in the many studios and one-bedroom apartments. At 250 Ashland Place in Brooklyn, for example, where James and Harrison live, 60 percent of the 282 affordable apartments are studios and one-bedrooms, most of which are for households earning more than $70,000 annually.

It is further not surprising that James has never visited Kathe and Mike in their market-rate apartment, as the structure and the design of the building – as demonstrated in Chapter 4 – do not encourage such mixing.

Everyone I interviewed in New York City living in studios or one-bed apartments were either singles or couples in their early thirties, and at the beginning of their careers. None of them had children. On a methodological note, this might also have to do with the fact that it was easier for me to get access to these kinds of people through word of mouth, or that this particular demographic might be more open to and interested in academic research. Yet it confirms my findings on the lottery regarding who primarily benefits from these newly-built, "affordable housing" units. However, further research on the socioeconomic status of people living in "affordable housing" in New York City is needed.

"It Is Better to Buy as Much as You can in the First Place": Residents' Experiences on the Affordability of Their Shared Ownership Homes in London

The findings in London are similar. According to one report, most people entering shared ownership are "typically aged between 16 and 45, and most enter the sector either as new households or from private rented housing (Clarke et al. 2008). It further shows that tenants in intermediate housing are singles or couples without children (ibid.). This is also reflected in my selection of interviewees: from all the tenants I interviewed living in one of the newly-built mixed-income development buildings, most entered the shared ownership scheme to get onto the house-buying ladder. All were first-time buyers and in their late twenties or early thirties. One of my interviewees, who lives in a one-bedroom with her husband in Islington, described the situation in her building as follows:

> In my case, as you can see with our neighbors, we're all the same age. So obviously, it's like young couples with one kid or without kids at all, looking for something that they can afford to start with. So, I would call it more starting flats for young couples rather than affordable living.
>
> (Interview with Clara 2015)

Clara and her husband, who immigrated from the Czech Republic a couple of years ago, own 100 percent of their apartment in the shared ownership scheme. They initially bought 75 percent of their apartment and were able to "staircase" to 100 percent within a year. According to Clara, it was the "best move" (Interview with Clara 2015) to buy 75 percent right at the beginning, as the price of the additional share depended on the future overall market value. When they bought the 75 percent share of the apartment in 2013, the price of their 55sqm one-bedroom apartment was £275,000. A year later, when they wanted to buy the remaining

25 percent share, a surveyor from the Housing Association came in to evaluate the property and told them that the value of the property had risen to £305,000. The value of the property had increased by £30,000 within 12 months. That is an increase of around eleven percent of the original price.

Clara's example relates to the second factor that I call market dynamics. Clara continued by saying that "it is better to buy as much as you can in the first place" (Interview with Clara 2015), not only because the price of the property was likely to go up in the future but because there were several additional costs that one has to pay when buying another share:

> It's like every single time you go to apply for another mortgage, you take this bank fee, which is like £1000. The surveyor is £500 or something and there are other costs.
>
> (Interview with Clara 2015)

As such, people who are able to quickly buy their full share of the affordable apartment make a good investment, while people who need several years to stair-case to 100 percent very likely have to pay more. The shared ownership scheme, thus, tends to give an advantage to people who are on the upper end of the allowed income band or at the beginning of their careers. Clara, for example, states that it is primarily people at the beginning of their careers who seem to have discovered the shared ownership scheme as an investment:

> We have lots of friends who are bankers and some of them are in the shared ownership scheme as well, which is quite funny because they are bankers and everyone knows that bankers have the best salaries ever. But if it's just one person applying for the program and she's not yet working in a bank for more than a year or something, she would exactly fit within the salary range, so she could apply. […] And within a few months they buy the whole thing, they put it on the market and they sell it off and that's it, end of the story. And within two years, you have the property gone.
>
> (Interview with Clara 2015)

In this way, "affordable housing" is lost quickly as the property owner can sell the apartment on the open market after several years. This means that there is no long-term protection of the newly-created "affordable housing" units, which I identified as the third problem of limited affordability. In other words, it is a form of privatization of "affordable housing," similar to the Right to Buy council housing program that was introduced under the Thatcher Administration. While the Right to Buy council housing program was implemented for those living in a council flat and wanting to buy their apartment, the shared ownership scheme is catered more to helping people with moderate incomes of up to about £66,000 to get on the housing ladder. Similar to the Right to Buy council housing program, however, it leads many to use "affordable housing" as an asset rather than a place to live, and, in turn, leads to a housing shortage for people on lower incomes.

For people like my interview partner Tom, the hope and joy he had when buying into the shared ownership scheme has slowly vanished and turned into something close to hopelessness. Tom might be one of those tenants for whom the shared ownership scheme was officially designed: first-time buyers who are not able to afford a full mortgage. He used to live with his wife and his parents in a small, former council flat and was delighted by the thought of being able to buy his first property together with his wife. However, as it turns out Tom might never be able to own the apartment. Although he and his wife have a steady income and, as he points out, can call themselves lucky in this regard, the price of Tom's and his wife's apartment in Peckham, in the London borough of Southwark, has gone up by about two-thirds of the original price. While the property value was £180,000, when they bought the first 25 percent share, a few years later, the price had already risen to £300,000. Tom described his feelings of anxiety and frustration in relation to "staircasing" as follows:

> To make sure I can afford to buy the whole place one day, I have to think about it and I have to keep track of it. So, every month, I am doing the calculations on a spreadsheet. And every month I realize it will be harder to ever buy another part of my apartment.
>
> (Interview with Tom 2017)

As the valuation of shared ownership schemes is determined on 100 percent of the current market value, even if the tenant only buys a share of the apartment, "staircasing" can and may very well be unaffordable for tenants like Tom. While their rent is still based on up to 80 percent of the market value, his "affordable" home is no longer affordable. This is especially frustrating to him when he realized that his neighbors, such as Patricia, are more quickly able to "staircase" to 100 percent ownership. Patricia lives with her husband and little daughter in a two-bedroom apartment in the same building as Tom. They were – similar to Clara – able to buy the whole apartment within a couple of years – something Tom could only dream of at the moment. In addition, the lease makes the shared owner the homeowner of the apartment – even if it is only partially – and, thus, responsible for all the repairs and maintenance in their home. This issue relates to the fourth factor that I call contractual obligations. While the Housing Association remains responsible for repairs and maintenance on the structure of the house, the shared owner is responsible for anything inside their own home. This further adds to the costs of a shared ownership apartment.

Another aspect that both Clara and Tom shared was the issue of changes in life circumstances, primarily with respect to family planning. For Clara, it was clear that she did not want to live in her apartment forever: "Obviously these flats are small. You don't want to live here until you're 70 or so" (Interview with Clara 2015). But while for Clara, it seemed a rather minor factor and not coupled with uncertainty or family planning, Tom expressed himself differently. Even though he and his wife wanted to have kids, Tom stated that "family planning is totally out of the question right now" (Interview with Tom 2017).

Tom's situation can be described as a form of housing deprivation, which is generally defined by inadequate basic housing conditions, such as poor physical standards, overcrowding, insecure tenures or living in unsafe areas (Stone 2006: 154). Even though he has no problems paying his rent and mortgage, Tom feels stuck in his "affordable" one-bedroom apartment that he will very likely never own. According to Stone, one could argue that Tom accounts for those "households that seem not to have an affordability problem (as measured by some standard), yet do experience one or more other forms of housing deprivation" (Stone 2006: 154). To that, the London Tenants Federation already remarked in a report in 2011 that,

> given that evidence showed from the start that intermediate housing was pretty much unaffordable even for those for whom it was apparently designed, the strategy was unsustainable in this form.
>
> (London Tenants Federation 2011: 6)

Gentrification of "Affordable Housing"

What has become evident in this chapter is that the term "affordable housing" ignores the individual experience or context of the people eligible for "affordable housing." In this regard, the term "affordable housing" becomes meaningless: just because one is eligible for "affordable housing," does not mean that one is able to get an 'affordable housing' apartment or that one finds it particularly affordable.

As I have shown in the first section of the chapter, the lower the rent, and, therefore, the lower the income of the applicants, the more people applied per apartment. In other words, developments like 461 Dean Street hardly provide any meaningful affordable housing for those on the lower end of the income spectrum. This erodes the potential for lower-income households to ever access "affordable housing." Furthermore, my findings of the NYC lottery process show a tendency to reject those who do not meet a narrow set of criteria to access "affordable housing" despite being eligible. In this way, housing associations individualize a structural problem.

The main role of housing associations in this context is not to prevent displacement but to indirectly facilitate it by funneling the displaced or soon-to-be displaced into "affordable housing" lotteries where they have little chance of getting "affordable housing."

In the second section of this chapter, I showed that even people with moderate incomes may face affordability issues. People like Harrison or Tom, both with moderate incomes, expressed affordability problems. For people like them, the term "affordable housing" has become rather meaningless as they face challenges to balance the actual or potential costs of their "affordable housing" apartment with the constraints of their incomes.

The shift of "affordable housing" strategies towards meeting the needs of moderate- and middle-class households rather than those most in need is evident not only in terms of "affordable housing" percentages and targets – as I have shown in chapters one to three – but also in the individual experience of "affordable housing" residents and those eligible for "affordable housing." Thus, my results suggest an element of exclusivity to "affordable housing" that is evident in both the limited access to "affordable housing" for lower-income households as well as in the perceived unaffordability of "affordable housing" for households on the lower end of the required income spectrum.

This exclusivity of inclusionary housing leads to an influx of more affluent residents living not only in the mixed-income developments but also in the "affordable housing" segment itself, resulting in what can be characterized as the gentrification of "affordable housing." Rather than serving as a gentrification-mitigating mechanism, "affordable housing," combined with the new market-rate housing, thus, indirectly contributes to the gentrification and displacement of the surrounding community. This is brought about by the ten structurally embedded factors in the selection management of "affordable housing" as well as the financing schemes discussed above. Rather than counteract, this exacerbates the lack of genuinely "affordable housing" not only for the surrounding, oftentimes low-income community but for all Londoners or New Yorkers who are looking for meaningful housing affordability.

Interviews

Interview Executive Director. 2016. Interview with the Executive Director of a Housing Association in New York City, conducted on August 24, 2016, by Yuca Meubrink in New York City, USA.

Interview Clara. 2015. Interview with Clara, shared ownership resident, conducted on August 21, 2015 by Yuca Meubrink in London, UK.

Interview Harrison. 2017. Interview with Harrison, affordable housing tenant, conducted on September 22, 2017 by Yuca Meubrink in New York City, USA.

Interview James. 2017. Interview with James, affordable housing tenant, conducted on September 5, 2017 by Yuca Meubrink in New York City, USA.

Interview Jenna. 2017. Interview with Jenna, affordable housing applicant, conducted on September 14, 2017 by Yuca Meubrink in New York City, USA.

Interview Max. 2016. Interview with Max, affordable housing tenant, conducted on May 1, 2016 by Yuca Meubrink in New York City, USA.

Interview Tom. 2017. Interview with Tom, shared ownership resident, conducted on March 23, 2017 by Yuca Meubrink in London, UK.

E-Mail Harrison. 2018. E-mail exchange with Harrison. Received by Yuca Meubrink, June 14, 2018.

Fieldnotes

Meubrink, Yuca. Participant observation of an informational meeting for the "affordable housing" lottery for 461 Dean Street, Fort Greene, Brooklyn, London May 16, 2016.

Meubrink, Yuca. Fieldnote to the interview with the Executive Director of a Housing Association, Brooklyn, New York City, August, 24, 2016.

Notes

1 For more information see the official website: https://housingconnect.nyc.gov
2 A large part of the argumentation and reasoning in the subsections 6.1.1. through 6.1.3. have already been published in German in the form of an article here: Meubrink, Yuca. 2018. "Hitting the Jackpot. Die New Yorker Wohnungslotterie als Erfüllung des Amerikanischen

Traums?". In: Kuckuck. Notizen zur Alltagskultur, 2018/2, 12–16. http://www.kuckuc-knotizen.at/kuckuck/index.php/2-18-gleichheit/175-2-18-gleichheit-leseprobe.
3 All names are kept anonymous or have been changed in this chapter to protect the identity of the individual.
4 Excluded from this assumption are, of course, individual live changing circumstances such as job loss or illness.

References

Bellafante, Ginia. 2017. "At $3,700 a Month, 'Affordable' Apartments Go Begging." *The New York Times*, November 17. https://www.nytimes.com/2017/11/17/nyregion/at-3700-a-month-affordable-apartments-go-begging.html.
Clarke, Anna, Alex Fenton, Sanna Markkanen, Sarah Monk, and Christine Whitehead. 2008. "Tenure Aspirations and Shared Ownership." Cambridge: Cambridge Center for Housing and Planning Research. https://www.cchpr.landecon.cam.ac.uk/Research/Start-Year/2006/Understanding-demographic-spatial-economic-impacts-future-affordable-housing-demand/Paper-Five/Report.
Florida, Richard. 2013. "Renting the American Dream." *Bloomberg.Com*, April 23. https://www.bloomberg.com/news/articles/2013-04-23/renting-the-american-dream.
Jobs, Sebastian. 2014. "American Dream." In *Metzler Lexikon Moderner Mythen*, Stephanie Wodianka and Juliane Ebert. Stuttgart: J.B. Metzler, 18–21.
Laterman, Kaya. 2016. "Ashland Comes to Brooklyn." *The New York Times*, July 8. https://www.nytimes.com/2016/07/10/realestate/ashland-brooklyn.html.
London Tenants Federation. 2011. "The Affordable Housing Con." London Tenants Federation. http://www.londontenants.org/publications/other/theafordablehousingconf.pdf.
Meubrink, Yuca. 2018. "Hitting the Jackpot. Die New Yorker Wohnungslotterie Als Erfüllung Des Amerikanischen Traums?" *Kuckuck. Notizen Zur Alltagskultur*. 18 (2): 12–16.
Minton, Anna. 2017. *Big Capital: Who Is London For?* UK: Penguin.
Navarro, Mireya. 2015. "88,000 Applicants and Counting for 55 Units in 'Poor Door' Building." *The New York Times*, April 20. https://www.nytimes.com/2015/04/21/nyregion/poor-door-building-draws-88000-applicants-for-55-rental-units.html.
New York City Health. 2015. "Community Health Profiles 2015. Brooklyn Community District 3: Bedford Stuyvesant. New York City Department of Health and Mental Hygiene." New York City Health. https://www1.nyc.gov/assets/doh/downloads/pdf/data/2015chp-bk3.pdf.
Oder, Norman. 2016. Atlantic Yards/Pacific Park Report. https://atlanticyardsreport.blogspot.com/2016/01/atlantic-yardspacific-park-in-2016.html.
Stein, Samuel. 2018. "Progress for Whom, Toward What? Progressive Politics and New York City's Mandatory Inclusionary Housing." *Journal of Urban Affairs* 40 (6): 770–81. https://doi.org/10.1080/07352166.2017.1403854.
Stone, Michael E. 2006. "What Is Housing Affordability? The Case for the Residual Income Approach." *Housing Policy Debate* 17 (1): 151–84.
Watt, Paul. 2018. "'Social Housing Not Social Cleansing': Contemporary Housing Struggles in London." In *Rent and Its Discontents. A Century of Housing Struggle*, Neil Grey. London: Rowman & Littlefield, 117–35.
Weaver, Shaye. 2016. "City's Affordable Housing Lotteries Favor Young Single People, Stats Show." *DNAinfo*, November 16. https://www.dnainfo.com/new-york/20161116/upper-east-side/affordable-housing-lottery-demographics-winners-new-york-city.
Zimmer, Amy, and Nigel Chiwaya. 2015. "MAP: What Are Your Chances of Winning an Affordable Housing Lottery?" DN*Ainfo*, October 27. https://www.dnainfo.com/new-york/20151027/midtown/map-what-are-your-chances-at-spot-affordable-housing.

Conclusion
Inclusionary Housing as Part of the Problem, Not the Solution to the Housing Affordability Crises

The production of affordable housing itself has led to a process of gentrification. This is what this book has shown in a nutshell. The purpose of this book was to advance the critique of inclusionary housing policies and practices in New York City and London. To this end, I examined inclusionary housing in New York City and London in the broader context of austerity urbanism and new-build gentrification. By comparing and contrasting the socio-spatial practices and effects of inclusionary housing in these two cities, I revealed important similarities as well as differences between them. Despite differences in national context, planning systems, housing policies and conditions in cities and neighborhoods, I gathered evidence that shows inclusionary housing is largely ineffective in creating socially-mixed communities and truly affordable housing for low-income New Yorkers and Londoners.

The overwhelming conclusion is that to cope with the austerity measures imposed on them, local authorities in both cities have promoted inclusionary housing as a planning instrument to create "affordable housing." In doing so, they have often actively engaged in entrepreneurial activities that support urban growth over the production of truly affordable housing. I introduced the concept of *gentrification through the back door* to better describe the policy of inclusionary housing in both cities and presented empirical evidence in each chapter of the different ways that inclusionary housing provides a "back door" to gentrification.

Gentrification and displacement are obviously not the stated goals of inclusionary housing policy. Nevertheless, as it currently exists in both cities, this is what inclusionary housing more or less achieves: a "back door" to neighborhood upscaling through which wealthier people move into poor urban areas, and, in turn, directly or indirectly displace the residing low-income community. In the following, I look across this study to draw out my key results and highlight their implications by illustrating five interdependent tensions in inclusionary housing practices and outcomes in New York City and London.

First, inclusionary housing *heightens the negative effects of austerity urbanism while being hailed as a progressive housing policy.* Although city governments assumed more steering roles in the drafting of inclusionary housing plans over time, thereby highlighting their priority of creating affordable housing, their plans have increasingly catered to middle-income households as well as to the promotion of private real estate development. In tracing the evolution of inclusionary housing in

DOI: 10.4324/9781003468479-7

New York City and London in the context of austerity urbanism, I have identified long-term trends and multiple shifts in its development. I have shown in particular how inclusionary housing more closely reflects the continuity of austerity urbanism than has commonly been assumed, despite some significant changes in the way it has been approached by each mayor in question. While the planning tools that purport to create affordable housing for the common good have changed over time, they have remained market-driven and urban growth-oriented and, therefore, fail to provide real solutions to the prevailing housing affordability crises, which have been amplified by decades of national austerity measures. I have further shown how local governments and planning authorities use inclusionary housing as an instrument to justify their adoption of entrepreneurial strategies in urban development. In this way, I have advanced the debate not only on the socio-spatial practices of inclusionary housing, but also on the "local realities" of austerity urbanism and the ways in which these affect inclusionary housing approaches.

Second, inclusionary housing has been applied primarily in low-income and gentrifying neighborhoods rather than in more affluent neighborhoods, where the high return rate for market-rate apartments helps cross-subsidize affordable housing, *creating tensions between the city administration and local communities where to increase the housing supply – both affordable as well as market-rate units*. I demonstrated in the book how locating "affordable housing" increasingly in low-income neighborhoods, city and local planning authorities engaged in the financialization of land and non-market housing despite massive protests from the local community. In New York City, authorities initiated large-scale rezonings in gentrifying areas or in areas that had not yet experienced gentrification to trigger MIH, which sped up the process of creating "affordable housing" by attracting real estate developers to invest in the areas. In London, local authorities adopted a stronger steering effect on urban regeneration schemes by acting as developers. In the case of the Central Hill housing estate in the London borough of Lambeth, Lambeth Council re-assumed control over the decision-making process of the redevelopment of its own housing estate by transferring the control to a council-owned SPV, which enabled the council to act as a commercial and speculative developer. The decision to demolish the estate rather than to refurbish was justified by the creation of 'affordable housing' and newly socially mixed communities. And even though, the decision to demolish Central Hill Estate was paused by Lambeth Council for the moment, this does not (yet) change the Council's course of allocating affordable housing in primarily low-income neighborhoods. In both New York and London, I have pointed out how city and local governments' planning decisions to invest in low-income neighborhoods had less to do with creating truly affordable housing for residing communities in fear of being displaced, than with attracting real estate developers to invest in those neighborhoods. This reveals how inclusionary housing paves the way for gentrification and displacement, thereby failing the trust local low-income communities have put in their elected officials.

This has, third, also created *tensions between city and local governments or governmental agencies*. I examined the decision-making process of developers' planning applications, and how local authorities have adopted different entrepreneurial and pro-growth strategies depending on the wealth of a neighborhood by placing inclusionary housing requirements on developers. While city governments generally pushed for development approval regardless of whether the affordable housing targets were met, local authorities or agencies in low-income areas were generally more committed to increasing the affordable housing percentage due to their obligations to their constituents. City and local governments in wealthier communities took losses in providing "affordable housing." The "affordable housing" agreed upon in lower-income communities, has, however, generally remained unaffordable for a large portion of the local community. Nonetheless, in most cases, local governments took the necessary steps to ensure that the development project can proceed. Thereby, developers as well as city and local governments have played a pivotal role in accelerating gentrification and displacement processes in low-income neighborhoods.

Inclusionary housing practices have further created tensions between its own two goals: the provision of "affordable housing" and the fostering of "social mixing." In spite of aiming at fostering social inclusion, inclusionary housing practices have, fourth, *spurred new developments that are designed in ways that have separated affordable housing tenants from market-rate residents.* I discussed three design practices that have been used in both cities that leave low-income tenants either segregated through separate entrances and tenure types, segregated beneath and behind waterfront condominiums, or separated through differing levels of access to amenities. In all three urban design practices, verticality plays a pivotal role in advancing a vertical enclosure movement, which I call vertical segregation by design. Inclusionary housing, thus, gives lower-income tenants access to spaces from which they are typically excluded while at the same time excluding them from communal spaces and magnificent views of the city. In this way, mixed-income housing serves as a "back door" to gentrification by indirectly displacing the low-income tenants housed in "affordable housing" units.

Fifth, inclusionary housing practices create further *tensions between competing affordable housing tenants or those eligible for affordable housing,* leading to a certain exclusiveness that serves as a barrier to people in certain income percentages and government targets. The example of the New York City Housing Lottery illustrated that not only one's eligibility for "affordable housing" but one being selected or "pulled" in the housing lottery does not necessarily mean that one can get an "affordable housing" apartment. The lottery's interview process and narrow set of criteria provided limited possibilities for many low-income households to ever access an "affordable housing" apartment. I showed how even households on moderate incomes face challenges in balancing the actual or potential costs of their "affordable housing." These and other barriers that low-income households face when trying to access "affordable housing" leads inevitably to an influx of more affluent residents living in "affordable housing," which can be characterized as a form *of gentrification through the back door.*

These tensions, examined within the book, have provided a rich, differentiated picture of planning practices, austerity measures and gentrification processes. By studying socio-spatial practices and outcomes of inclusionary housing across

New York City and London, I illustrated how new-build gentrification, through local government planning, is part of a broader politico-economic process. In this way, the complexity of the mechanisms involved and the interdependencies of those politically responsible come to light.

Each of the five areas of tension described above requires, of course, further research, in particular with regard to other neighborhoods and cities that have also enacted far-reaching inclusionary housing programs. I further propose to closer examine the maybe not-so-obvious link between austerity urbanism and gentrification, as it has rarely been discussed in the literature. As one can see from this book austerity has produced new forms of gentrification and displacement. And these new forms must be explored further as well as the ways to resist them. In this context, the systemic role of racial and gender discrimination should also be further explored, as they appear both in the context of inclusionary housing and more generally in the field of housing policy and practice.

Now a final question: what wider use might the concept of *gentrification through the back door* have in other contexts of social mix or "affordable housing" policy? On the one hand, I would argue that the concept's utility is quite specific to inclusionary housing due to it being based on so-called "poor door" practices and the experiences of residents at risk of being displaced by inclusionary housing practices.

On the other hand, *gentrification through the back door* is a conceptual offer for more research. It shows the need for much more diverse understanding of neighborhood change and urges academics, politicians as well as city planners to pay more attention to specific forms of gentrification and displacement and how they come about. The concept has been useful to understanding how and why inclusionary housing policies in both cities have consistently been allocated in ways that reinforce socio-spatial inequalities. It may, thus, be helpful to evaluate other social mix policies in terms of their impact on the urban and social fabric through its greater focus on the local state or other actors driving gentrification processes. State-led gentrification emphasizes the role of the (local) state as an instigator, catalyst or promotor of the socio-spatial restructuring of the city. While *gentrification through the back door* also pays a great deal of attention to the role of the local government or other semi-private or private actors in furthering the interests of developers, it primarily looks at the socio-spatial practices that lead to neighborhood transformations under the guise of seemingly benevolent housing programs. And that is exactly what local governments and planning authorities as well as mainstream scholars should do more of: they should be looking more critically at the socio-spatial practices and the effects of the housing policies under scrutiny. That is what makes the concept relevant in both academic and political contexts: a concept that may provide a useful starting point in the study of the relations between housing and planning policies and new-build gentrification processes and one that may help to draw a more nuanced picture of the complex mechanisms at play in the contemporary production of affordable housing.

Afterword

The COVID-19 Pandemic as a Transformative Moment of Inclusionary Housing?

At the time of writing – roughly four years after my fieldwork – the world is slowly emerging from the COVID-19 pandemic. New York City and London have both been epicenters of their countries' outbreaks, where tens of thousands of people have died as a result of the virus. Following the lockdowns necessary to contain the virus's spread, thousands of people have lost their jobs or faced cuts in income, many local businesses have gone bankrupt, and households have faced dramatic housing insecurity, being unable to make rent or mortgage payments. Put simply, the pandemic has exacerbated the ongoing housing crisis in both cities. The full impact on housing and renters is still hard to put into figures. Clearly, neighborhoods with poor housing conditions have been hit particularly hard. Overcrowding and poverty in deprived areas have created the ideal conditions for the virus to spread, which in turn has accelerated low-income tenants' housing insecurities in these areas. According to a report by the ANHD, as of 2022, about 600,000 households in New York City have fallen behind on rent, and 110,000 eviction cases have been filed by landlords (Block 2022). Similarly in London, over 400,000 households are expected to be significantly behind on rent and about 10 percent of private tenants are projected to be unemployed, which is about double the average rate, according to a report published by the London School of Economics in 2021 (Whitehead et al. 2021). The New York State Legislature, as well as the central government in the UK, enacted emergency eviction notices to ensure that people impacted by the pandemic in both cities can remain in their homes. However, in 2021, those emergency suspensions on evictions and foreclosures have come to an end, and, thus, a backlog of people has remained threatened.

In addition, the high levels of expenditures needed to cope with the pandemic have plunged both city governments into fiscal deficits and debt. New York City has experienced the worst fiscal crisis since the 1970s, leading the press to draw analogies to the fiscal and urban crisis and its aftermath of 1975 (i.a. Ferré-Sadurní et al. 2020, Maisano 2020; Yablon 2020). Just as in the 1970s, New York City today faces the challenge of solving its fiscal problems and generating sufficient revenues to sustain the public sector. Just as then, the city is in many ways dependent on the New York State governor and the state legislature as well as federal spending to close its budget deficits.

DOI: 10.4324/9781003468479-8

Since the Trump administration had already signaled that federal spending would not be forthcoming, in the summer of 2020, New York City's Mayor de Blasio called on the state to give the city long-term borrowing authority and to raise taxes on the wealthy to avoid laying off 22,000 workers in the city and help avoid cuts in welfare spending. The governor, however, was reluctant to assert borrowing permission or to raise taxes on the rich (Maisano 2020).

The change in national office made federal spending possible. The Biden administration issued an emergency stimulus package of $22 billion for New York City to mitigate the immediate negative effects of the pandemic (Haag and Rubinstein 2021). Given the urgency of the situation, the New York State legislature has ultimately raised taxes on millionaires, which, among other things, helped to win funding for schools (Phillips-Fein 2021). Nevertheless, providing housing for people on low incomes remains one of the biggest challenges for the New York City government.

Similarly, London's boroughs have been hit particularly hard by the pandemic. After more than a decade of austerity, already under-funded local governments in London now face financial ruin (Gallardo 2020). The Councils of Croyden and Bexley have already received bailouts from the central government. The total COVID-19 shortfall of London councils is estimated to be £1.4 billion (London Councils 2020). Even though London received some emergency funding from the central government, it has proven insufficient in covering the costs of key public services in the city's boroughs. Thus, in December 2021, the Mayor proposed to raise the council tax by £31.93 to cover key public services such as the police, transport, and fire brigade. He further announced that building "affordable housing" was one of his core priorities (Mayor of London 2021).

The question arises as to whether the pandemic will make a difference in how national and local governments approach the creation of "affordable housing." In what follows, I briefly discuss the latest developments and (prospective) shifts of inclusionary housing policies in each city in the wake of the pandemic and comment on their potential to support the growing need for affordable housing. I further comment on the periodic phases of inclusionary housing outlined in Chapter 1 and ask whether recent approaches in both cities might represent something like a fourth phase of inclusionary housing.

The End of Section 106 in England: A New Fast-Track Route for Developers or a New Way to Deliver Affordable Housing?

On the back of the pandemic, the Ministry for Housing, Communities and Local Government (MHCLG) published a White Paper in August 2020, called Planning for the Future. The report included proposals for fundamental structural changes to England's current planning system.

The report, however, faced fierce criticism. During the consultation phase that ended in January 2021, 44,000 responses were issued (Cuffe 2021). In particular, the move to abolish Section 106 agreements and the Community Infrastructure Levy and replace it with a new national Infrastructure Levy sparked concern among local authorities and housing organizations. The idea of the White Paper was that developers pay a fixed proportion of a scheme's value to the local authority, which in turn can then fund a range of local infrastructure including "affordable housing." The main criticism related, among other things, to the threshold for developer contributions and the planning "permission in principle."

In relation to the threshold, the government proposed to exempt developments of less than 40 or 50 residential units from developer contributions, which is an extension of the former exemption of fewer than 10 units. According to the White Paper, this exemption was thought of as a short-term measure to make it easier for developers to "bounce back following the COVID-19 pandemic" (Ministry of Housing, Communities and Local Government: 2020: 68). In other words, all developments that are smaller than 50 units would not need to contribute to "affordable housing." The Royal Institute of British Architects (RIBA) dismissed the proposed reforms as "shameful" as they "do almost nothing to guarantee the delivery of affordable, well-designed and sustainable homes" (Royal Institute of British Architects 2020). RIBA further adds that

> [i]f the government is serious about addressing the dominant position of large housebuilders and the lack of quality social housing, the Secretary of State needs to make changes to the tax system, look at why land approved for development lies untouched for years, and give local authorities power and resource to promote and safeguard quality.
>
> (SPV Royal Institute of British Architects 2020)

Furthermore, in relation to the planning permission "in principle," it would allow development proposals, mostly on urban and brownfield sites, to directly receive planning permission if they meet certain criteria. The in-principle matters would relate to the location, use, and amount of development on a site, thereby leaving aside the question of whether housing development should be approved at all.

After a long process of revisions and consultations, the ideas put forward in the Planning for the Future White Paper led to the Levelling-up and Regeneration Bill that was introduced to Parliament in 2022 and became law in December of 2023. While the act took up some of the critique expressed during the consultation phase, concerns remain over whether the new infrastructure has the potential to address the housing shortage in England. According to a report done by the Centre for Social Justice in 2022, big questions remain over (1) the quantity and type of affordable housing it will provide, (2) the delivery of on-site affordable housing, and (3) the geographical distribution between low and high land values (Center for Social Justice 2022).

First, in terms of the quantity of affordable housing provided, there is a danger that the developer contribution will be set too low. As the amount to be paid by developers is on completion of the project and not at the time of planning permission, it is likely that this will result in fewer affordable homes. In that way, the new infrastructure levy is also linked to the market in a similar way to Section 106 obligations. As there is no guarantee that developers will not be able to negotiate down their obligations on the grounds of financial viability, as they have previously done in their Section 106 agreements.

Second, there is a clear risk that a fixed contribution by developers is less likely to result in on-site affordable housing, which, in turn, will lead to fewer mixed-income developments.

Third, local authorities are expected to set their own rates of the infrastructure levy for different types of development. This means that the rates in areas with low land – and development – values will be lower than in areas with high land and development values, which inevitably will further manifest geographical inequality (Center for Social Justice 2022).

With respect to London: The Mayor of London, Sadiq Khan, criticized the bill as an "unworkable proposal" as it creates "uncertainty and eat[s] up resources from a planning system that is already struggling" (Jessel 2023). Instead, he would rather like "to work with the council and the housing sector to improve the current developer contributions system" (Jessel 2023). This critique was expressed shortly after Sadiq Khan announced in May 2023 that he had fulfilled his promise to start building 116,000 affordable homes between 2015–2016 and 2022–2023 as part of his Affordable Homes Programme (Mayor of London 2023). This was widely celebrated as a success and attributed in part to his influence on the planning system to increase the proportion of affordable housing on major developments (Fowler 2023). However, as I have shown in this book, the definition of affordable housing is very broad and in this case includes the Mayor's new categories: London Affordable Rent, London Living Rent and London Shared Ownership. All of these categories still remain significantly more expensive than Social Rent and, therefore, unaffordable for many low-income communities in London.

It is therefore still unclear to what extent these changes to the English planning system and the abolition of Section 106 will be able to address the lack of affordable housing or of whether this will just be another tool to entrench economic and social inequality in London or elsewhere in the country. What is clear, however, is that the proposed planning reform translates into a "fast-track" system for developers that contributes to urban growth. What remains to be seen is to what extent this will lead to more "affordable housing" for low-income tenants or whether it will be at their expense.

A Glimpse of Hope in New York City?

At the end of 2021, in the midst of the COVID-19 pandemic, the New York City Council approved two large-scale rezonings: one in the Gowanus neighborhood in Brooklyn and the other in the SoHo-NoHo area in Manhattan. So far, these are the eighth and ninth neighborhood-level upzonings of the 15 neighborhood-specific rezonings planned across the city by the de Blasio administration's housing plan. The plan aims to create and preserve 300,000 "affordable housing" units and to facilitate the implementation of the city's MIH program, as described in Chapter 1. However, it is the first time that the de Blasio administration received approval for upzonings in predominantly white communities with incomes well above the city's average. Up until then, the de Blasio administration had only advanced neighborhood rezonings in areas currently experiencing gentrification or that had not yet undergone gentrification. As illustrated in chapter two, the earlier rezonings thereby indicated to potential developers that these neighborhoods were worthwhile to invest in, thus, spurring gentrification rather than the creation of housing affordable for the residing low-income community.

The Gowanus rezoning plan envisages the construction of about 8,300 apartments of which 3000 would be considered "affordable housing" created via the city's MIH program. The rezoning plan was the first to have undergone an independent racial impact study, which is mandatory for all neighborhood rezonings starting in 2022. The study concluded that the rezoning would be "positive for racial equity, increasing racial integration and countering local exclusionary development trends" (New York City Council 2021). Neighborhood groups, however, remained opposed to the plan, citing concerns over the placement of "affordable housing" on the most polluted sites in the area, the feasibility of the flood protections at the Gowanus Canal, the changing character of the neighborhood and – pointing to the unfilled "affordable housing" promises of previous rezonings – whether the city will uphold its "affordable housing" targets (Brand 2021a).

The last two concerns have also been the main reasons for the resistance to the SoHo-NoHo rezoning plan, which is expected to add 3,000 new apartments to the area, including about 900 "affordable housing" units. The local community board rejected the proposals completely. Local community board members in particular feared the erosion of SoHo's historic artistic and cultural identity as well as its fashionable shopping district. SoHo has undergone considerable gentrification since the 1980s when artists moved into lofts in the former manufacturing zone, transforming the area into one of New York City's whitest and wealthiest communities. It is this very community who are now concerned that big developers will destroy their little galleries and shops by bringing in taller buildings and big department stores, calling it a "give-away to developers" (Brand 2021b).

Nevertheless, both rezonings have been widely celebrated as a success by city authorities, planning officials, and affordable housing advocates. In particular, the Gowanus rezoning plan has been seen as a successful community planning effort by local leaders and the Department of City Planning. In contrast to the rezoning processes in lower-income areas such as Inwood or East Harlem, local politicians in Gowanus and planning officials seem to be more willing to work with the local community and integrate comprehensive community planning into the rezoning. Valerie E. Stahl, who compared the rezoning processes in East Harlem and Gowanus, pointed out that these disparities in collaborating with the community are "set against the context of differences in each neighborhood's racial and socioeconomic demographics, with Gowanus having higher rates of homeownership, housing costs, median income, and a larger non-Hispanic white population" (Stahl 2020: 237).

Local community groups that opposed the Gowanus rezoning, however, felt they had little say in the process. Not only did they feel that the virtual public hearings held during the pandemic were not as accessible as in-person public events, especially for the lower-income residents (Kully 2020), but they also disputed the city's data that presented Gowanus as an overwhelmingly white and wealthy neighborhood. They argued that the data used had actually presented the demographics for all of Community Board 6, a much larger area that also includes the more affluent neighborhoods of Cobble Hill and Park Slope. While these areas are hillsides, the area to be rezoned lies in the lower part of the district around the contaminated Gowanus Canal into which the city has been dumping millions of gallons of raw sewage every year (Shuk et al. 2020). According to the environmental organization Riverkeeper, this canal is one of the most polluted bodies of water in the country due to it once being the location for numerous industrial facilities, such as manufactured gas plants, cement factories, oil refineries and a chemical plant (Riverkeeper 2010). According to these local community groups, it is primarily low-income people of color that live in the area around the canal (Shuk et al. 2020). They presented data that showed that the respected area is less than 35 percent white with an annual median household income of less than $50,000 (ibid.). In this sense, the Gowanus rezoning appears to continue the trend of de Blasio's administration's targeting of low-income neighborhoods of color for largely luxury real estate development. It remains to be seen to what extent the new Mayor of New York City, Eric Adams (since 2022), will continue this trend of rezoning with his "City of Yes for Housing Opportunity"[1] proposal, which aims to encourage the development of affordable housing throughout New York City through changes to city's zoning code.

The city is, however, not alone in combating its housing affordability crisis. The state governor and state legislature not only released financial aid programs to mitigate the effects of the COVID-19 pandemic on housing and renters, but also proposed reforms on two programs that would immediately affect New York City's inclusionary housing program.

One program that is often assumed to be necessary to make MIH work is the 421-a program, described in the Introduction. The program is implemented at the state level but only applies to New York City. Over the decades since its inception in 1971, it has become a central public subsidy for developers to finance their development projects, provided that they meet certain requirements. Many of the MIH developments are heavily subsidized through this tax exemption program. At the time MIH was crafted, policymakers thought of MIH as working in conjunction with the 421-a program. According to a report by the NYU Furman Center, the availability of the tax exemption "greatly increases the value of additional zoning density and its potential to cross-subsidize affordable units" (NYU Furman Center 2015: 15).

The program, however, was often criticized by affordable housing advocates as "a give-away to developers" (Stark-Miller 2022) since it essentially exempted developers from paying property taxes for 35 to 40 years while producing little "affordable housing" in return. After it expired in 2016 and was renamed the "affordable housing" NY Program in 2017, the program was once more up for renewal in June of 2022. The new Governor of New York, Katy Hochul[2], thus, saw the opportunity to

> enact a different kind of abatement program that can continue to incentivize rental housing construction across New York City while creating permanent and deeper affordability and spending taxpayer money more efficiently.
>
> (New York State Governor 2022: 133)

Hence, she proposed a new program that she called the Affordable Neighborhoods for New Yorkers Tax Incentive, or 485-w, that aimed at reaching deeper affordability requirements, slightly increasing wage requirements and creating an affordable homeownership option. Hochul's version would, for example, delete the 130 percent AMI threshold for "affordable housing" units, requiring all "affordable housing" units to be targeted at less than the Area Median Income.

The proposal received support from political leaders such as the new Mayor of New York City, Eric Adams, the Assembly Housing Committee Chair Steve Cymbrowitz as well as the powerful Real Estate Board of New York, whose president argued that it "provides the private sector with an important tool for producing rental housing at deeper levels of affordability permanently" (Kinniburgh 2022).

Housing advocates and organizations, however, have criticized Hochul's proposal for not creating an entirely new program that would "prioritize other ways of making housing more affordable to lower-income New Yorkers, including vouchers, which organizers, researchers and even major landlord groups agree are the quickest way to prevent evictions and get people off the streets" (Kinniburgh 2022). Cea Weaver from Housing Justice for all, the leading statewide coalition of over 80 organizations that represent tenants and homeless New Yorkers, argues that amid a surging COVID-19 pandemic that left many New Yorkers in rental debt, "Hochul is continuing the worst of Cuomo's legacy. [...] By continuing programs like 421-a and offering property owners tax rebates, while ignoring rental assistance and the looming eviction crisis, Governor Hochul continues to ignore, as Cuomo before her did, those New Yorkers who are most negatively impacted by the housing affordability crisis" (Housing Justice for All 2022).

Hochul's proposal, however, did not receive broad support in the Democratic-controlled legislature, whose members were reluctant to extend a program that had been criticized as a lucrative tax break for the real estate industry, especially with an election looming (Haag 2022). In 2023, she launched a pilot 421-a program for projects within the Gowanus rezoning area in Brooklyn that were already vested in the tax abatement program when it expired. In January of 2024, she announced that she would – again – propose a new tax abatement for new rental construction to replace the expired 421-a program (New York State Governor 2024).

While some experts claim tools like this program are necessary to make new "affordable housing" financially possible in more affluent neighborhoods, just like the recently rezoned areas in SoHo and Gowanus (Kinniburgh 2022), others claim the additional density obtained through the rezoning in these higher-rents neighborhoods has the capacity to cross-subsidize new "affordable housing" units without direct subsidies (NYU Furman Center 2015). Either way, even if this program does create some deeper affordability, it still exempts developers from paying millions in property taxes, thereby stimulating private luxury development projects rather than housing truly affordable for the people most in need. And as I illustrated in Chapter 3, developers – in particular in high-rent neighborhoods – tend to negotiate a reduction in or find ways to get out of their "affordable housing" obligations on-site.

Another reform that Hochul has proposed in 2022 (New York State Governor 2022) and will propose again in 2024 (New York State Governor 2024) is to remove the limit on the floor area ratio of residential developments that are currently set at 12.0 in high-density residential areas, affecting predominantly high-rise districts in Manhattan or Downtown Brooklyn. By removing this threshold, developers would be able to build more densely in these areas that currently have no ability to increase residential density through rezoning and, therefore, trigger the Mandatory Inclusionary Housing Program that would bring more "affordable housing" to these high-rent areas.

It is evident that the city's rezoning of more affluent areas and the state's proposal of these reforms have strengthened their role in these market-based programs with the intention of maximizing the production of "affordable housing" amidst the COVID-19 pandemic. But in all three cases, the city and state governments have relied on rezoning as the principal tool to address the predominant housing crisis – the same tool that, as I have shown throughout this book, is fueling gentrification and heightening displacement pressures rather than providing truly affordable housing. While it remains to be seen whether these state's proposals – if implemented – will produce more "affordable housing," it is clear that developers would seriously benefit from them. They would not only get the chance to build more market-rate apartments in the city's most lucrative neighborhoods, but they would also be exempt from paying property taxes for the next three to four decades. And since the majority of the units in new developments will be market-rate, the tiny percentage of "affordable housing" to be built will reduce their profits only slightly.

Concluding Remarks

It might be premature to begin thinking more expansively about inclusionary housing in terms of periodic phases. That said, it is clear that the federal funds issued to support recovery will not be there forever, raising the question of how both cities will be able to support the needs of their residents in finding a home in the future. In the 1970s, the New York City government only obtained federal aid by agreeing to sharp budget cuts. As a result, the city government dramatically cut its spending on a range of public services, ushering in the age of austerity. Similarly, the financial crisis of 2008 brought about a new round of austerity measures, thereby intensifying neoliberal urban governance and practices in both New York City and London. Whether the COVID-19 pandemic can be seen as a transformative moment to form a more equitable London or New York City or whether it is only the beginning of another round of austerity politics remains to be seen. Looking back over the last 50 years, however, it is likely that another crushing round of austerity will follow.

Either way, what has become evident in both cities is that inclusionary housing is now entering what I call its fourth phase, which combines an increased steering role for local authorities with the consolidation of pro-real estate and pro-gentrification politics. Even if the "rules of the inclusionary housing game" were adjusted in each city in response to exacerbated housing affordability problems, as in New York City, or were significantly altered, as in both London and England, this would mean nothing but *continuity despite change* – an outcome I have already drawn from the three periodic phases of inclusionary housing described in Chapter 1. So far, it is evident that the COVID-19 pandemic has not brought about a transformative change in the way both cities create "affordable housing" or attempt to solve their housing affordability crisis. While creating more "affordable housing" remains high on the agenda for both, each city relies on the same strategy of "building their way out of the crisis" as before (refer Chapter 1). Until this changes, "affordable housing" will remain out of reach for a great many in both cities.

Notes

1 Details of the proposal have only been released at the time of writing in September of 2023. For more details see the website of the Department of City Planning: https://www.nyc.gov/site/planning/plans/city-of-yes/city-of-yes-housing-opportunity.page.
2 The Democrat Katy Hochul took office as a governor of New York City in August of 2021, after her predecessor Andrew Cuomo resigned due to allegations of sexual harassment.

References

Block, Lucy. 2022. "New York's Pandemic Rent Crisis." *ANHD – Association for Neighborhood & Housing Development*. https://anhd.org/report/new-yorks-pandemic-rent-crisis.
Brand, David. 2021a. "NYC Council Approves de Blasio's Massive Gowanus Rezoning." *City Limits*, November 23. https://citylimits.org/2021/11/23/nyc-council-approves-de-blasios-massive-gowanus-rezoning/.
———. 2021b. "Manhattan Community Board Votes to Reject SoHo-NoHo Rezoning." *City Limits*, July 27. https://citylimits.org/2021/07/27/manhattan-community-board-votes-to-reject-soho-noho-rezoning/.
Center for Social Justice. 2022. "Levying Up. Ensuring planning reform delivers affordable homes." *Center for Social Justice*. https://www.centreforsocialjustice.org.uk/wp-content/uploads/2022/12/CSJ-Housing_Paper.pdf.
Cuffe, Grainne. 2021. "Pincher: Replacement of Section 106 to Put 'More Ammunition in the Hands' of Councils." *Inside Housing*, November 3, 2021. https://www.insidehousing.co.uk/news/news/pincher-replacement-of-section-106-to-put-more-ammunition-in-the-hands-of-councils-73170.
Ferré-Sadurní, Luis, Jeffery C. Mays, and Jesse McKinley. 2020. "Virus Forces N.Y.C. to Consider Tactic That Nearly Led to Ruin in '75." *The New York Times*, May 29. https://www.nytimes.com/2020/05/29/nyregion/budget-borrow-coronavirus-ny.html.
Fowler, Ryan. 2023. "Mayor of London meets promise to start 116,000 affordable homes for Londoners." *The Intermediary*, May 15. https://theintermediary.co.uk/2023/05/mayor-of-london-meets-promise-to-start-116000-affordable-homes-for-londoners/.

Gallardo, Christina. 2020. "British Council Faces Financial Ruin Due to Coronavirus." *POLITICO*, May 21, 2020. https://www.politico.eu/article/british-council-faces-financial-ruin-due-to-coronavirus-covid19/.

Haag, Matthew. 2022. "Why a Lucrative Tax Break for Developers Is Likely to Die in Albany." *The New York Times*, May 26. https://www.nytimes.com/2022/05/26/nyregion/tax-exemption-housing-development.html.

Haag, Matthew, and Dana Rubinstein. 2021. "New York is Getting $22 Billion in Federal Aid. How Should it Be Spent?" *The New York Times*, June 16. https://www.nytimes.com/2021/06/16/nyregion/de-blasio-coronavirus-pandemic-aid.html.

Housing Justice for All. 2022. "On Housing, Governor Hochul Continues Worst of Cuomo's Legacy, Abandoning Renters and Homeless New Yorkers Amid COVID Surge." *Housing Justice for All* (blog). January 5. https://housingjusticeforall.org/on-housing-governor-hochul-continues-worst-of-cuomos-legacy-abandoning-renters-and-homeless-new-yorkers-amid-covid-surge/.

Jessel, Ella. 2023. "London mayor joins calls to scrap 'unworkable' new infrastructure levy." *Planning Resource*, July 26. https://www.planningresource.co.uk/article/1831326?utm_source=website&utm_medium=social.

Kinniburgh, Colin. 2022. "Hochul's Proposed 421-A Replacement Is in For a Fight, Key Lawmakers Signal." *New York Focus* (blog). February 7, 2022. https://www.nysfocus.com/2022/02/07/421-a-replacement-in-for-a-fight/.

Kully, Sadef Ali. 2020 "For City's Public Meetings, Shift to Virtual Format Has Meant Attendance Boost—& Complications." *City Limits*, December 14. https://citylimits.org/2020/12/14/for-citys-public-meetings-shift-to-virtual-format-has-meant-attendance-boost-complications/.

London Councils. 2020. "London Councils warns of £1.4bn funding gap threat to post-Covid renewal." *London Councils* (blog), September 24. https://www.londoncouncils.gov.uk/press-release/24-september-2020/london-councils-warns-%C2%A314bn-funding-gap-threat-post-covid-renewal.

Maisano, Chris. 2020. "New York City's Fiscal Crisis Can't Be Solved on the Backs of Its Working Class." October 29, 2020. https://jacobinmag.com/2020/10/new-york-city-fiscal-crisis-unions-working-class-covid-19.

Mayor of London. 2021. *"Mayor Publishes Budget to Build Fairer City Despite Impact of Pandemic."* London City Hall. December 22. https://www.london.gov.uk//press-releases/mayoral/mayor-publishes-budget-to-build-fairer-city.

———. 2023. *"Mayor Hails Record-Breaking Housing Delivery as He Meets His Promise to Start 116,000 Affordable Homes for Londoners."* London City Hall, May 15. https://www.london.gov.uk/mayor-hails-record-breaking-housing-delivery-he-meets-his-promise-start-116000-affordable-homes.

Ministry of Housing, Communities and Local Government. 2020. "Planning for the Future." Government UK. https://www.gov.uk/government/consultations/planning-for-the-future.

New York City Council. 2021. "Gowanus Neighborhood Plan: Racial Equity Report on Housing and Opportunity." *New York City Council*. https://council.nyc.gov/land-use/plans/gowanus-neighborhood-plan-racial-equity-report-on-housing-and-opportunity/.

New York State Governor. 2022. "Governor Hochul Announces Sweeping Plans to Address Housing Affordability Crisis in New York State." Office of Governor Kathy Hochul, January 15. https://www.governor.ny.gov/news/governor-hochul-announces-sweeping-plans-address-housing-affordability-crisis-new-york-state.

———. 2024. Governor Hochul Announces Next Phase in Long-Term Housing Strategy Will Focus on Increasing Housing Supply in New York City. Office of Governor Kathy Hochul, January 9. https://www.governor.ny.gov/news/governor-hochul-announces-next-phase-long-term-housing-strategy-will-focus-increasing-housing.

NYU Furman Center. 2015. "Creating Affordable Housing Out of Thin Air: The Economics of Mandatory Inclusionary Zoning in New York City." New York City: NYU

Furman Center. http://furmancenter.org/files/NYUFurmanCenter_CreatingAffHousing_March2015.pdf.

Phillips-Fein, Kim. 2021. "Opinion: We Are Facing a Turning Point for New York City." *The New York Times*, June 1. https://www.nytimes.com/2021/06/01/opinion/new-york-city-covid.html.

Royal Institute of British Architects (RIBA). 2020. "'*Deregulation Won't Solve the Housing Crisis' – RIBA Criticises Jenrick's Planning Reforms.*" Royal Institute of British Architects. https://www.architecture.com/knowledge-and-resources/knowledge-landing-page/deregulation-wont-solve-the-housing-crisis-riba-criticises-jenricks-planning-reforms.

Riverkeeper. 2010. "*Campaign: Stop Polluters - Gowanus Canal.*" Riverkeeper. 2010. https://www.riverkeeper.org/campaigns/stop-polluters/gowanus-canal/.

Shuk, Elyse, Nora Almeida, Jack Riccobono, and Katia Kelly. 2020. "Opinion: Councilmember Relies on Misleading Data in Push for Unjust Gowanus Rezoning." *City Limits*, October 8. https://citylimits.org/2020/10/08/opinion-councilmember-relies-on-misleading-data-in-push-for-unjust-gowanus-rezoning/.

Stahl, Valerie E. 2020. "Zones of Resistance: Local Participatory Institutions in Two New York City Neighborhood Rezonings." In *Zoning. A Guide for 21st-Century Planning*, edited by Elliot Scar, Bernadette Baird-Zars, Lauren Ames Fischer and Valerie E. Stahl, 223–245. New York: Routledge.

Stark-Miller, Ethan. 2022. "Fate of State Affordable Housing Subsidy Remains in Limbo." *Politics NY*, March 16. https://politicsny.com/2022/03/16/fate-of-state-affordable-housing-subsidy-remains-in-limbo/.

Whitehead, Christine, Kath Scanlon, Ann Edge, Nancy Holman, Martina Rotolo, and Fanny Blanc. 2021. "*Homelessness and Rough Sleeping in the Time of COVID-19.*" London School of Economics. https://www.trustforlondon.org.uk/publications/homelessness-and-rough-sleeping-in-the-time-of-covid-19/.

Yablon, Alex. 2020. "Austerity Is Coming for New York City. It Doesn't Have to." *Slate*, September 25. https://slate.com/business/2020/09/new-york-city-austerity.html.

Index